D1154424

COLLEGE TEACHING

A Psychologist's View

COLLEGE TEACHING

A Psychologist's View

BY *Claude E. Buxton* YALE UNIVERSITY

Harcourt, Brace and Company · New York

Copyright, © 1956, by Harcourt, Brace and Company, Inc.

All rights reserved. No part of this book may be reproduced in any form, by mimeograph or any other means, without permission in writing from the publisher.

[a·8·56]

Printed in the United States of America

PREFACE

What began for me as an uncommonly strong interest in teaching has gradually developed into the avocation of trying to improve college instruction. During the ten years since I first offered a seminar on teaching I have presented it in four major universities and have discussed such matters with faculty members from just about all the disciplines there are. I do not suggest that there is any magic general formula for teaching. What is good teaching depends upon many things. Many of them are discussed in this book, and some have even been the subject of research investigation. Yet, although there presumably are principles of good teaching, some being statable on the basis of research and some being merely plausible extensions of standard psychological theory, the number of such principles operating simultaneously and the interactions among them simply make it impossible as yet to draw generalized conclusions about how to teach. It all depends: on who the instructor is, on the conditions under which he teaches, and on other related circumstances.

The problem of the individual instructor is to adapt, so far as this is required, and to exert his individuality, so far as this is desirable, by being attentive to everything that goes on in himself, his students, and his classroom. If he is analytical and flexible and well motivated, he can learn to teach better. This book is intended to suggest things he may look for, attitudes he may adopt, aspects of sheer technique he may try out, and even some of the goals he may try to achieve. But he will have to do the trying for himself. If he will try, and if he can recognize his successes and admit his failures, he will gradually shape his performance to be satisfyingly effective in his own eyes and the eyes of his students. As one of my correspondents has said, "Whenever a teacher tries something that is suited to his style, so that it 'pays off,' he may be counted on to continue using it just as surely as Pavlov's dog drooled."

The initial chapters in this book deal with the nature of higher education and with its strengths and its weaknesses, thus providing a background for later discussion. The experienced college teacher may wish to skim rather quickly through these chapters. Attention is then given to education in psychology and to the role of the individual faculty member. A discussion of the major techniques of teaching follows, and finally a discussion of student characteristics helps to explain why techniques have the effects they do.

It is difficult to analyze the research on teaching at the college level. It is relatively scanty and often not very well done. Some of the studies which are technically best deal with unimportant problems, while important problems are left to be attacked with the aid of only experience, or what one psychologist calls "wisdom research." Wherever possible I have combined pertinent research materials with discussions of technique, and I have not hesitated to refer to subjectively based essays whenever objective material was lacking. The subjective material in many instances comes from only one source: me. I have felt it important to try to articulate what is so often inarticulate. Being explicit in order to make it possible for someone to check on a claim or a belief about teaching is so desirable that being wrong every now and then is worth the risk.

It is obvious that teaching problems are different in the various disciplines. But just how different they are depends upon how dissimilar the disciplines are. Thus, although the teaching of physics inevitably requires a somewhat different approach than the teaching of psychology, these two, as empirically based disciplines, are taught in a more nearly similar fashion than are the classics and psychology. Teaching problems in psychology and sociology, or other behavioral and social sciences, tend to have much in common. I am convinced that an attempt to work out problems in any one field can be suggestive in others, particularly when these are closely related.

I have not dealt with certain topics which may be important to particular individuals. For example, the teaching of special topics or courses is not discussed except in one instance: there is a brief treatment of the experimental psychology course in an Appendix. This is included because there is promise of increasing generality in the use of the experimental approach for teaching many subject matters and because this problem is of particular interest to me. Nothing is offered on problems of graduate instruction, although I believe that much of what is said can be applied to it. Omitted also is any treatment of demonstrations, motion pictures, and other more or less mechanical aids to classroom instruction. The principles of instruction there are largely the same as for any other kind of material introduced into the classroom; furthermore, the use of such materials is so varied and so dependent upon a particular set of circumstances, that it is somewhat pretentious to try to state ideas peculiar to this set of techniques. (The intensive research on educational films now taking place, especially in the military laboratories, may soon change my views on this.)

The evolution of the manuscript for this book was greatly aided by criticisms made by Professor Frank W. Finger's seminar on teaching at the University of Virginia, and by students in my own seminars at Yale. To other psychologists with whom

I corresponded concerning the material in the Appendix (where they are named), I express my thanks. To three other scholars —the psychologist Professor Ernest R. Hilgard, the sociologist Professor Robert K. Merton, and the economist Professor Albert Gailord Hart—I am indebted for another kind of assistance. They suggested modifications in the presentation that make it easier for the scholar in related disciplines to examine what is said here and to note cross-references to writings on teaching by specialists in his own field.

I must also express my gratitude to Mrs. Susan R. Henry and Mrs. Dorothy L. Badger for their labors at the typewriter.

CLAUDE E. BUXTON

New Haven, May 1956

CONTENTS

1

THE DEVELOPMENT OF AMERICAN HIGHER EDUCATION

A complete understanding of present-day college education is presumably not to be achieved in a lifetime. Certainly, experiencing college for four years or graduate school for three does not guarantee such an understanding. Yet the beginning college teacher needs to know as much as he can about college education in general and, equally, about the place of his particular discipline in it. We shall therefore try to contribute to his understanding of education by analyzing its historical development as well as its current strengths and weaknesses. We shall discuss higher education in general, but make special references to undergraduate education; we shall then discuss the contributions the teaching of psychology can make to both.

The way such a discussion is written will obviously be influenced by the fact that a psychologist is doing the writing. Yet I hope that any reader who is not a psychologist will find relevance when he asks, "How does this apply to my own field?" The more closely related the reader's field is to psychology, the more easily will the question receive a meaningful answer. But it often happens that an understanding of a particular educational development is useful not only to a psychologist but also to a teacher in a field quite far removed from the social sciences.

MAIN TRENDS OF DEVELOPMENT

Any analysis of American higher education since the founding of Harvard in 1636 will show changes of many kinds, changes that are in many respects interrelated or interdependent, and that are to a great extent reflections of changes in our society. There is no simple way to categorize these changes, and we shall follow a somewhat arbitrary plan of presentation, stressing three trends.

Religious to secular. In many respects early collegiate-level education in this country, like many of its contemporary institutions, was dominated by Protestant sectarian beliefs and practices. As time went on new or different kinds of institutions were founded, society itself changed, and the religious influence gradually decreased, although not without struggle. It is preserved in a good many institutions still, but has in most colleges much less significance than it once had.

One way of documenting this change is to examine the intentions of the founders of the different institutions of higher education. It has often been remarked, for example, that the early privately founded institutions such as Princeton or Yale were intended to produce men fit to serve church and state, with service to the church being, if anything, the dominant note. It is now clear [137, p. 5] * that these early institutions were not seminaries. Nor did they require conformity to religious tenets for

* The bracketed numbers indicate original sources; see reference list on p. 381.

admission. Nevertheless, many different religious sects founded their own colleges and retained a controlling interest in many aspects of college affairs for generations thereafter. Even when the era of the publicly supported institutions began, some state universities came initially under the *de facto* domination of particular sects, rather than under public, nonsectarian control.

The success of the founders in providing for the religious ministry is perhaps best marked by the fact that in the early history of Harvard and Yale as many as 70 per cent of the graduates each year went into the ministry. And the change with the ensuing years is equally demonstrated by the drop of this proportion to approximately 10 per cent by the early nineteenth century.

By the middle of the eighteenth century society's respect for political or religious authority as such had decreased, and in education there developed increasing emphasis on practicality and professional specialization. Associated with such general changes was the establishment of special theological schools, either as subdivisions of what had previously been a college, or as a new type of independent institution. The sectarian need to create colleges was thus diverted and a new kind of founder motivation became increasingly evident: the feeling on the part of municipalities or states that they were responsible for providing educational opportunity at the college level to ensure its availability to all qualified persons. In the mid- and later nineteenth century this trend was marked, and many new institutions were created, not to serve religious needs but to further the exploration and communication of many kinds of knowledge.

Another sign of the decreasing significance of religion in college education has been the change in the place and function of extracurricular religious life on the campus. In the early days of the American college much of the campus life and most of the academic study was organized about, or was planned in the service of, churchly or at least Christian themes. Attendance at religious services for the student body was typically compulsory. In all ceremonials there was a strong religious note. But by the latter part of the nineteenth century, with the increasing rebellion against religious formalism or stricture noted above, religious domination of campus life decreased.

It should not be assumed that this came about without struggle. Just the opposite is true. Pierson, for example, records changes in the significance of chapel and reactions to these changes at Yale:

"Yale had lost all traces of monasticism at least as early as the Civil War. And its faith now had some rather special qualities. The chapel requirement, for example, had come into question. Despite an improved rotation of effective preachers, the Sunday services were not always inspiring; and it was noticed that the heartiest expression of religious feeling was apt to be the Doxology. As for daily chapel, that seemed hardly a religious service at all. A stranger would witness a gathering of some twelve or thirteen hundred students—the most massive congregation of young men in the country. But most of these worshippers shot into the aisle and rushed into their seats between eight and ten minutes past eight. Some kept their overcoats buttoned to conceal the fact that they were still only half dressed. Nearly all would have brought their books for their first recitation. And not a few, unless too near a faculty sentinel, would proceed to consult these texts, or the morning paper, during the service. As was whimsically recorded: 'If a sociable dog is lingering about Chapel between 8:05 and 8:10, the chances are against his being outside after 8:10. Nobody in particular calls him in, but there is a general air of hospitality through all the stream of worshippers, and he will flow innocently along with them and into the centre aisle.'

"Now much of daily chapel could offend a sensitive stranger. Indeed there were men at Yale who argued strenuously against such an abuse of religion. But more still defended. Chapel brought the whole College together under the President. It emphasized man's dependence on God, and the idealistic purpose of the institution. It also got every undergraduate out of bed. And the strongest consideration of all was the fact that the Seniors, after having been through it all, always voted that the custom should be continued." [211, pp. 12-13]

It is of course true that on many smaller campuses, and especially those still associated closely with a particular church, religious activities are today a prominent aspect of campus life. Interestingly enough, in certain places, including Yale, such activities have become endowed with the prestige that makes them desirable to socially and politically ambitious undergraduates. Yet it may safely be said that in the colleges in general religious life is of much less importance than it was in an earlier day. Of course, the degree of interest expressed in matters religious, or the extent of actual participation of students in such affairs, does fluctuate as a function of social climate (especially social stress, as in war or depression). Expressed religious interest also reflects the search for fundamentals of education by a faculty or student body, and is influenced by the way in which local tradition, alumni pressures, or boards of control change in character.

It was clear, within the curriculum of the early college, that American higher education reflected Protestant beliefs about what an educated man (one fit to become a minister) should know. This curriculum was largely centered about the classics, although, beginning around 1800, more and more stress was placed upon the sciences, mathematics, and other disciplines. Such subjects were listed as entrance requirements, and college consisted largely of an extension of the education begun in high school. It has been pointed out [137, pp. 11-17] that this general type of curriculum, given a treatment and an interpretation in the light of existing religious beliefs and aims, was well calculated to produce orthodoxy of belief and to turn out men who possessed a body of knowledge possessed by other men who were educated by the standards of the times. In a sense, it was assumed that there was a body of Christian knowledge, the prime responsibility of the college being merely to get it into the student, usually by rote learning and recitation methods. The crowning feature of the process of producing the Christian gentleman and scholar was typically the course in moral philosophy, taught to seniors by the president of the college, himself often a clergyman. This series of discourses upon Christian conduct and views upon life and society was presumed to complete the contribution of the curriculum to preparation of the individual for a life of social and moral responsibility.

As religious influence on the campus declined in other respects, so it declined in the curriculum which has just been described. Again, it was not without conflict and soul searching that educational requirements of religious sorts were removed, but the rebellion against such prescriptions and the pressure to permit individual reactions to religious questions were gradually effective. By and large, religious study in the usual college curriculum is now afforded by way of historical and comparative studies in the various religious beliefs. The typical curriculum committee would now shy away from the inclusion in the curriculum of subject matter for which emotional fervor or indoctrination was a dominant note. This intellectualizing of religious questions or problems seems to characterize even the recent proposals for educational programs to revive or return to religious considerations. Religious participation or practice is left largely to the extracurricular realm, and detailed studies of a religious sort are regarded as the responsibility of the theological school.

A final aspect of the gradual change of higher education from religious to secular may be found in the administration, control, and faculty-selection processes of American institutions. For example, the boards of control of the early colleges were mostly clergymen, but by 1860, McGrath [184] found, only about two-fifths of the members of boards of control of private institutions were clergy, and in 1930, about 7 per cent (see table below).

Proportions of Members of Boards of Control Representative of Various Occupational Groups

	PRIVATE INSTITUTIONS		PUBLIC INSTITUTIONS	
	1860	*1930*	*1860*	*1930*
Clergy	39	7	4	2
Businessmen	23	32	24	24
Bankers	5	20	4	13
Lawyers	21	21	39	30
Educators	5	10	9	4
Farmers	2	0	15	9

Selected data from McGrath [184]. His data are based on a representative group of institutions of the two types. His values are here rounded to the nearest whole number.

In the same period in the same institutions the total proportion of business-oriented board members rose from 28 to 52 per cent. While the clergy evidently have never been heavily represented in the boards of public institutions, the dominance of the business-oriented board member, established early, has increased somewhat. The more recent data of Beck [22] are consistent with the impressions given by McGrath's data.

These changes in the occupational origins of board members reflect of course the tremendous growth and increasing financial and social importance of banking, business, and industry. Gradually, men regarded as leaders in such fields came to be regarded as capable of leadership in others. In addition they possessed money which they might give and time which they could afford to give to the institutions to whose boards of control they were invited. In the extreme case, of course, this has led to the situation where every member of a board of control knows how to meet a payroll but few know much about education. Even in the less extreme cases however, and in institutions where such persons were invited to membership in boards of control precisely because they had long acquaintance with and deep knowledge of problems of education in addition to their competencies in business or industry, it has been inevitable that secular interests would in time come to distract from religious interests.

Another example of administrative change over the years may be found in the presidencies of colleges. Originally, of course, almost all presidents were clergymen, but gradually the practice of appointing clergymen waned, until by the end of the nineteenth century prominent presidencies were occupied by persons of many other backgrounds, among them a psychologist, a geographer, and a physicist. It should be remembered with respect to boards of control and chief administrative officers that there was a significant trend away from privately controlled and toward state or publicly controlled institutions. These, of course, were much less likely to depend upon sectarian leadership and in many instances were legally held to a clear separation of church from college. It is an interesting commentary upon our own times that in some instances a re-emphasis on the role of religion in higher education comes not from clerical but from lay leadership in important educational posts, as witness the expressed views of President Pusey of Harvard [218].

In summary, higher education has gradually changed from being purely private and sectarian to acknowledging public and general responsibility, except for certain institutions, the Roman Catholic in particular, which remain strongly sectarian to this day. Along with the change in the sphere of felt responsibility there has come a change in acceptance of control by forces or persons other than the sectarian ones of the early founding days.

At the present time there are certain interesting questions related to this acceptance of the secular role, or public responsibility and some degree of public control. One question which causes much debate is whether, in a time when private institutions are in difficult financial straits, they should seek the financial support of state or federal agencies. This question is not an appropriate one for full discussion in the present context, except to say that while much alarm is expressed at the possibility that accepting such money may mean yielding control of the private institution's affairs, much federal money has in fact been accepted in the form of veterans' allotments, research contracts and subsidies, subsidies for fellowships and training programs, and the like. The pressures on the accepting institutions appear to be no greater than those already exerted by alumni groups or wealthy prospective individual donors or those likely to be exerted by the large corporations organized for systematic giving to higher education, whose support is so eagerly sought.

Another question has to do with the wisdom of placing in control of educational institutions persons who do not know intimately the problems of such institutions. Such persons are sometimes found in high administrative posts and more often in boards of control. It has been pointed out [137, p. 129] that control over the educational profession in this country is an odd arrangement, compared to control over other professions. Educators from the beginning have had little to say about the management of the institutions in which they work, and thus about the management of their own careers. This differs sharply from the kind of control exhibited in the legal or medical professions, where it would hardly be regarded as appropriate for a controlling body of laymen to judge what was fitting and proper conduct. It is true that sporadically in some institutions, e.g., Harvard, according to President Lowell [169], faculty representatives have sat on boards of control, but this is not generally the case. As a consequence, there are difficult problems of communication between faculty and board, or between president and board, even though in many instances boards of control must directly or indirectly pass upon the merits of educational questions, as when financial decisions affecting educational programs are made. Perhaps the problem was illustrated most graphically in recent times by the dismissal of George D. Stoddard from the presidency of the University of Illinois. The successful surprise motion for a no-confidence vote at a meeting of the board of trustees was made by a former All-American football player who had been elected to that board. After Mr. Stoddard's forced resignation was denounced by various persons, including some twenty department heads of his own university, the Governor of Illinois explained [202] in justification of the board's action that Mr. Stoddard had become prone to make educational policy, which usurped the functions of the (lay) board of trustees.

Elite to popular. As secularization in American higher education has increased, there has been an accompanying increase in the degree to which education has been intended not for the few but for the great body of youth.

We have noted that the early curriculum was primarily classical in character, consisting of such subjects as Latin language and literature, Greek language and literature, perhaps Hebrew and some mathematics, with such later additions as geography, higher mathematics, history, and English grammar. This kind of curriculum was not closely related to the economic or the practical life of the seventeenth or early eighteenth century. It was sought in the main by students whose families could afford the luxury of having a son study matters which would not yield a direct increment to family income or resources. The curriculum, in fact, did not even relate very closely to the personal as distinguished from the vocational life of the so-called educated man, either during the college years themselves or in later life, so that the expression "gentleman *and* scholar," with its implication that the two were different aspects of the same individual, was unfortunately reinforced.

There were, however, many pressures against the restrictive

concept that higher education was intended for an elite group. For example, the expansion of American society, with increasing differentiation of occupations and professions, tremendously increased the need for knowledge of all rather than just the classical kinds. This need for knowledge, and the multiplying examples of the value of knowledge, led to a higher valuation upon all kinds of education, and not merely for a select group of individuals. As American society expanded there was a tremendous push for social, political, and geographic mobility which led to the creation of many new institutions, among them increasingly more that were controlled by municipal or state bodies. These many new institutions tended to reflect the characteristics of their founders, the needs of the place and times, and the demands of the students. A wider group had to be served with an education dedicated in part to the prevalent push for mobility.

It is an interesting commentary on our history that competition, both between states and between communities with real-estate or trade booms or aspirations, was an important factor in the founding of many colleges and universities. This at once reflects the prestige value which gradually became attached to education as such and suggests the kinds of pressures upon educational programs which were exerted from the date of founding of these institutions.

It further became clear, in the growth of our particular society, that what has been called American pragmatism was to be a significant force in education as well as in politics and other aspects of life. Usefulness was not an important standard for the early classical curriculum, but it gradually became an important criterion for many people both inside and outside the institutions of higher education. The range of subjects made available for study therefore multiplied even faster than did the number and kinds of educational institutions, and in some instances reached the point of absurdity. Flexner [109] in 1930 had considerable fun compiling and remarking upon some of the course titles and research topics he was able to find in educational literature, and the situation is probably much the same today.

In association with the pragmatic tendency in our society and in our educational systems, it is the belief of Hofstadter [137, pp. 109-14] that there is another American tendency which has been of peculiar significance in shaping our educational pattern. This is what he calls "youth cultism": the tendency to look upon the period of youth as a golden era in life, of wishing generally to be youthful, and of encouraging youthful behavior. Such attitudes or motivation in the culture lead to high valuation of the college years as providing opportunity for favorable and protected development and maximum encouragement to the youth of the nation. This particular influence upon education will, of course, work in precisely the opposite manner from a value upon maturity, stability, and fixity of purpose, and in Hofstadter's view it has increased the utilitarian and popular character of education.

Another kind of pressure upon education to break away from its limitation to an elite group and a particular classical curriculum came from the increasing industrialization and urbanization of our culture. Particularly was there an increase in technological knowledge and an insatiable demand for more such knowledge. In the mid- and later nineteenth century, responding to this demand and creating it as well, there came great developments in science in this country and even more in Europe. Thus there was available for importation and exploitation a tremendous flood of pure and applied knowledge not included in the old curriculum or directly sought by most persons who studied that curriculum. Many American scholars studied in Europe and brought back the new interests and knowledge. Inevitably much of the new knowledge was incorporated in programs of higher education and was sought by many aspirants to upward mobility in the social and business worlds. This trend was accentuated by the formal inauguration of the land-grant college system with the passage of the Morrill Act in 1857 and the ensuing development of state-supported institutions catering to as many residents of the state as were minimally qualified for an interested in the newer programs of education.

It is generally remarked that the great growth in size and numbers of American institutions has been made possible in part because in this country there has been more of an economic margin to be devoted to the development of education than has been the case in many other countries. This point is reinforced by citing the proportion of school graduates who go to college, in this country and elsewhere, and by citing comparisons of total numbers of institutions or total numbers of students. Yet in 1850 President Wayland at Brown University was pointing out that colleges of that era had lost the support of the public and had chosen to go begging for the money on which to operate [137, p. 25]. Wayland frankly said that in his view the colleges should "adapt the article produced" to the needs of the community, i.e., arrange the program of the student at least partly with a view to his future participation in the vocational and governmental life of his community. Thus, to gain support from the public, even the private and well-established institutions had begun to conform to the pressure to serve a wider population and, through educational programs, to meet needs that were not met by the classical curriculum.

Perhaps the most impressive way of indicating the great shift from elite to popular higher education is simply to cite enrollment figures. The accompanying data from surveys of the United States Office of Education make it abundantly clear that of the group judged most eligible (by age) for college education, the proportion actually resident in an institution of higher education is steadily increasing. According to Conant [77] this proportion is presently higher than in any other country except Canada.

Year	*Enrollment*	*Percentage of population aged 18 to 21 years who were resident in college*
1890	156,756	3.04
1900	237,592	4.01
1910	355,213	4.84
1920	597,880	8.14
1930	1,100,737	12.37
1934	1,055,360	11.46
1938	1,350,905	14.38
1942	1,403,990	14.25
1946	1,214,772 (nonveterans)	12.74
	1,676,851 (including veterans)	
1950	1,730,023 (nonveterans)	19.27
	2,659,021 (including veterans)	
1952	1,878,268 (nonveterans)	21.92
	2,301,884 (including veterans)	

Some veterans were in the 18-21-year group; the estimated percentages of the population resident in college for 1946 and later are therefore underestimates. Data taken from [268].

General to specialized. The early curriculum may be spoken of as general in character, on the basis of at least three different interpretations. First, it encompassed most of the kinds of knowledge regarded as fitting signs of education. It was thus general to the expected intellectual world of the individual receiving it. Second, it could also be called general, by intention at least, because the doctrine of formal discipline underlay educational practice in a very systematic and pervasive way. Thus it was felt that the exercise of the supposed mental faculties, such as reasoning or memory or imagination, by study of the difficult disciplines of Greek or Hebrew, fortified the mental powers of the individual so that he was prepared to deal with problems he might confront as lay or clerical citizen. It is true that the initial pressures to expand the curriculum led to the introduction of history, more modern literatures, and so on, but these subjects were carefully scrutinized to discern their supposed disciplinary value. In the third place the early curriculum was general in the sense of being largely prescribed and taken in common by all students in the college.

Against this conception of the proper education for a gentleman were many of the pressures already referred to as stemming from an expanding and differentiating society. Of particular relevance here were certain influences not discussed explicitly earlier. One of these was the fact that as the range of knowledge, especially that in science and technology, increased in scope it was progressively more difficult for a single individual to be a general scholar, or even a general scientist—the fields of learning became progressively more fractionated and specialized. As special areas of interest developed, they tended to become professional fields in their own right, and those who concentrated in them developed deep personal identifications with them. Parallel to this development, in a sense producing it, was the development and wider acceptance of the concept of inquiry, of research. According to this idea, knowledge was not merely to be acquired in rote fashion from materials already set down in the book, but was something to be sought, to be expanded, or to be created by the educated person. The university idea of a community of scholars gave strong impetus to development of the spirit of inquiry in this country's institutions. And finally, in Pierson's judgment [210], there were pressures for freedom in education which were but part of a broader change toward freedom in economic enterprise, universal suffrage, and the elimination of social and class barriers. These influences all caused the early curriculum to be regarded, by the mid-nineteenth century if not long before, as narrow and restrictive in its influence, and as giving an incomplete picture of the available learning.

One of the first adjustments made to this situation by college authorities was a reduction of the degree of prescription in the programs of advanced students. First the seniors, and, gradually through the years to the beginning of the twentieth century, the earlier classes in the college, were permitted progressively more free electives in their programs. This change too was not something which came about easily, but rather involved many a hard-fought battle in faculty meetings, and many a frustrated student petition for variety in the curriculum. Many college programs changed very little in the direction of free electives, as Pierson indicates, or practical problems made such change slower than might have been wished. One view of the wisdom of permitting the student to elect courses, from an institution which took the lead in adopting the elective system, is that of President Lowell, writing in 1887: "For a score of years the college has been surrendering the selection of the studies to be pursued by undergraduates more and more into the hands of the students themselves, and in so doing it has, in fact, made three assumptions, upon the correctness of which the wisdom of this policy must depend. The first assumption is that the student will work harder upon a subject selected by himself than upon one which has been prescribed for him by the faculty. The second is that he will choose a course of study corresponding more closely with his individual needs than any curriculum that can be fixed by the college, and the third is that the responsibility cast upon the student and the experience which he will gain by exercising it will be themselves potent factors in his education. The first of these assumptions is, no doubt, correct, but the second and third are true only in case the student has knowledge enough of his own mental strength and weakness and sufficiently clear views upon the general principles of education to make a really wise selection, and in case he is willing to give the subject a serious and careful consideration." [169, p. 3]

The misgivings of President Lowell were reflected in many colleges by a reaction against the concept of extended free elections which took the form of a system of majors, or majors and minors. This kind of system, familiar in most institutions today, ensures certain common elements of education, usually in the first two college years, requires a certain degree of concentration, usually in the last two years, via a major subject or program, and controls the extent to which elective studies are permitted to fill in the gaps in this program. Thus, while American institutions have not retained in original form the idea that a prescribed and general course of study was appropriate for all students, it is fairly clear, and emphasized by contemporary adherents to certain forms of general education program, that an element of the idea remains: We should like to permit allowance for individual differences in student interests and capabilities, and still retain an unambiguous conception of what an educated man is. Furthermore, it cannot be said that the mental discipline view has been entirely abandoned, for it lingers on in discussions of general education and elective systems.

A second kind of development away from the early notion that one general kind of higher education would do for all was the growth, especially in the latter part of the nineteenth century, of specialized schools associated with the earlier college, or arising in the newly founded universities or land-grant institutions. Schools of commerce, forestry, home economics, veterinary medicine, and so on, are now commonplace. Such an institution as Harvard created schools of business and graduate study, and had previously created special schools of medicine, dentistry, law, and theology. Cornell University was founded to meet the needs of any citizen qualified to enter. Some of the new institutions, among them Stanford, Chicago, and Vanderbilt, were founded as universities and contained from the start special branches offering curriculums adapted to particular interests or groups of students. By 1910, the university idea, at least in its American form, was well established, and all kinds of education for all kinds of people was the American pattern.

As is to be expected, the fragmentation of institutions of higher education into a multitude of special schools (as well as departments of instruction, research institutes, and so on) exerted an influence upon the college. The specialized branches of the university, and of knowledge, made available much new material and many new kinds of scholars for roles in the college curriculum. And, in clear conformity with the American pragmatic tendency to shape education to socially useful, and especially to vocational, ends, pressure increased upon the college to permit its students to study those aspects of knowledge which would prepare them for so-called real life, especially the world of business and the special professions.

Summary. We have, today, a situation in which higher education has developed manifold branches and forms, so that while the classical curriculum may still be offered in some manner or other in many institutions, it tends to be embedded in or overshadowed by a very great variety of educational offerings and programs. The modern institution has developed to the point where it feels that it has public responsibility. It is sensitive to the needs of the local and national community and adaptive to the welfare of not merely a religiously oriented elite group but rather a wide variety of persons in a largely secular culture. The strength of the modern college or university lies in its close kinship to the aspirations of, if not all the people, a considerable segment of them, and in the degree to which, whatever its faults, it has been able to aid so many of the people in so many ways.

PSYCHOLOGY'S PLACE IN HIGHER EDUCATION

Against the background of what has happened in education as a whole in this country, especially during the past 70 years or so, it is interesting to review what has happened in psychology. We can go no further back than approximately 1880, since that is the beginning of the period in which scientific psychology was taught in recognizable or formally labeled fashion in America. Prior to this, of course, psychology was always taught as an aspect of philosophy, either in special courses or as a component of, particularly, the mental or moral philosophy course. However, most present-day psychologists are inclined to think of the psychology thus presented as prescientific, at least preexperimental, and thus more closely kin to British associationism and other philosophical schools of psychology than to the kind of science-oriented discipline in which we like to claim our roots are to be found.

It seems to be very clear that psychology was one of the very disciplines to which we have referred previously as being involved in the inrush of science and technology, especially from Europe, toward the latter part of the nineteenth century. Wolfe [284], for example, wrote in 1895 urging the appropriateness of the "new" psychology for inclusion in undergraduate programs. French [112] wrote in the same general vein in 1898, but was not positive enough, in Cattell's view [65]. As is well established, the most important early scientific psychology in this country was Wundtian and introspectionist in character. It continued to be so, in spite of functionalist reaction here and there, through at least 1910, when Mary Whiton Calkins could still write that no matter why any student should wish to study psychology, the purpose of the study should be to give him a firm scientific introduction to himself through (almost exclusively) introspective methodology [244]. This view was quite congenial to Ruckmich [229] also. In 1891 Krohn [160] and in 1894 Delabarre [83] published summaries of information secured through the use of questionnaires, showing that the prime interest of American psychologists was in establishing laboratories, putting psychology on a firm scientific footing, and getting research and advanced study under way. As progress was made in these respects, undergraduate offerings became more numerous and psychology courses, particularly in the upper college years, became one of the more attractive electives. In due time psychology achieved the at times dubious honor of being required for graduation.

The content of those early courses is of contemporary interest. Krohn's report indicates, for example, that at the University of Chicago in 1891 a twelve-week introductory course was offered, meeting five times per week. It dealt with the anatomy and physiology of the nervous system and the sense organs, plus William James' *Briefer Course.* Following this there was a reading course for two terms, using James' *Principles of Psychology* and having an accompanying laboratory. At Clark there was a so-called practical course, in which some 300 experiments on classical topics were performed, these presumably being introspective and demonstrational in character. The class met for three afternoons per week. There were also lectures on physiological psychology throughout the year, and these were related to the practical course. In addition, Clark offered a course dealing with such topics as instinct, dreams, hypnotism, and psychological aspects of anthropology, as well as a weekly conference which apparently could be adapted as students and instructor saw fit. Harvard at that time was offering a one-term introductory course and a so-called beginner's course meeting three hours per week throughout the year, with weekly demonstrations to groups of approximately ten students. Wisconsin appeared to have one of the most complete formal curricula. It offered courses in general psychology (the mind-body problem, mental disease, sensory processes, psychic phenomena, etc.), experimental psychology (five hours per week, two terms), advanced experimental psychology, comparative psychology, abnormal psychology, and anthropological psychology. (It is somewhat difficult to determine, from some reports of courses, whether they were all open to undergraduates or whether some of them were reserved only for graduate students.)

Both Krohn's and Delabarre's reports make it very plain that psychology was from the beginning a specialized discipline. It was intent on making obvious its separation from philosophy, the discipline with which it was most often fused in the beginning, and from education, with which it was often fused administratively. It was an appealing entry in the list of free electives, appearing to promise a means of satisfying student curiosity about various previously unstudied topics. To illustrate, the material on abnormal psychology, psychic phenomena, and dreams, offered in courses at Wisconsin, Iowa, Clark, and elsewhere, in the early days, must have been viewed as a rather special supplement to the previously orthodox or even austere curriculum of those institutions. At Iowa, furthermore, there was a one-term course on memory, consisting half of theory and half of special practice. By providing such materials and serving the varied interests of students, psychology, like so many other disciplines, had certain utilitarian aspects along with its stern and generally uncompromising scientific rigor.

Another kind of parallel between psychological developments and those in undergraduate education generally may be found in the influence of the graduate school upon undergraduate work. The men who founded the laboratories, who fought the fight for independence from philosophy and education, and nurtured the special science of psychology in its infancy, were also the men who wished to train more psychologists to carry on the work. It was almost inevitable, then, that graduate or professional standards should govern much of what was done at the undergraduate level. Thus our courses even at the present time carry, in many instances, the labels of professional subfields as these first developed in psychology: for example, educational psychology, or experimental psychology, or individual differences. Here and there over the country undergraduate psychology offerings at all levels are planned independently of requirements for entrance to graduate school or independently of the standards of the psychological profession at large. But it is safe to say that national and graduate standards and the national professional societies, in psychology as in chemistry and other scientific fields, have greatly influenced both the kind and level of work offered to undergraduates, particularly in all courses beyond the most elementary ones.

Psychology has always been one of the disciplines appealing to popular tastes, and within the colleges and universities it is typical of the disciplines that contribute to mass education. Perhaps psychology cannot be said to have come along in time to have contributed much to the revolt against the elite concept of education, but it has indeed played a part in the exposure of a large proportion of our population to both science and a more or less practical subject matter. Reference was made above to signs of this in even the earliest psychological course offerings. The move toward popular education in psychology has, however, gone further in recent years in the deliberate attempt, as illustrated by Ruch's very successful introductory text [228], to find out from the students what they most want to learn and then give it to them. Following Ruch's very successful effort many other texts or courses were modified in this direction. This popularization tendency presumably contributed in goodly measure to the tremendous enrollments in psychology courses, especially following World War II, when in various institutions of the country lecture classes reached almost preposterous dimensions, some of them containing more than 1,000 students. It has at the same time caused much concern among psychologists over whether educational standards in psychology have been lowered unduly.

It is noteworthy that psychology also contributed to the extracurricular aspects of development in colleges and universities, especially in the realm of services to students or faculty. Testing skills and services were made available for many purposes; counseling services and therapeutic services were developed. These and many other psychological influences helped to shape the character of the institution of higher education. In laying a groundwork for the so-called student personnel point of view, psychology has had a very great but not as yet adequately evaluated impact, particularly in the publicly supported institutions.

Finally, it should not go unnoted that the break of higher education away from the conception that generality of education was achieved through mental discipline was in large part reinforced or accelerated through the research findings of psychologists who were themselves teachers.

For the present it will serve our purposes to summarize these comments about psychology's role in the development of American higher education by saying that it, like the rest of education, has been or is almost altogether secular in character (with a few exceptions, especially in the Roman Catholic institutions), that it has contributed to the widespread movement to bring education of all kinds and degrees of purity or practicality to masses of people, and that it has shared in the tendency to be specialized, compartmentalized, and professionalized in its presentation and orientation at the undergraduate level.

OTHER SOCIAL SCIENCES IN HIGHER EDUCATION

Developments in psychology have not been unique; comparable trends have been noted for all the closely related social science disciplines. For example [267], the period in which psychology had its rapid initial development in this country, from about 1880 on, marked also the beginnings of instruction in sociology. The first course in this subject was offered at Yale in 1876; the first professorship was created at Indiana in 1883; and the first formal department of sociology was formed at Chicago in 1893. Anthropology began to be recognized in almost exactly the same period, with a chair being created at Harvard in 1885 and the first active department at Clark in 1888 [270]. Economics can be said to have been offered first at William and Mary in about 1790, when Adam Smith's *The Wealth of Nations* was used as text material in a course on moral philosophy [267]; it appears, however, that only a few institutions began work in economics during the next three-quarters of a century, so that it, like the other social sciences, had its great initial development in the last quarter of the nineteenth century.

In each of these disciplines, and in political science as well, there was a notable influence of German training and scholarship before and after the turn of the century, just as in psychology. There was also a notable increase in specialization, as reflected in numbers and kinds of courses offered. For example, Bernard [28] indicates that in a sample of 219 institutions, there were 718 sociology courses in 1909, but 2,683 in 1940-44. There was a fivefold increase in the number of hours of economics offered in colleges and universities, between 1910-11 and 1925-26 [261]. In anthropology there appears [270] to have been an increase from some 57 courses offered in this country in 1901 to a total of 1,930 offered in this country and Canada in 1948-50. And in addition to becoming progressively more specialized or fractionated, these fields, like psychology, served continually increasing proportions of the total undergraduate population at the expense of classical subjects, in both elementary and advanced courses. In many colleges, the social science departments assumed a dominating position because of the sheer size of their faculties and the student load they carried.

2

CRITICISMS AND ISSUES IN HIGHER EDUCATION

For many people in recent years it has been a pastime, for some almost an avocation, to criticize education. The general public has exhibited dissatisfaction with secondary education, and the college faculty has joined in complaints that too little, and much of that the wrong sort, is accomplished there [32, 242]. Both alumni groups and faculty members have been quick with critical comment concerning higher education, as in the enjoyable, yet pointed, book by Barzun [20]. For various reasons the public has been concerned with the possibility that higher education contains or conceals influences harmful to our national security or way of life. Perhaps it is reasonable to say that such criticism, particularly when thoughtfully given, is always healthy, and may merely reflect conservative opinion about the challenging ideas of educators engaged in the free pursuit of truth. Certainly it is to be expected that such criticism, thoughtful or not, will reflect in both amount and fervor the temper of the times generally, and since these are troubled times we should expect concern about such a significant phase of the national life as education.

In reviewing these comments, we shall note that criticisms from various sources are not always consistent. Part of the trouble is that the critics honestly stand for different values in education, and part is that the criticism would not be made were the critic more familiar with the object of his concern. This latter statement applies of course to the lay critic, but may apply perfectly well also to the professor in the graduate school who objects to undergraduate programs, or to the professor in a given specialty who is dissatisfied with what appear to him to be the pretensions of persons in another specialty. We must therefore examine the criticisms thoughtfully, search for the relevant replies, and then determine how the results of our analysis apply to what has been done in the name of psychology.

Complexity and diffuseness of purpose. One of the first criticisms, which Jones has graphically described in detail [151, p. 217 and following], is that in its tremendous growth spurt the American educational institution, especially the college and university, has lost its identity. Just exactly what it is, is difficult to determine. Condensing Jones' comments we may note, for example, that institutions vary in size from more than 40,000 students down to a thousandth of that number. The number of faculty members available to work with these students may be large enough to permit much attention to individual work, in such large institutions as Harvard or in certain smaller colleges. It may also happen that no individual attention is possible at all, in certain large institutions or in small understaffed colleges. Financial resources are not closely correlated with size of institution, nor is the kind of name attached to it. Universities are sometimes small institutions offering only the bachelor degree, and colleges are sometimes large institutions offering the Ph.D. and other specialized degrees. In many instances the word university, or college, is used to name an institution which is almost solely vocational or trade oriented in character, or which "educates" by mail in a short period, or which offers in residence intensive short courses or other special programs different from the usual four-year bachelor's degree program. Just to confuse things properly, at Yale the word college has a still different meaning, according to which it designates what would be called dormitories in other institutions in this country, although to be sure Yale's colleges are not quite dormitories either, for they in various ways have developed limited educational programs and extensive and organized extracurricular programs. With all these variations in institutional nature, it becomes obvious that a college degree, particularly at the bachelor's level, has no standard meaning.

The immediate significance of all this lies in the fact that in ways almost too complex to analyze, the good and the bad, the worthwhile and pointless, the genuine and shoddy, the intellectual and other, are mixed in contemporary education. Only the most thoughtful and systematic of faculties, with the consent of the wiser boards of control, have kept their programs straight and describable, their objectives clearly stated, their degree-granting activities unambiguous. There is, of course, merit in the statement that what an institution is called, or how it is organized or run, does not matter so long as it gives something of value to students who come to it. The unfortunate fact in American life is, however, that college degrees have high social and financial value. Through a sort of halo effect, the academic label is far too often presumed to indicate a person educated to various kinds of competence, adequate to the assumption of various kinds of responsibility, and capable of living a rich as well as a useful existence. The existence of such unjustified presumptions shows it to be essential that the objectives of various kinds of higher education be clarified, and that purposes and methods be understood by a wider range of the public. Most important of all is the obvious need to re-examine the concept of education itself and to decide where it fits within our culture. We shall discuss this question more fully in the next chapter.

Utilitarianism. We have referred earlier to the force of the demand for usefulness in education. In America, learning has not, on the whole, been fostered for its own sake or for its contributions to the enjoyment of life. Instead, particularly during the period of expansion of educational institutions and in the present, it has been fostered because it led to other ends, such as making a living, becoming politically or socially effective, or being technologically or professionally competent. Furthermore, most of these goals have been regarded as justifying any means by which they may be reached. Within this kind of logic it is simple to expect that education, along with family upbringing and other institutional experiences, is to be dedicated to utilitarian ends. Indeed, it is sometimes believed even now that a college faculty should be dedicated, not to a search for truth and the communication of this search and its product to each new generation, but rather to maintaining such specific socially accepted ideas as that of free enterprise. In this instance, of course, indoctrination is proposed to be a primary aim of education (see further discussions of this problem, p. 83 and p. 279). The dangers of this view are illustrated by the role of demagoguery and propaganda in the German education of the 1930s.

There is a widespread belief that education should be responsive, especially in the tax-supported or land-grant institutions, to the demands of the public. This has led to what Flexner [109] calls the service-station concept of education, according to which everything is taught or done for some group which is sufficiently vocal or sufficiently large to press for it. In addition, of course, the service-station concept in many of the larger institutions has led to the auxiliary provision of extension services, short courses, specialized conferences, soil-testing or animal-clinic services, and an entire host of arrangements which while truly serving the people confuse our concept of an educational institution. To confuse matters further, the tendency in certain traditional college-level disciplines has been to search out and offer courses with vocational uses, to stress the choice of a major as related primarily to vocational plans, and to regard as educationally significant that which is in reality merely practical. A side effect of all this is to compound the numbers of courses and objectives in the college, adding to the diffuseness of purpose.

Another aspect of the demand for utility is the belief that everyone in a democratic society should have schooling. In many states this has led to the belief that anyone who can manage to go through high school should be permitted to go to college and should find something there of use to him. Unfortunately, legal requirements of attendance at school up to a certain age have resulted, in a great many school systems, in an automatic kind of promotion by which the student who has not made much progress is nevertheless moved forward so that in due time he may be declared a graduate. One can easily say this is the fault of the schools. It is perhaps more to the point to say that it is the fault of a society which places high value upon school experience but does not permit its school systems to divert, drop, or reclassify those pupils who are not reasonably adequate to respond to stimulation of such a level that all remaining pupils would make fast educational progress. Be that as it may, the effect of the pressure to keep most youngsters in school and to provide them with a variety of programs to serve their probable future needs has been to lower the standards of achievement in many of the disciplines which should serve as a basis for higher education. In addition, many individual programs simply do not include any instruction in those disciplines, even for students who will later present themselves for admission to college. In the opinion of many college faculty members, the push of school education to satisfy immediate and expressed demands for usefulness has led to a definite lowering of college-level educational standards. This is illustrated by the necessity for the colleges to use part of their available program to make up deficiencies in the preparation of their students.

All these trends are expressions of the pressure toward usefulness defined in a particular way. We must not overlook other definitions. No one would criticize the utilitarianism implied in the development of competent professional training in medicine, or law, or divinity. Nor can one criticize the development of the strictly trade or vocational school, with its lack of pretension to any objectives other than preparing an individual to earn his living in a particular way. Because usefulness can be defined in various ways, then, to meet the criticism that utilitarianism weakens modern education a necessary step will be to distinguish between the different kinds of usefulness in education, to designate clearly just which programs or institutions have set which kinds of goals, and then to attach discriminable labels to them. At that point society may begin to learn how much value it should attach to the different kinds of approach. Utilitarianism in what is probably its worst meaning, that of short-sighted attention to narrowly defined and practical objectives, is to be found in varying degrees everywhere in American education, and any proposed revision of educational offerings to avoid such a problem will encounter inertia, if not distress, among many faculty members.

It is possible to analyze the role or function of psychology in the college in light of the criticism of utility for its own sake. It can be said immediately that most psychology teachers are aware of the student pressure for usefulness ("When will we get to something practical in this course . . . ?") and many of them are strongly motivated to accede to this pressure, if only as a device for getting hold of and later turning to other, presumably educationally sounder, purposes the initial strong student interest. As stated in Chapter 1, there is no doubt that many heavily practical courses have been invented and offered by psychologists. Yet it is clear that on the issue of utility psychologists are still very much in conflict among themselves.

I have referred elsewhere [55] to the view of people like Berrien [30], Remmers [222], and Pressey [215] that psychological teaching is always to be assessed in large part for its direct usefulness to the student, whether that student will become teacher, homemaker, or business man, and Ericksen [102] has considered it essential that at least one senior course be devoted to such ends. In contrast, Keller and Schoenfeld [154], in describing their teaching at Columbia, evidently are not greatly concerned with practicality. The trend in elementary textbooks, as mentioned previously, clearly exhibits conflict both among authors and within the writings of most authors. While there is an effort to provide materials meeting the student's particular standards of usefulness, there is at the same time a recurrent attitude that some more general goal, such as an understanding of science, is simultaneously being pursued (if only to pacify the instructors who might adopt the text). One attempt to solve this problem is that of Wolfle and his associates [288]. Their particular proposal is to label certain kinds of psychology courses as vocational or practical in character, and set them apart from other aspects of the program. Their further intention is that the vocational or practical courses would not be elected by the majority of students, but rather that this majority would be brought (largely by the quality of instruction, we may infer) to accept the objectives of other, more liberally defined kinds of courses. Whether such a proposal can be made to work in an institution which itself reflects mainly utilitarian goals is a question which remains to be answered.

It may be remarked also that, although graduate and professional education in psychology for a variety of reasons are directed much more than undergraduate education toward certain kinds of utility, there nevertheless has been a conflict at the graduate level between these objectives and those of science. The socially acceptable compromise has been to declare that even in the Ph.D. programs which are typically applied in their intent, as in clinical psychology in most universities, the scientific approach is to be stressed. Rogers [226] has written both keenly and movingly about this conflict for the person oriented toward the practice of psychotherapy.

It is not only in psychology that utilitarianism has been a matter of concern or even conflict, for the other social sciences have had the same problem. For example, political scientists have reported that their students seemed to aspire primarily to practical learning, particularly in relation to vocation [267]. The first ten objectives listed by students included preparation for law, politics, public relations work, government service, graduate study, business, and so on, and, in fifth place, preparation for citizenship. The faculty members polled very clearly put general preparation for citizenship in a higher position among their objectives. It is true that they recognized the importance of usefulness of what is taught, but the difference in emphasis between students and faculty reflects and helps determine a difference of opinion among political scientists themselves about their primary teaching aims [6].

Perhaps the most general way of expressing dissatisfaction with the urge for utility which characterizes so much of college education is to say that in time of social stress we begin to realize clearly that the kind of utility achieved in the service-station development of higher education is not necessarily the kind of utility most important for the life of a citizen or for the welfare of a democratic society. The widespread sentiment, for example, that moral considerations must again become paramount in questions of diplomacy, or in relationships between individuals, leads directly to dissatisfaction with the dominant utilitarianism in education. The majority of psychologists are probably serene in the face of such problems and firm in their belief either that science and scientists are not concerned with them, or that it is more realistic to teach what can be instrumental in a relatively immediate or obvious way in the life of the student. To the extent that these criticisms are valid, present-day psychology is not meeting directly the problems residing in the relation between education and society. (Many activities of members of the Society for the Psychological Study of Social Issues are exceptions to the state of affairs here criticized.)

Lack of coherence. It is said that education in many institutions is now measured by accounting methods. That is, the definition of the bachelor's degree is that so many courses have been passed, and that they have been distributed over the available curriculum according to formulas which require courses chosen from certain groups of disciplines (usually, from among their elementary courses only) or certain varieties of skills. The rules do not necessarily require that anything learned is to be remembered for long, or to be related to other bits of learning. There is perhaps considerable hope that somewhere in the learning is something practical. Under the conception that knowledge comes ready-made in course-sized packages, the student can concentrate his efforts upon passing term examinations and securing term marks, typically in a goodly number of subject matters in any given term, with little chance or stimulus for discovering relationships which are not purely intradisciplinary.

Such an education is organized around nothing in particular. There is no framework upon which to place and consider the ideas encountered. Conflicting ideas tend to be accepted in turn, without full attention to the conflict or its significance. The contribution of specific disciplines or experiences to a more general set of attitudes and ideas which will help the student meet new situations or information is not worked out. The fact that reality or the world is whole, not broken down into convenient or arbitrary segments corresponding to college courses or disciplines, is simply not appreciated. The student does not even know what he does not know.

It is true that in an earlier era the Christian religious theme provided a central organizing concept. Other kinds of organizational concepts have been tried as the religious one was found wanting, among them the theme of society's needs, the theme of the individual's needs, the theme of Western cultural and social tradition, and so on. And at a less ambitious level, the patterns of interrelationship within small groups of disciplines, or pairs of disciplines, have more commonly been sought in jointly offered courses or courses under a departmental label by a person with interdisciplinary interests. These themes or organizing concepts or searches for communality of ideas have evidently developed in response to a felt need for integration, a word for which no good substitute has yet been found. But by and large this need is not now met at the college level.

The mass production methods necessary in so many institutions carry with them many of the shortcomings mentioned above. Mass production also can place certain additional obstacles in the way of coherent or integrated educational development. One is that any system for dealing with large numbers of students runs the danger of becoming impersonal. This impersonality, particularly as it refers to lack of contact between student and teacher, makes it especially difficult for even the able student to shape his education into a meaningful and connected pattern. Books can, after all, only facilitate integration. Each student must personally and finally achieve it according to the way in which he has already started to view the world, the resources he has to command, the way he assimilates what he has experienced, and so on. Contact with instructors who can analyze his problems and adapt to them where written materials cannot, surely must be important in the student's attempts to see for himself an orderly and meaningful world.

In addition, one of the most unfortunate aspects of mass

production methods, administered with the aid of rules printed in college catalogues and without much leeway for individual interpretation of the rules, is their rigidity or uniformity. It is surprising to learn that in a large institution with a very wide variety of offerings and seemingly great variety in student programs, the students graduate in clusters of dozens or hundreds from programs in which particular course sequences or patterns are largely the same for all because these appear to be the ones available, or the ones expected in satisfaction of degree requirements. Since the election of such programs occurs largely under impersonal circumstances and with no particular organizing theme (except the vocational one, perhaps) it is highly unlikely that these students will later exhibit the superior retention and more effective functioning of college learning which is presumed to result from a coherent or interrelated learning experience.

Within the discipline of psychology it is clear that the charge of lack of coherence is generally applicable. It applies to the elementary course which, if it follows leading texts such as Munn [200], Ruch [228], or Hilgard [136], teaches a little bit of almost everything but does not hang it on any clear-cut theoretical, scientific, or other framework. That I am not original, and possibly not altogether fair, in charging such texts with lack of coherence is shown by the reaction of William James a goodly number of years ago: he found it necessary, in the preface to the abridged version of his *Principles of Psychology* to note that "my critics . . . have been unanimous in one reproach, namely, that my order of chapters is planless and unnatural. . . . The order of composition is doubtless unshapely, or it would not be found so by so many. But planless it is not, for I deliberately followed what seemed to me a good pedagogic order. . . ." [149] Yet books such as the one by Keller and Schoenfeld [155] or Muenzinger [199] are written partly as a reaction against heterogeneity.

The charge may equally well be made upon examination of

almost any undergraduate curriculum in psychology. Such an examination readily shows (see Chap. 4) that there are no organizing principles or dimensions cutting across more than a few courses, and perusal of textbooks prepared for the various courses shows that the student can in ten undergraduate courses acquire slightly different and therefore maximally confusing conceptions of psychology and of the inherent sense of the discipline. More than this, the psychology offerings typically do not have a clear relationship to what the student learns in other departments. And perhaps the most common instance of lack of coherence is found where the instructor in the individual course feels a pressure to introduce the student to everything the instructor knows or that the student might encounter in that special field of psychology, and so covers many topics without regard to whether they have been or can be understood as conceptually interdependent.

Imbalance. As indicated in the previous chapter, the elective system was introduced to give the student more opportunity to follow his own interests and fit education to his own needs as he interpreted them. The restraints upon unbridled election typically have taken the form of requiring that a definite proportion of college work be devoted to the mastery of some one discipline. This requirement, together with distributional requirements of various kinds, is practically universal at the present time and, in many instances, has been given a vocational slant. It does not remove the possibility that in a system of majors, with some distributional requirements and some free elective hours, the student will spend too much of his elective time taking additional work in the major subject, or closely related to it. If he does, he will be following a program which is narrow or out of balance in relation to the world in which he will live. McConnell reports that in the College of Sciences, Literature, and the Arts at the University of Minnesota in 1939 and 1940, some students took as much as half their college work in a single department [180]. Those who majored in English literature, for example, took an average of 73 quarter hours in that department, in addition to an average of 16 hours in composition. (Presumably about 180 quarter hours were required for graduation.) Majors in political science had an average of some 52 quarter hours in that field, but concentrated 106 hours in the social sciences generally.

McConnell notes that the students majoring in English had such a narrow concentration that, although they had an average of 25 hours in languages, they had only 13 hours in history, 6 hours in philosophy, 1.5 hours in music, and 1.9 hours in art. They took little natural science—mainly in psychology. The average amount of physical science was 3.8 hours. McConnell makes a clear point in saying: "One may suspect that the anti-scientific bias of many humanists is due to their lack of scientific knowledge and understanding." [p. 66] The point is probably equally well made in reverse, however, for it is to be suspected that the student concentrating in science is little exposed to, and is suspicious of, the seeming intangibles encountered in literature, the arts, and the social sciences.

Imbalance in educational development evidently must be dealt with by and within the faculty. As Faust makes clear in discussing the College of the University of Chicago, responsibility still resides with the supposedly experienced and knowledgeable faculty to guide the student toward a broad yet thorough understanding of himself and the world so that the necessary specialization for disciplinary or occupational ends is seen in unbiased and sensible perspective [213]. In particular, imbalance can occur in academic settings where the faculty is not alive to the dangers of narrow and thereby prejudiced views in a supposedly educated man, or where the faculty does not have the courage (or capacity for overcoming vested interests) to say just what, from all the knowledge available, is so significant that it should come within the compass of undergraduate education. The focus of these problems is typically the major and its relationship to the remainder of college work, for it is there that professional specialization, strong vocational motivation, immunity to communication with other disciplines, and overconcentration in search of academic security or advantages in competition all tend to focus.

As we have said earlier, psychology came on the scene as an undergraduate discipline after the elective system had begun, and it has been specialized from the beginning. Like other disciplines, it has tended to permit overconcentration by majors, although not perhaps to the extent permitted in such a subject as chemistry. Consistently, the urge to teach as though our students have the same kinds of vocational ambitions that we have, or the same conception of their reasons for studying with us, has been very strong. And as might be expected, the tendency to let the student take all the psychology courses his program will allow has been evident quite often. However, to do justice to them, there are a good many psychologists who do not believe in overconcentration. They feel that the objectives of undergraduate education and of psychology itself are better served if the undergraduate spends a goodly proportion of his time in studies which are related to and serve to illuminate psychology.

It still must be admitted that to psychologists this typically means ensuring that the student is exposed to sociology or anthropology, and to physics, mathematics, and biology. The psychologist does not ordinarily think of the humanities and the arts as significant also in their contributions to the general development and understanding of his students. We may illustrate the point further by remarking that, for example, the field of the psychology of religion has been moribund for many years, with only scattered signs of attention to it as in the pamphlet by MacLeod [171] or the writing of Allport [4]. Furthermore, although we are quick to object to the misuses of psychological concepts by Hollywood or the misreading of Freud by contemporary novelists, psychologists have left the important substance of literature to the psychological amateur. Esthetics goes relatively unnoticed, in either its philosophical sense or its directly expressive sense, as in the arts. It seems likely indeed that through accident or choice psychologists in general are continuing to show imbalance in their conception of what may be important educational material.

Irresponsibility. Implied in the foregoing discussion of educational imbalance was a criticism which deserves to be brought out openly. This is the commonly made point that American college education exhibits, and is conducive to, irresponsibility regarding those aspects of our society which must be protected and cherished if democracy is to survive. This kind of criticism is scarcely new, for in an earlier day education for the elite was criticized as not having sufficient contact with the economic and personal life of those exposed to it. At the present time, however, the charge is particularly serious and difficult to interpret.

Some of the signs of irresponsibility and irrelevance in college education are these: American college life is generally regarded as carefree and in many respects whimsical, kept in check only by rules, deans, and faculty restrictions. Riots in the spring, long football weekends in the fall, and proms in the winter are thought by many of the public, the students, and the alumni to be predominant components in collegiate life. In many institutions fraternity and sorority systems or other varieties of organization and secret society distract from the main line of education and in addition contain their own elements of stubborn insistence upon the right to immaturity. Perhaps the most objectionable element of irresponsibility in American institutions is overemphasis upon intercollegiate athletics, with the associated rationalizations about disregarded moral codes, distractions from learning, and sheer expenditures of time and energy, as well as the inequities in treatment of individual students produced by a huge athletic machine. And it should not go unnoticed that faculties themselves are prone to accept as fact the immaturity of college students and the necessity for a youthful fling, and then to reinforce student expectations by ruling them in a somewhat authoritarian way, with occasional inconsistencies which keep the situation unclear.

More serious, to many who have tried to analyze contemporary education, is the irresponsibility springing from sheer lack of experience in making decisions, from the failure to have formed attitudes, opinions, and values on important matters, from lack of proper informational background upon which to base decisions and opinions, and, most of all, from lack of motivation to regard independent and mature judgment and behavior as central to effective social existence. This criticism reflects a basic lack of confidence in college education or the students it produces. It is shown by the feeling of much of the lay public that a college educated person has not yet learned about the "real" world. Whatever the basis for the criticism, however, it is clear that the faculties who have tried to come to grips with this problem will need the aid and company of many other faculties for generations to come.

It is difficult to assess the position of psychology in relation to the criticism of irresponsibility, just as it presumably would be difficult to assess the position of any other specific discipline. It would appear that psychology has generally avoided, particularly until recent years, any direct concern for morals or conduct, on the ground that these were not proper matters of concern for a scientific discipline. Concerning the existence of such major diversions as athletics and fraternities, psychologists have probably been neutral, or at least not aggressively resistant. On the other hand, in one sense the utilitarian trend in psychology has been concerned precisely and responsibly with personal and social conduct, through the evident concern for the processes of adjustment, or the processes of interaction in the small group, through analyses of propaganda, and so on. Perhaps the effect on our students has been in part to impress upon them the consequences of thoughtless action or biased analysis. More likely, the typical undergraduate teacher of psychology has presumed that his students should make their own interpretations of what he offers, and has indicated that regardless of their responsibility for answering his way on examinations, they are entirely at liberty to develop their own personal codes and evaluations. This mixture of laissez-faire and authoritarian approaches has probably not resulted in a final contribution to the formation of responsible and mature behavior any greater than that coming from the humanities, where the amateur in things psychological has traditionally been concerned with values as he analyzes them in man's symbolic expressions and conduct. Clearly this is an aspect of utility and responsibility which needs further consideration by psychologists. The list of specific points to be considered, furthermore, must in my opinion sooner or later include questions of a more nearly absolute nature, such as what adjustments are good, and what values or goals in life are essential or important.

Failure to produce leaders. More and more the leaders of our society are drawn from the ranks of formally educated persons. But modern analyses suggest strongly that there is no reason to be complacent about this. For one thing, the leadership very often springs from social position or financial background rather than from the quality of education. For another, the very remarks that may be made about irresponsibility in education and educated persons apply with full force to the leadership qualities exhibited by all too many college graduates who happen to come into positions of prominence. The moral and conceptual qualities for the best leadership are lacking. And finally many people feel that modern education is still somewhat elite in the sense of failing to search out, stimulate, and prepare the full proportion of able persons for leadership. As is often suggested, the problem is partly a financial one.

What is involved here, in the opinion of the authors of the Harvard report [132], is what they term a Jacksonian-Jeffersonian dilemma. On the one hand, American education aspires to raise the general intellectual, social, and economic levels of the population. By its expansion and limitless variation it has indeed provided some form of educational opportunity for any man's child, and this is good and desirable. But the authors of the report, and many others as well [e.g., Aydelotte, 17], are inclined to believe that the Jeffersonian side of the dilemma, in which American education has sought to provide the best stimulation for the ablest persons, has in recent years received too little attention. The twofold problem of finding the right students and then giving them opportunity for the right kind of education will demand the best thought of college faculties and an increment in scholarship and other educational costs. This must be accomplished without cutting down on education for the whole population.

It is probably appropriate to say that if education fails to produce enough citizen-leaders, psychologists are neither more nor less responsible than their colleagues in the undergraduate faculty. The problem of leadership, it is true, has become an object of scientific study. So has the problem of identification and recruitment of professional or scientific talent, as in the Wesleyan and the Wolfle studies [159, 287]. But these are technical approaches, and we are far from being able to assimilate their significance into our own conception of the function of college education. It seems very likely that psychologists, in conjunction with behavior scientists from other areas such as political science, sociology, or anthropology, may jointly form a more adequate concept of leadership than we now have, and after that beginning may contribute more to the conception educated people or college faculties have about responsibility for and preparation for leadership in the society at large.

The evaluation of educational criticism. Some effort has been made above to consider not only general criticisms of higher education but some of the compensating arguments or extenuating circumstances. It is worth repeating that the validity of the evidence on which some of the criticisms are based and the total mass or strength of the evidence are not readily determined. Inevitably, therefore, faculties have made the best judgment they could in face of the difficulties involved. Since it is not common American educational practice to include in the plans for educational innovations any devices or criteria for eventual evaluation of them, we shall presumbly have to get along for some time to come on the same subjectively based judgments that we have made to date.

There is currently another complication for which we must allow in assessing education. This is what has been termed anti-intellectualism, and it has been exhibited in many places in our culture. In its baldest form it appears in the encouragement of nonintellectual or extracurricular activities as the real purpose of college attendance. In less obvious manner, it exists in the student who seeks both a quiet gentleman's C and a practical education in the bargain. In another way it shows up in the culture at large in the suspicion expressed concerning theoretical, general, or abstract ideas, or those who deal with or teach them. In a most significant way it shows up in the willingness of the general public or of alumni to accept the notion that Congressional investigating committees, sports editors, or boards of control have the right to bring intellectually "errant" faculty members into line, to catch out students thought to be radical in their search for truth, or, indeed, to decide upon lay grounds whether professionally competent books should be permitted in the presence of the "immature and irresponsible" student.

Anti-intellectualism must be understood as a pervasive influence both inside and outside the faculty and both inside and outside the student body. Criticisms of education and attempts to reformulate educational programs or objectives have to be thoroughly examined in the light of the existence of this tendency as well as the existence of factually based, sincere, and constructive comment.

3

LIBERAL AND GENERAL EDUCATION

We turn now from the general characteristics and weaknesses of higher education to more specific questions about exemplary programs and the problems encountered in them. Our concern continues primarily to be the liberal arts college for, as Jones [151] makes clear, this category of institution has the most members, many more than any other kind if university colleges are included, and this is also the type of institution which has reacted most immediately and urgently to the critical comments about education. Educational reform is most likely to occur in times of social stress. Two of the great sources of impetus to revision and experimentation in liberal education were the great economic depression of the 1930s and the drastic consequences of World War II.

The fully satisfactory definition of liberal education has not yet been written, as one may observe by reading the many essays written in the past two decades. Yet perhaps the final language of definition need not concern us overmuch, since there are many essential elements of agreement among those who have considered critically the nature of liberal education and two associated concepts, general and special education. For purposes of further analysis a working viewpoint concerning these concepts will be formulated below, with no presumption that it is perfect or would meet with widespread agreement. Specific programs and their problems will be considered, and then we shall discuss briefly the place of psychology in all of this.

The nature of liberal education. The first question about the meaning of liberal education has to do with the word *liberal* itself. In this context the word may in effect be replaced by the word liberalizing or liberative. And the general significance of the word liberative, to choose one of the pair, is something like this: Liberative education is intended to free the individual from rigid, habitual, or biased modes of thought, to help him to explore many realms of knowledge and activity, and to lead him to cherish the pleasures and responsibilities of such freedoms. Those aspirations reflect certain distinguishable objectives of liberal education. Of course, the translation of the objectives into a concrete intra- and extracurricular program of education is difficult and often feebly done, but on the objectives themselves there is substantial agreement.

The current notion of how concepts are formed leads us to expect that detailed statements of these different objectives are the best operations to define the thing to which they compositely and generally refer. For present purposes we shall say that the first objective of liberal education is to provide the student with methods and skills useful in confronting not only the disciplines he encounters in college but also the circumstances and activities he encounters upon leaving college. The most important methods or skills are those involved in the thinking process. It is commonly stated, for example, that a liberal education should enhance the capacity for analysis and for criticism of self or others. Also, it is commonly hoped that a liberal education will increase the capacity for dispassionate judgment which characterizes the wise individual, and beyond this that it will make available to the student, as part of his intellectual resources, the techniques involved in creative thought, or constructive imagination, or planful contemplation. In a somewhat different category, but in their way essential as methodology for an educated person, are the skills, the tool-subjects, by which disciplines are opened to him and their fullest use realized: languages, mathematics, linguistics or logic, and, almost always singled out for special attention, effective English communication. Writing in reasonable form and with maximum communication value receives most emphasis, but in many instances the spoken word comes in for its fair share of attention also. This objective and the two still to be described are not achieved in a course or in a particular discipline, but in many aspects of the college program and in all the four years.

A second defining objective of liberal education is the pursuit of knowledge as such, the mastery of information of many kinds, with the intention of broadening the student's grasp of reality and thereby reducing the provincialism of a partly informed mind. The many disciplines studied are themselves the major means for reaching this objective, as are the methods and skills referred to above. But rather than naming disciplines as objectives in themselves, which in a sense would confirm and fix their actually arbitrary or conventionalized separation into special fields, those who have tried to rethink liberal education typically have sought to designate broad areas of human knowledge or experience which in their judgment are representative and in that sense essential to the student. The most common classification is perhaps a three-part one into the humanities and arts, the social sciences, and the natural sciences. Depending upon the institutional program one examines, one may find that history, philosophy, religion, the literatures, or perhaps various representatives of the sciences may receive formal mention, or the number of categories which receive general emphasis may be four or some other number. This number in itself is not important, but the defining feature appears to be that in fixing upon knowledge requirements for a liberally educated individual, it has been found necessary to organize, group, redistribute, or combine the particular disciplines in some manner which ensures that the student will touch upon or develop some reasonable degree of mastery of representative fields of knowledge.

The remaining objective which defines liberal education will be described here rather more in the psychologist's language than in the language commonly used to define it. To the methods and knowledge objectives must be added a third one which is motivational in character. It is commonly said, for example, that a liberally educated person is one who has examined, or begun to examine, his own values and those of his society, in order to judge which ones are important or worthy of support. It is also commonly said that these values are in large measure moral ones, related to personal and societal conduct. Furthermore, the liberally educated individual is often said to be one whose tastes have been cultivated, whose opinions are analytical, whose attitudes are well grounded. All this language comes under the motivation rubric, though to be sure the exact fit is not always clear. Perhaps we may state the objective this way: Liberal education, in all its methods and content, is intended to strengthen certain motives, such as those related to responsibility for society and self; to strengthen or inculcate other motives, such as those related to esthetic judgment and satisfactions or prospective occupational choices; to teach new incentives as objects for existing motives, as when the rewards of scholarship are realized to be pertinent to the needs for expression and self-esteem; to teach new means of achieving previously learned incentives; and so on. It becomes clear from such statements that liberal education is in its own way calculated in part to ensure certain lines of development or conduct rather than others, this policy being based upon the assumption by the faculty that it has professional and individual personal responsibility for making such judgments and carrying them out. (This kind of analysis, and the assumption of responsibility by the faculty, is seen as a sharp contrast to the more common and less reasoned adoption of a laissez-faire attitude with respect to the impact of education upon student motivation, described in the previous chapter.)

Against the background of these three objectives for *liberal* education it is now proper to ask, what is *general* education? Initially we may say it is part of the process of meeting the objectives of liberal education, but in itself is not the whole process. It has been described, typically, as education pertinent to those aspects of life which all people must face in common. McDonald, in an excellent essay, epitomizes the problem in this way: "We are standing, as it were, with one foot in the twenty-first century of scientific application and the other foot in the eighteenth century of social-moral application" [182, p. 33]. As Faust has said [213, p. 6], general education is not usually concerned with the problems peculiar to the business of being a chemist or a carpenter or an architect or a housewife, but rather with the problems our whole society faces. It assumes that educational preparation for these problems is good for that society and the individual within it. Problems of this kind would be, for example, war or criminality or economic fluctuation and the attendant social and political ills, and the general preparation for facing them would include not merely the disciplines dealing directly with them but all disciplines which indirectly, by producing wiser and more broadly developed persons, may make a contribution. More than this, each individual member of our society without exception has to formulate a personal philosophy, an outlook upon, or ways of dealing with, the world, and although the solution is in each instance peculiar to the person, such problems are given attention in a program of general education because it may be assumed they exist for all maturing individuals. McGrath and his associates [185] have suggested that general education does not attempt to level all individual differences but rather to seek maximum development of the individual as this may be consistent with the general good.

It is clear that while general education may help maximize the differences among individuals, in order that each may be of greatest significance as a member of society, this cannot really be its major concern. Instead it must search out the common problems, heritages, and aspirations of the society and the individual and seek to deal with these. To fulfill the objectives of a more completely defined liberal education, therefore, it is necessary that there be another major component, *special* education. By this term we refer to that aspect of liberal education in which the individual, through special studies carried to a high level of mastery, pursues his own particular and more narrowly defined educational interests and prepares himself for graduate or professional training, or learns through his own achievements at that high level of mastery the satisfactions of persistent and intelligent scholarship. Vocational results may come as by-products, but they are not the prime objective of special education properly understood. Since the major is the most typical instrument of special education, we shall deal with it in a separate chapter on the psychological curriculum (Chap. 4).

General and special education are intentionally represented here as complementary parts of liberal education, contributing in different ways to the achievement of its general objectives. Both general and special education, properly planned, can contribute to maturity, to good attitudes toward the intellectual life and the life of the citizen, and to the capacity for good judgment which society so badly needs. One must always remember, however, that it is exceedingly difficult to evaluate those contributions, especially in the context of improving existing programs [90, 91, 92, 118].

VARIETIES OF GENERAL EDUCATION PROGRAMS

There are many ways of defining what seem the most important common problems of college-educated persons, and there are therefore many different kinds of general education programs. There is no objective evidence as to the relative merits of these programs, so that we can only learn their main features and then form any subjective judgments we can. (Problems of general education—in science in particular—receive valuable discussions in the books by Cohen and Watson [70] and Conant [76].)

Distributional programs. Some kind of distribution program was established or retained in most institutions, paralleling the system of majors as this developed historically. As concern for the objectives of general education increased in recent decades, perhaps the most common faculty reaction was to re-examine, modify, or make more stringent the distributional requirements on their rule books. Under a distribution system a student typically is required to sample courses from groups of disciplines outside the one in which he majors; there is very great variation in the degree to which that sampling is itself controlled, directed, or restricted. Typically, distribution requirements should be fulfilled within the first two years of college and definitely completed within the third year. A distributional version of general education in effect assumes that the right material is already available in the curriculum and merely needs re-ordering, or scheduling, to ensure its getting to the students.

An analysis of the weaknesses of this kind of program will perhaps illustrate the kinds of problems we should expect to encounter in other more tightly worked out programs, whether or not there are data indicating the difficulties encountered in the latter. First, distribution programs tend to be planned from strength, that is, from vested interest. The departments having the longest tradition of lower division courses, or the most insistent voices in faculty meeting, typically tend to work their materials into prominence in the listing of courses acceptable for distribution. (Ward [272] cites a teacher in a social science survey course who told him, "I have only one injunction from my department as their representative in this survey—'Maximize the segment devoted to sociology.' ") Vested interests, allowed to function in this way, in effect prejudge what is essential in education, and this is prejudgment from a special rather than a broad educational point of view. Second, courses in distribution are typically elementary courses. This has several consequences, among them the oft-mentioned one that a collection of miscellaneous knowledge or viewpoints is hardly an organized education. There is also the result that progression to higher levels of difficulty or mastery, and therefore of challenge to the student, is not possible in view of the heterogeneous backgrounds of the students in any given course. It is in this kind of course that one so often finds a good many floundering freshmen, many sophomores, a few juniors, and a sprinkling of bored seniors. A third comment on the distribution-course system is that such courses, recognized by student and faculty alike as something to be ticked off under what we have called an accounting method of measuring education, are typically regarded as of secondary importance—as something to be endured before beginning the major. Intellectual motivation is therefore at an unhappy low in all distribution courses, but especially in one which is regarded merely as the lesser of the available evils in its required group.

For the teacher who wishes to maintain good standards of achievement, the teaching of a distribution-requirement course tends to be frustrating, for he finds that since such courses are not taken in predictable patterns, proportions, or sequences, he cannot diagnose the kinds of interrelationships with other disciplines or concepts that his students may be ready to grasp. He thus cannot attempt, except in a superficial or formal way, to root his material in what his students already know, or show its connections with other materials. Finally, because of the tendency to assign introductory (and thus distributional) courses to younger teachers more recently out of specialized graduate school, and because it is the easy way out for even veteran teachers, the courses taken in distribution are typically taught as a prelude to a major. In fact, their supposed general or distributional character is often resented by their instructors, who make it clear in no uncertain terms that the student who wishes to do well in the course had better approach the material in the spirit of one who just might major in it.

The integrated-studies program. Among the many varieties of general education program there are several which attempt to assist the student to see interrelationships among ideas and fields of knowledge. Each program in addition has unique features, but the three described below all are relatively conservative, in that they are concerned with teaching basic materials which were largely in the curriculum prior to creation of the special program, with the commonly stated objective of acquainting the student with the major fields of knowledge about his world and society and himself. The materials are regrouped or reworked to make the integrated character of knowledge apparent and effective wherever possible.

At the University of Wisconsin, the College of Letters and Science provides a special program of limited enrollment in the first two years [281]. In the first year the undergraduate studies Greek and Roman culture, early man and his society, the physical universe, theory and practice of writing, medieval and Renaissance culture, the transition to industrial society, earth science, and the nature and function of language. In the second year he studies European culture, modern American industrial society, biology (including some psychology), American culture, and the international scene. In each year there is provision for an elective, to give flexibility and to protect the student who needs particular courses as preparation for entrance into certain major departments after the first two years. Except for this elective, the program is prescribed, which is a sharp contrast with the distributional type of arrangement. The courses offered, themselves partly familiar and partly new, seek out the interrelationships of knowledge. The stated objective of the program is to provide a broad general education through the integration of subject matter, and we may well expect that careful planning by the faculty, limitation of enrollment to a distinctive group of relatively small size, and introduction of a large degree of communality into the programs of the students could lead to considerable success in attainment of that objective.

The program of the widely known University of Chicago College [37, 66] may, for our particular purposes, be classified as an integrated-studies program, although that hardly does justice to its many unique features. To itemize some of these, the College for many years included the last two years of high school along with the first two years of the typical college; it has used placement examinations to ensure the student's being put to the level of work for which he is prepared, and to enable him to bypass formal courses if he can demonstrate that he has mastered the equivalent in some other way; it has used comprehensive examinations at the end of large units of work, rather than examinations in course, in order to facilitate broader review and study, or a broader view of any area; it has used an integrated system of courses, most of them being prescribed rather than freely elected by the student. Integration is achieved not only by carefully planned sequences of courses, but to a large extent by interdisciplinary scholarship within courses, many of them being taught by persons trained in several related disciplines. The major fields of knowledge to which courses are devoted are natural science, social studies (the social, political, and economic order), the inheritance of Western civilization (art, literature, philosophy), and communications (writing, language, mathematics). In addition, history is taught as an integrative discipline, and there is a special course in the organization and methods of knowledge. Stress throughout is not on rote learning but rather upon understanding. Much attention is given to training in intelligent reading, reflection, and analysis. The objectives of teaching in the College focus on the techniques and the knowledge regarded as desirable for meeting common social problems. To the extent that those objectives are met, students may be enabled to solve personal problems wisely, achieve their ambitions in an occupation or profession, and contribute to the life of the nation.

In the Chicago program the natural and social sciences are very important areas of study, and the faculty recognizes that this emphasis is desirable in an age in which science is socially of such great importance. The study of psychology is included in one part of the biological science component of the natural science division of work. The materials there covered, to judge from published reading lists [67], are concerned with major systems or viewpoints in the field, for the authors mentioned are Titchener, Koffka, Hull, Tolman, Spearman, and Freud. Psychology is also involved to some extent in a course concerned with personality and culture, in the social science division of the program, but the psychological materials all appear to be embedded in an anthropological and sociological context.

One of the liveliest programs at Yale is Directed Studies, a two-year course of study to which men are admitted on application at the beginning of freshman year. The purpose of the program is said to be to explore the values, for the student and for the university, of a carefully organized combination of specially designed courses as a common intellectual basis for the work of the last two years [291, p. 14]. In freshman year the student takes three prescribed courses (philosophy, literature, and history of art) and, depending on his preparation and aims, mathematics or physics as a fourth course and language or ROTC as a fifth. In sophomore year the three prescribed courses are philosophy, studies in society, and history; two other courses are elected from among the languages, sciences, or ROTC. The distinguishing features of the program are as follows. Philosophy, as a discipline, stands at the center of the program, and the philosophers who teach in the program have something of an integrative function. Most of the courses are taught in small, discussion-size groups, and the relatively large staff necessary to provide this kind of instruction is a closely knit group with much intercommunication. There is much emphasis upon the development of the student's ability to express himself, to challenge and discuss intelligently, to search out suitable sources, and so on. Psychology is represented only in the sophomore work in studies in society, being taught as social psychology. Among both faculty and students there is an unusual degree of enthusiasm for what is being done, and an impression that superior educational results are being obtained. A dash of cold water must be thrown on this impression, however, for to date, in terms of the available indices (honors earned at graduation, marks relative to ability level, etc.), Directed Studies students are not distinguishable in any clear way from their peers during the last two years of college [51].

Student needs. The distributional and integrated studies programs may be said to stress the problems and characteristics of the world into which the student will go, and to a lesser degree the satisfaction of the student's personal and peculiar needs for preparation to enter that world after college. The two illustrative programs we describe now seem to shift the balance of emphasis more clearly to a concern for the student as an individual.

At Michigan State College there is a Basic College encompassing the first two years of college work and providing for all students the prerequisites for entrance into the many specialized schools of the institution or into advanced work in the arts and sciences [196]. Within this Basic College program the student is required to take one-year courses in communication skills, natural science, social science, and the humanities. Each of these courses is to some extent interdisciplinary and integrated; there is a planned sequence in the way the subdivisions of each course develop. In addition to these courses, the Basic College student takes work in various introductory, exploratory, and elective courses taught by the staffs of the various specialized schools. The stated objectives of the Basic College program include the intentions to aid each student to develop into a more wholesome individual and a more effective citizen, to acquire better study and learning skills, to develop more effective personal traits, to become more able in personal, social, civic, family, and leisure time activities, and so forth. Professional counseling and remedial services of various kinds are made available in an extracurricular way. The effect, then, is to orient the whole Basic College program rather definitely toward what might be called the common personal needs of the students. Psychology as a discipline is involved in the professional services made available. It is also prominent in the social science course, where the objectives of the three successive academic quarters center in problem areas, such as how to orient new members of the group to prevailing patterns of behavior, how to satisfy human needs and wants, and how to control human behavior.

The program at Sarah Lawrence College [237] is illustrative of programs of general education which are even more specifically intended to meet the needs of individual students. (It goes so far in this direction, in fact, as to make somewhat inapplicable the earlier statement that general education is concerned with *common* needs or problems.) It is assumed in the Sarah Lawrence program that the educational purpose of the college is to aid the student in planning the general conduct of her adult life, as an individual, as a partner in marriage, and as parent and citizen. These objectives are to be reached by an educational plan which is concerned with the whole life of each person taught: to help each student discover her own abilities and the best uses of them, to understand her relationships with others, and to establish personal and social values. The Sarah Lawrence faculty recognize that students mature in very different ways and at very different rates, and for this reason have made the formal aspects of the educational program extremely flexible, so that the best plan can be worked out for each student at her particular stage of development. There are no formal grades, but there is an extremely detailed report system, with careful reviews of progress by the faculty. There is no major, in the conventional sense, but instead a course program planned around principal areas of interest and individual need. Small classes only are offered, and regular conferences occur between student and instructor.

It is interesting to note that psychology is an active contributing discipline at Sarah Lawrence. It is involved in both the natural and the social science aspects of the program, with the choice of psychological materials clearly being governed first of all by the expressed objectives of the college curriculum rather than by specialized or professional objectives. Thus attention is given to such course topics as marriage and the family, the psychology of art, and the preschool development of children, as well as to certain of the courses more common in other colleges.

PSYCHOLOGY IN GENERAL EDUCATION

It should by now be apparent that psychology as a discipline, particularly as a labeled branch of study, does not enter in quantitatively important ways into many general education programs. At this level "the proper study of mankind" is more likely to be carried on in the traditional humanities climate than in the more recently developed scientific atmosphere. Furthermore, psychologists have not planned materials, or stated teaching objectives, or concentrated enough on the educational problems involved in general education, to justify any complaint of discrimination. Berrien [30], in particular, makes this clear. Yet, as the Sarah Lawrence College and other programs show and as a number of psychologists have indicated [130, 288], psychology, among the many relatively more recently developed disciplines, has rich possibilities for contributing to general education objectives. (We shall discuss this further in the following chapter.)

PRACTICAL PROBLEMS IN GENERAL EDUCATION PROGRAMS

Although there is little dependable evidence to aid us in evaluating the results of various forms of general education programs, there are some generally recognized difficulties in planning them. These in part resemble the difficulties mentioned in connection with the distributional form of general education, but in part come from the special character and status of the more fully developed programs.

There is what is sometimes called the sharpening-leveling problem. This is the question of whether the stress in general education should be upon bringing all students to the same minimum level of competence in various matters, as prescribed-course programs imply, or whether education and society itself are better served by permitting programs which enhance the strong points and disregard the weak points, at least to some degree, of each individual student, on the assumption that a wide range of kinds of persons is necessary in a democratic society.

The problem is illustrated by the fact already discussed, that carefully planned general education programs have varied all the way from nearly complete prescription to rather free election from specially planned or even regular departmental courses. At present one can only guess, with the authors of the Harvard Report [132], that more careful integration of a general education, calculated to make people alike in certain significant ways, with a special education intended to give free expression to differences, is likely to be preferable to a solution by means of the general education program alone.

There is also the problem of how much the extracurricular life of the institution should contribute to general education objectives. Properly handled, it is clear that sports, dramatics, and many other aspects of extracurricular life can be of much educational value. Many faculties, however, have been unwilling to rely very much upon such programs, if only because they felt they had no real control over the activities. Certain non-credit activities, however, may be planned to be an important part of the over-all educational program. For example, the faculties may count heavily on remedial, counseling, and other services staffed by professional personnel and administered in such a way that referrals from the faculty as well as standardized testing, placement, and allied functions are intelligently handled.

Although it is generally agreed that greater coherence and integration of knowledge are desirable attributes of general education programs, precise definition and illustration of these objectives remain difficult. Integration, presumably, must finally be something that occurs in each individual mind, whether this is the mind of a faculty member or a student. In all likelihood we cannot truly cause integration in our students, but we can make it easier or throw barriers in the way of it. A major problem therefore occurs in the development of integrated or interdisciplinary courses. If integration be interpreted here as the development of a concept structure in which, without regard to origins or kinds of knowledge, the relationships between concepts are inherent in the structure itself, it becomes clear that this is, from the specialist's viewpoint, an advanced stage of the development of knowledge. Presumably it is reached only after mastery of the disciplines or concepts separately. And yet within certain disciplines, or certain groups of disciplines, from the very beginning of the student's experience, concept structures can be created or utilized which *draw upon* scholarly and high level integration. Thus it appears to be possible that certain segments of sociology, cultural anthropology, psychoanalysis, and experimental psychology (learning theory) fit naturally together in a theoretical scheme which carries its meaning with it and does not depend upon "interpretation" or "integration" from outside or above [178]. Parts of biology and psychology seem to have fitted together naturally at Antioch [105, 164], and a working union of anthropological, psychological, and sociological materials has been developed at Northwestern [27, 292, 293]. In a number of institutions across the country, there appears to have been derived for history, politics, and economics a concept structure which functions in this same general way for even the beginning student, and this is also true of certain combinations of literature, philosophy, and the arts. But in many other areas of knowledge, some of which have been created by fiat in planning general education programs, the basic scholarly work has not been done, or insufficient time has been allowed for it. Further, faculty members assigned to the task have sometimes been motivated, not by the desire to achieve this kind of scholarly result but rather the usual specialized results, with the consequence that survey courses, sheerly verbal integrations and other sharply criticized educational solutions have developed.

There is also the problem of correlating what is to be done in general education at the college level with what is done in the preparatory schools. In recent years considerable concern has been shown in this matter, with the Harvard Report [132], the so-called Andover Report [73], and the report of the President's Committee on General Education at Yale [75] all directing attention to it. Involved are such questions as whether the schools are providing the proper background for general education in college, and how to set admission requirements which will ensure that the student's preparation is the best possible foundation for getting maximum profit from the college offerings. There also is the problem of proper placement, and of making suitable arrangements for the able or well-prepared student to avoid wasting his time through repetition of material already studied. It has apparently been the unfortunate experience of several institutions, notably the University of Chicago, that a lack of co-ordination with school programs, however reasonable the rationale for that lack of co-ordination, creates difficulties at the college level [158].

Perhaps the most serious problem in planning general education, serious enough to merit repeated mention, is that of the vested interest. The departments of instruction are typically concerned with enrolling sufficient students to justify retaining their present faculty and with having those students experience and appreciate the values of their particular discipline. Those concerns tend to become competitive and in the process sometimes become more important than considerations of the welfare of the student. It takes reasonableness in the departments plus strong administrative leadership to avoid power struggles among the departments. But such avoidance is essential to permit the development of a program reflecting the faculty's most rational judgment about how to achieve intellectual development in the student.

4

PSYCHOLOGY IN THE CURRICULUM

In the preceding chapter special education was referred to as that aspect of liberal education in which the individual, through special studies carried to a high level of mastery, is enabled to pursue his own particular and more narrowly defined educational interests, or to prepare himself for graduate or professional training, and to learn through his own achievements at that high level of mastery the satisfactions which can come from persistent and intelligent scholarship. In special education as in general education, the intent is to contribute to the same liberalizing objectives of increased methodological and skills sophistication, increased knowledge, and enhanced motivational structure.

Except for certain interdepartmental or combined programs, in most colleges special education is carried on within the departments; we shall therefore examine here some of the issues related to the departmental curriculum in psychology. Later in the chapter we shall make the assumption that departmental offerings too may be analyzed into components which correspond to general education (service) offerings and special education (major) offerings, and in this way establish a clear continuity with discussions in the preceding chapters.

CRITICISMS OF THE TYPICAL CURRICULUM

Objectives. Typically the objectives of the psychology curriculum go unstated, in the bulletins or catalogues which describe the course offerings and in the minds of faculty and students as well. The common presumption as to aims is probably something like "to teach psychology, naturally." Certain curriculum objectives may be apparent by inference, as when particular courses are labeled as reserved for honors students, or for majors, or others are planned for a mixed graduate and undergraduate group. Beyond such inferred statements of objectives there is only the fact that our collections of courses typically bear labels reflecting divisions and subdivisions of the psychological profession and science, so that the student must form his conception of psychology by sampling from offerings which are not explicitly planned to give him a representative view.

Talking about formulation of objectives is sometimes regarded by psychologists as talking about mere form. The simple fact, however, as can be testified by those who have tried it, is that the statement of one's teaching objectives is a difficult exercise and, once accomplished, has a powerful effect on one's teaching. It seems only reasonable to think that psychology departments would have a much clearer idea of what their respective curriculums were intended to contribute to the college program, and how such contributions might be made, were the formulation of any program preceded by the careful statement of objectives. After such a careful formulation the difference between "cultural" and "pre-professional" majors might turn out to be something more important than the present frequently found practice of permitting the cultural majors to by-pass statistics, and the difference between honors and pass students might turn out to be something more important than whether the honors students have a discussion-type course in senior year, while the pass students always have lecture courses.

Overlap, repetition, and boredom. Wolfle [286] has convincingly demonstrated that the typical undergraduate curriculum in psychology leads to a great deal of waste motion on the part of the student and the faculty as well. For example, he found that texts commonly used in elementary educational, child, social, and applied psychology courses treat the same general set of topics (except that applied psychology has the largest number of topics peculiar to it). Of 31 topics analyzed, nine were covered in all five courses; 21 topics were discussed in at least three of the five courses. This kind of duplication of effort is likely to be found no matter which of the common texts in each field is used, for to be commercially competitive with one another it appears to be assumed by both authors and publishers that the texts must cover much the same ground.

Certain consequences of this weakness of the psychology curriculum usually follow. One is the uneven motivation of students. This will always occur to some extent, but as they too often encounter materials studied previously the repetition becomes boring. Another consequence is that within the whole lower level of the departmental curriculum the student tends to move merely from one elementary course to another, without being carried into more general, more difficult, new, or more stimulating topics (an analogue of the criticism of distributive systems as provision for general education; see Chap. 3). A third and related expectation which is almost always borne out is that there is no helpful sequence in the courses which a student takes, no possibility that he can build later knowledge upon a foundation laid earlier. Ordinarily, carefully planned repetition and review provide an opportunity for fixing our mastery of any subject matter. But it may be expected that unplanned or unwitting repetitiousness and duplication, far from having the desirable effect of increasing mastery through added or intensive study of the same material, are likely to prevent departmental work from ever appearing as an organized or coherent whole to the student and, because after the first course nothing very different or new ever happens, to give him a false feeling of mastery of the field.

Organization of the curriculum. It has been pointed out on numerous occasions [e.g., 56, 286] that while the psychology offerings may be made ineffective in part for lack of stated objectives and because of duplication, they also exhibit no over-all plan or organizing principles. There are courses organized around such themes or objectives as method (experimental, testing, interviewing, personnel selection, statistics); the organism studied (animal, comparative); the process (learning, perceiving); the age of the organism (child, adolescent, old age); professional situations (educational, clinical, industrial); and so on. Perhaps it is fair to say that, like the divisional organization of the American Psychological Association, the undergraduate curriculum represents the evolved interests of different psychological groups and the corresponding individual faculty members, rather than a considered plan for a coherent experience of what psychology has to offer.

It must be admitted that there is no clear-cut evidence that the present helter-skelter organization of the curriculum is entirely bad, but we can suspect that it contributes to both overlap and lack of coherence. For example, a course defined by the age of the organism (child or adolescent psychology) is almost certain to overlap with one defined by the professional situation (educational psychology, with emphasis on the school years). In contrast, a course on the process of learning, particularly if taught from the usual scientific-analytical viewpoint, rarely makes coherent contact with the course on educational psychology, and the latter develops its own conception of the learning process for application to the complex skill and personality learnings with which the school teacher must cope. Such examples could be multiplied and would make more impressive the need for re-analysis of our curriculum and the text materials created for it.

Professional and graduate influences. Although it is common practice to remind ourselves [55] that only a few of the students who take elementary courses with us will major in psychology, and of the majors not a great many will go on to graduate school and into the profession, it is a matter of common knowledge that the undergraduate courses reflect the standards, habits of thought, language and choice of content which are important at the graduate and professional level. This is especially apparent when graduate and undergraduate students share the same classes, but is nevertheless common elsewhere, including the independent liberal arts college. (In fact, since post-college success of students is sometimes a principal reward of college teachers, and this success is more obvious if more of the students go to graduate school in psychology, the independent college teacher may be among the most firmly professional in his orientation. For a responsible expression of the recruitment interest see McClelland [179].)

Thus it may be that a course in abnormal psychology gives overemphasis to the psychiatric nomenclature of mental disorder, thereby reducing time available for the analysis of cultural and learning influences which might be more appropriate for the non-professional student. Or, an introduction to statistics may pay separate attention to many forms of correlation, rather than stressing the general properties of this form of statistical analysis and its significance as a particular instance of quantitative thought. A laboratory course may insist upon the compilation of large quantities of routine data, in order to achieve stable or representative means in the several experiments a student performs, rather than making clear to him the general reasons why matters of this kind, along with others, are of importance in the scientist's way of doing things. A course in child psychology may be overconcerned with normative statements about development, as these stem from professional or practical concerns for assessing early stages, rather than with the complex causal interpretation of behavioral changes observed in the young child. And, in any course, mastery of a largely technical vocabulary might be required.

There is a difficult but essential distinction to be made here. On the one hand, it is possible to plan and teach undergraduate courses as an exposition of the field of psychology as defined by the professional psychologist. The content of the field then governs the content of the undergraduate program. On the other hand, it is possible to plan and teach undergraduate courses according to the considered educational needs of the students, in which instance the instructor will choose or the curriculum will contain those research materials, those methods and those procedures for teaching which advance the student toward a higher intellectual level as an individual. As I have said elsewhere [55], it appears that the latter position is the one that justifies the existence of psychology offerings in the liberal arts program. While there may be disagreement about just what the needs of students are, or about the best pedagogical devices for meeting these needs, it would seem that these, rather than the needs of the instructor for professional self-respect, or the desire to mirror the field of psychology in the undergraduate curriculum, should dominate curriculum planning.

Again we may note that the problem being discussed is not peculiar to psychology. In economics, for example, it has been said: "The general trend . . . placed heavy emphasis on the development of analytical thinking and method of analysis. Preparation for citizenship and general cultural values received surprisingly slight support . . . the majority of teachers of economics believe that theoretical analysis is the primary objective of the elementary economics course." [261, pp. 53-54] (Further questioning showed that current economic problems and institutions were also regarded as significant topics for presentation.)

Stereotyped approaches. While psychologists have been venturesome in many things, especially in recent decades and at the graduate level when their discipline has been expanding in manifold directions, it can scarcely be said that they have ventured in many new directions in planning their undergraduate offerings. Rather, inertia has been a major factor in curriculum developments, especially in the larger institutions or departments. The examples set at Colgate [29], Harvard [247], and Columbia [154] are exceptions, but the curriculum has continued to grow and become more specialized by a process of accretion, rather than by a process of careful planning with regular pruning of the course list. I find, for example, more than 30 psychology courses listed in the undergraduate catalogue of one of our important departments. (No student could take more than 10 or 12.) This is rather typical of the way in which various interests of faculty members with a background of specialized Ph.D. training, identifying with the specialized profession of psychology, are reflected in undergraduate course offerings. As new specialties develop, new courses are added; rarely is an old course dropped. Indeed, to suggest pruning course lists is to threaten the average department head with reduction of his staff, for the opportunity to express one's own interests through the offerings of a specialized course has commonly come to be regarded as not merely legitimate but also as more essential to one's career advancement than teaching courses planned primarily to meet an explicitly defined educational need of students.

There is some justification for regarding the sameness of the curriculum from one psychology department to another, or in a given department from one year to the next, as a premature rigidity of our teaching practices. Since we do not know in any very complete way what kind of curriculum will help psychology make its best contributions to liberal education, we should perhaps hope at a minimum for quite different kinds of programs in different institutions. This would give an initial basis for curriculum revisions or for more systematic study of the principles according to which our curriculum should be planned. Particularly does it seem desirable for psychology departments to break away from the inflexible assumption that textbook education is the only or the best kind, and to try out curriculum plans which permit supervised and independent direct experience with behavioral material, unconventional syllabi, reduction in number of specialized courses in favor of general or basic courses, and new or modified teaching objectives.

UNSOLVED ISSUES IN CURRICULUM PLANNING

The psychologist who would improve the curriculum is confronted not only with problems or criticisms of the kind just discussed, but also with a number of issues which demand some kind of resolution no matter what the objectives of the over-all program in psychology may be. An analysis of these issues in psychology affords a kind of case study which could be replicated in any other social science.

Methodological questions. Four different aspects of psychological method may be regarded as possible or essential components of the experience of the student whose special education (field of concentration, major) is in psychology. With respect to none of these have we reached agreement concerning the amount of emphasis which is proper, or the time or the place at which they are to be introduced into the curriculum.

There is, first, the perennial problem of what to do about statistics or, more generally, quantitative thought. There are still psychologists who believe that statistics is a technician's area, not necessarily suitable for inclusion in undergraduate experience. To them it appears that much of psychology can be taught to students without direct attention to the quantitative aspects of methods by which that psychology is developed or tested. Probably the great majority of psychologists, however, believe that one of the keys to understanding or representing the modern discipline is its quantitative approach to so many of its problems. They find only challenge in the sorrowful fact that some college students are not easily taught anything involving numbers or numerically founded concepts. They most of all want to discern how to make the quantitative approach plain to these and all other students. Yet if we endorse this aspiration, there is still the problem of whether statistics is best taught as a separate discipline, with psychological applications—that is, as method, psychological content being introduced only for exemplification—or whether it should be taught in the context of a subject matter of some other kind (such as experimental psychology or general psychology) and definitely treated as only a means to an end of understanding that other subject matter. There is also the question of the level at which quantitative teaching should begin. If it could begin in the very first course there would be a great gain in efficiency in teaching later courses, and a reduction in the degree to which statistical concepts have to be duplicated in various courses after the elementary one. Quite clearly, however, there are many other things to do in the first course, and perhaps there is not the proper student motivation there anyway to permit sufficiently thorough treatment of quantitative methods. Finally, there is the question of just what quantitative ideas are the important ones. Fundamental concepts of measurement may be regarded as more significant by some instructors than particular forms of correlation, or heavy stress may be placed on sampling problems to the exclusion of other concepts. It is clear that decisions about the teaching of quantitative method must be correlated with decisions about the teaching of other courses or topics. Only in this way will it be possible to ensure proper attention to such concepts at the right time and with certainty that a useful level of mastery is attained.

Second, there is the problem of experimental method. Although it is almost uniformly regarded as necessary for a psychology major to become familiar with experimentation, there is great variation in attitude toward the method and the teaching of it and toward the degree to which it should be stressed in elementary courses. There are those, for example, who feel that experimental methods are overly technical in nature for undergraduate teaching purposes and that the return they yield in understanding does not justify the time necessary to master them thoroughly. There are others who regard experimental methods as unnecessarily rigid, limited in scope, and simply not suitable for attacking many kinds of important or pressing psychological problems. It seems to me that an overly narrow conception of experimental method is implied in the latter views. In this narrow conception, experimentation is regarded as consisting mostly of such laboratory specifics as lifting weights, constructing apparatus, recording after-images, and caring for animals. Were this all there is to experimental method, and there is no denying it is about all some students have been exposed to in the past, one could hardly justify stressing it in an undergraduate program. On the other hand, the more up-to-date and representative view of experimental method is that it involves general principles of design, of analytical thought, of conclusion drawing and of sampling, which are of significance in many realms of psychology and far beyond it. If stress in teaching experimental method is laid upon what is transferable or generalizable, the material can truly be regarded as appropriate for inclusion in liberal arts education.

We may grant such an opinion but still find ourselves confronted with certain problems in the teaching of experimental method. Perhaps the most pressing one is whether there should be a separate course in experimental psychology, or whether, as Wolfle and associates suggest [288], since so much of modern psychology is experimentally oriented, the method should be taught in a topical context, as an aspect of any (or of a particular) course dealing with psychological content, such as learning or perception. Even if the decision is to offer a separate course, there is the pedagogical problem, as for statistics, of how to provide enough content and of the right kind to make the methodological learning fully meaningful. And also, as with statistics, there are problems in deciding just what aspects of experimental method are the basic ones, or which forms of method are easiest to begin with, and so on [8].

It appears to be an efficient curriculum plan to allow for one major effort to teach experimental method, and similarly one major effort to teach statistics. In recent years there has been considerable attention to the possibility of combining the two courses. This would have the special advantage of permitting direct attention to the statistical aspects of experimental design. This does not resolve the question of what content to utilize, but if that question is answered by assigning any particular content more or less arbitrarily, and if adequate time is allowed, a highly meaningful kind of teaching appears to be possible. This kind of course may be an excellent solution for the major, and also an efficient and stimulating learning experience for the typical student who wishes to sample psychology briefly.

A third methodology which may be included somewhere in the undergraduate psychology curriculum is that of testing, typically of intelligence, interests, or aptitudes, but sometimes of personality as well. In recent years there has been a reaction against this kind of teaching, particularly as it may have contributed to the production of partially trained persons who have proceeded to do psychological work in a not very competent or fully ethical way, thus reflecting unfavorably upon the psychological profession in general and creating a threat to the welfare of the persons whom they appear to serve. Furthermore, training in testing, more than that in experimentation or statistics, has been regarded as more practical, more concerned with the uses of psychology than with the proper scientific understanding of it, and it has thus been deemed less suitable for liberal arts education.

It may be that a narrow conception of the purposes or values of training in testing is involved here. Perhaps it is true, as is sometimes said, that many tests have been developed without principle, used without validation, interpreted without insight; equally, one might argue, sophistication in all these matters has been developing rapidly and it should now be possible to find, in the field of testing methods, generalizable or transferable concepts. Particularly may it be possible to treat testing situations as special cases of observation or of experimentation and thus to link testing concepts with other aspects of method. To the extent such things are possible, testing methods may justifiably be regarded as undergraduate curriculum material. The specific skills which, e.g., a highly practiced Rorschach technician or Civil Service test constructor must have need not be taught at the undergraduate level, nor need the student have detailed experience in testing the mentally ill, where professional competence and responsibility are required. Instead, through limited, carefully selected and supervised first-hand experience with test behavior and through study of the methodological, ethical, and other questions posed, the student may acquire, as does the student in the laboratory, a more complete understanding of what psychological data mean. There will remain, however, the question of what content to utilize in teaching the method, although solutions to this problem may come more easily in testing this area than in such a subject as, for example, statistics.

The fourth methodological tool to which we call attention here because of its unclear status in the curriculum is that of interviewing. The technique may be concerned, of course, with occupational placement, public opinion, or with varying degrees and kind of personal problems, many of which cannot be approached by an undergraduate student for sheer lack of background. Psychologists often have felt that the techniques should not be introduced at the undergraduate level, partly because of the ethical or public relations problems involved, and partly because interview techniques are often regarded as a matter of merely practical concern (as in rule-of-thumb guidance of employment interviewing), or as not exhibiting generalizable principles of method. But sophistication in such matters has increased greatly in recent years, and the dynamics of this kind of interpersonal relation are the subject of study by many investigators. For this reason it may well be true that what is generalizable about interviewing methodology should be introduced in a concrete way into the curriculum, at least for the majoring student. Careful control over this learning would be necessary, together with full indoctrination with respect to the ethical questions involved.

The choice of curriculum content. In addition to the issues concerning method which we have discussed there are questions about just what psychological facts, laws, or concepts are to form the substance of the curriculum. These issues must be resolved in one way or another to create a curriculum at all. It may well be that if they were carefully and systematically resolved a curriculum could be created which exhibited little of the repetitiousness and inefficiency to which Wolfle has so pointedly called attention.

Presumably everyone would agree that the most basic of

psychological ideas should form both the beginning point and the main substance of undergraduate education. However, it is on the meaning of the word *basic* that a primary curriculum issue turns. One meaning is implied in the book by Wolfle and his associates [288] in their recommendation that certain core courses be offered. These authors suggest that the core courses should correspond to those aspects of behavior which are immediately evident to introspective analysis of the phenomenological type: motivation, perception, thought, and so on. In another meaning the word basic might refer to the major categories of causal factors in behavior, beginning with learning and growth and perhaps including also all the topics listed by the phenomenologically oriented curriculum builder, since those topics refer to processes which are both consequent and antecedent, depending on how they are viewed or at what moment. The word basic might also point to a concern for presenting the best available theoretical orientation and position, so that the largest number of facts and laws learned by the student can be seen in fullest significance. Finally, basic might refer to what is judged to be most useful in the personal life of the individual student. Pressey [215] and Berrien [30] have been especially articulate in arguing for this latter consideration, and the survey of Sanford and Fleishman [235] shows how widely the view has been adopted. It would be premature to argue that one of these conceptions of what is basic is the most appropriate one and equally premature to argue that all undergraduate curriculums should be exactly the same. Clearly, however, departmental group decision as to which approach to utilize in planning the curriculum is desirable so that the content will be reasonably coherent and will facilitate over-all mastery of the field by the student.

Implied in the foregoing comment concerning the problem of what is basic is a second, slightly different kind of problem, which requires some discussion here: that of deciding how and where to present psychological theory to students. The feeling of a goodly number of psychologists is that theory in psychology is chaotic, well calculated to convince students that psychologists mostly bicker among themselves, and not of sufficient integrating merit to justify taking much time for it at the undergraduate level. The elementary course is often taught with little concern for the nature and the role of theory in psychological thought. Indeed, the position may be taken that the student is not ready for theory until after he has had a thorough introduction to the empirical data of psychology. On the other hand there are psychologists who believe that not only are quantitation and theory necessary to give meaning to empirical data, but that some particular theory should be mastered in the student's very first introduction to psychology, if only to provide a framework within which to master or compare other theories at a later date ([154]; see the criticism by Wendt [275]).

The question of how much theory, and what kind, persists throughout much of the curriculum. It reaches acute form in relation to the common senior course in psychological viewpoints, which all too often consists of a motley set of views, some current and some outmoded, taught without full interconnection with materials learned in other and prior contexts. It seems essential that the curriculum be planned to ensure that the student does not go to the one extreme of regarding theory as useless or unreal in its significance, or to the other of regarding theory, even of the fantasy type, as all that counts, and rigorously achieved data as unimportant. It seems probable that psychology as a discipline is in a stage where theoretical tools are among our most powerful ones for producing scientific progress; we therefore do an injustice to students if this understanding is not part of their learning.

A third content problem requiring some policy decision has to do with our common demand that our students learn our technical language. It is relatively easy, particularly in elementary courses, to demonstrate that from 40 to 80 per cent of the examination questions are wholly or in part tests of vocabulary knowledge. This is often defended on grounds that the language is necessary for more advanced work, for intelligent reading or participation in class, for discriminating reading of popular materials on psychology, or for reading after formal course work has ceased. The difficulties with this defense are, of course, that many students do not take advanced work or read advanced materials in psychology, and that our technical language, after all, varies in usage and is sometimes downright fuzzy in meaning. One cannot easily take the position that technical language should be avoided in courses for non-majors but used in courses for majors, if only for the reason that in most departments the two groups have many course experiences in common. Perhaps the best to be hoped for is that students will be taught a sensitivity to the language problem, not only in psychology but in other disciplines, that they will gain such understandings as the operational approach to definitions and, indeed, any ideas helpful in resolving semantic confusions, and that in a course they will be expected to master and utilize only those technical language items which are likely to be of most general significance to them in their later work.

Fourth in our consideration of curriculum content problems is whether, or to what extent, content from related disciplines is to be taught. It is always possible, of course, to study our own staff specialties and courses and the offerings of other departments, and in this way decide on the most appropriate way of ensuring that our students learn any materials regarded as essential in, for example, biology, mathematics, philosophy of science, sociology, anthropology, or physics. We can insist on work in other departments and we can bring material from other disciplines into our own courses where it is most appropriate, although this must be done with due regard for the reactions of other departments about what they may regard as pirating! Perhaps the more difficult problem, and the scholarly one, is that of deciding just which material from the related disciplines is truly functional in enhancing psychological understanding. Psychology itself is divided on such problems, as is shown by our discussions of the relative merit of physiological-sounding intervening variables, or the merits of information theory for psychologists. The need is clear for the psychologist who plans a curriculum to include such content as he can believe in and can make come alive for the student. The need is equally clear to avoid having in the psychology curriculum materials which might be more effectively taught in other departments, or which fail to contribute to a better understanding of psychology as such.

A fifth issue in choosing curriculum content is closely related to the methodology of teaching and to the previously mentioned issue concerning the role of theory. This is whether content intended to facilitate synthesis of psychological knowledge into a comprehensive view by the individual student is best included after preliminary work of an analytical sort or should be included everywhere. To give a concrete example of this problem: Is it better to present initially in separate courses the material concerned with psychological processes such as motivation and perception, and concepts such as capacity or traits, and then later deal with personality as an integrative conception (as proposed by Wolfle *et al.* [288]), or is it better to present the concept of personality from the very beginning with the hope that it will provide direction and meaning for the detailed analysis of behavior? Some middle path may be the only realistic one. By turns, both analytical and synthetic pedagogical processes may be essential, within courses and from one course to another. Perhaps our resolution of this issue, then, should be to ensure that the student is not subjected to either the extreme of learning how to take man apart without ever putting him back together again, or the extreme of having always a naïvely global, not carefully detailed or analyzed conception of man and his behavior. Whether formal curriculum organization is utilized to achieve this end could become, then, a not very crucial question.

GENERAL EDUCATION IN PSYCHOLOGY

We have previously commented briefly (Chap. 3) upon the rather unimportant role psychology has played in formally organized general education programs. As did the Knox Conference [130], we may now inquire how psychology in its more common participation in distribution programs, or simply in liberal arts education in general, can or should contribute to such agreed upon and liberally oriented objectives as those formulated in that chapter. The present discussion is at once an attempted exemplification of what general education can mean, applied to a specific subject matter area, and an attempt to become specific concerning what objectives ought to be achieved in the departmental curriculum.

Methods and tool-skill objectives. As previously noted, it is generally agreed that the liberal arts student should become capable of more effective thought and judgment and possess the necessary intellectual tools to permit him to exercise his improved capacities for thought in new directions or at higher levels of competence. It is often said that teaching in psychology is in one sense in a favorable position to contribute markedly to achievement of such an objective. The relatively undeveloped state of our field and the nearness of the boundaries of sure knowledge make it easy to show the student how necessary is attention to method, but how readily, by acquiring certain tool-skills, he may move into new intellectual terrain.

Some of the contributions scientific psychology can make to thought processes are these: the central importance of accurate observation, of both self and events external to the self, can be made evident; the various operations or processes by which concepts attain empirical meaning, and the problem of avoiding semantic traps in making logical analyses, can be shown; through the study of experimental design and operations, broadly conceived, attention can be drawn to the necessities for and the skills of analysis, to the concept of causation, to the requirements of evidence and the rules governing the drawing of conclusions, to the problem of bias and prejudgment, and to the tendency to search for single rather than multiple explanations of behavior; in experimental survey testing and other settings, the problem of sampling can be stressed; the significance of the quantitative approach to empirical problems can be made very clear indeed; the uses of hypothesis, law, and theory in scientific and in social thought can be presented. In teaching to such objectives there is ample opportunity to show the significance of dispassionate and properly founded judgment, to encourage practice in the forms of creative and critical thought so necessary to the well-educated person, and to demonstrate convincingly the fruitfulness of the empirical and theoretical methods which science has developed for attacking many kinds of problems both within and without formal science.

Knowledge objectives. It was suggested earlier that a second objective of liberal education is the pursuit of knowledge as such, the mastery of information of many kinds, with the intention of broadening the student's grasp of reality. Perhaps the most general understanding which psychology can contribute here is the knowledge that behavior is lawful, approachable, or understandable, as is any event in the natural world. It is not something mysterious which will lose its essence utterly if subjected to scientific study, regardless of what some humanists say or fear. This general understanding will presumably be compounded out of specific realizations of the existence of sensible knowledge in many specific areas of human conduct, including the social aspects of behavior. Again we can itemize some of the particular kinds of knowledge which may be regarded as having general educational significance: an understanding of the psychological aspects of significant social institutions, such as the family, government, education, and religion; an enhanced understanding of interpersonal and intergroup relations, including attention to the dynamics of major phenomena such as war and peace, social pressure and unrest; the role of communication in social and individual phenomena of adjustment and in propaganda and opinion formation; a knowledge of significant processes in the individual, including growth, learning, adjustment, and the relation of these not only to individual conduct but also to social phenomena; a knowledge of individual differences, again not only in relation to an understanding of self but in relation to social variation and differences in social perception. In addition to materials calculated to reduce provincialism and to lead the student to new ideas or to different views of the world and of society, it may be regarded as desirable to include some treatment of the nature and status of psychology as a discipline, of its dual status as both social and biological science, and of its general place among the intellectual disciplines, the sciences, and the professions.

Motivational objectives. It is in this realm that the impacts of teaching are least well understood. It is not clear, for example, whether attitudes, values, motives, or standards of conduct are directly teachable in the ordinary (intellectualized) sense, or whether they must develop outside the context of formal teaching in a naturalistic (unintentional, casual, nonintellectual) way [34, 288]. Further, it is not clear just how far teaching may or should go in attempting to affect personal standards of students without becoming indoctrination in the nondemocratic sense, i.e., without taking freedom of choice from the student. The discussions of the role of liberal education in our society in recent years have made it plain, however, that permitting the student to develop his own standards in an unguided way not only confuses him but constitutes a refusal by the faculty to accept full responsibility for the contribution of education to the needs of society. In choosing a position between the laissez-faire and the indoctrination extremes, in other words, many who believe in democratic education now think that somewhat more indoctrination is essential, whatever the label it be given (see the related discussion in Chap. 3). It seems desirable for psychological teaching to contribute wherever it can to standards and modes of conduct generally regarded as appropriate in our culture. Obviously, one of the standards involved is protection of the individual who wishes to disagree with or differ from those standards, up to the limits that a democratic society can tolerate in its own best interests.

We shall discuss here four motivational changes which we might well hope for in our psychology students, all of them being regarded as objectives of liberal education. We may, in the first place, expect an increased tolerance for and acceptance of self and others, together with enhanced respect for the individual. Study of such topics as individual differences, psychological development of the individual, or the relation between social structure and behavior should increase the tolerance and acceptance which the student feels or expresses. Second, we might hope for increased feelings of responsibility for analysis and conduct of the affairs of society, whether through government, the educational system or some other aspect of community life. The study of the nature of leadership, of the roles of intellect and feeling in the development of social institutions and functions, of the family, or of intergroup relations should contribute toward such a development. As a third aspiration, we might look toward an enhanced capacity of the student for enjoyment of life. This may result from the development of new modes of response to esthetic experiences; through preparation for a career, or clarification of vocational choice; through increased self-acceptance and freedom from personal conflict, making increased energies available in other and outgoing activities; or through increased desire to explore and master new intellectual skills or realms of knowledge. All of these are references to motivational states, and admittedly it is very difficult to assign responsibility for their development to particular studies. It would seem likely, however, that the study in general of the dynamics of individual behavior and adjustment, of sensory and perceptual reactions, of capacities and abilities, or of new methodologies should be contributory. The fourth aspiration, which presumably characterizes all college teaching, is that of leaving with the student an increased awareness of knowledge itself as a human value. Our students may acquire this value in any instance of rewarded discovery of the reaches and uses of psychological knowledge or method, which leads us here to the belief that only to the extent that we are able to teach a truly substantial discipline are we likely to aid in the process of teaching respect for knowledge as such.

That psychologists are by no means unique in aspiring to achieve objectives of the kind discussed above is illustrated by a survey of sociologists' opinions about their objectives in teaching [267]. The first ten aims listed, in order of frequency, were these: to help the student understand his society; lead him toward objective thinking about social situations; acquaint him with technical terms and concepts; assist him to analyze his own experiences through sociological concepts; acquaint him with the sociological approach to social problems; teach him the scientific approach; stimulate attitudes of social responsibility; present verified knowledge designed to change student attitudes; prepare for advanced courses; elaborate the principles of social behavior. These aspirations appear to be close to the methods, knowledge, and motivational aims of psychologists.

Liberal arts teaching. Evidently, if we wish to accomplish results of the kind just described, and if we are to accomplish them even with students who study with us for only a term or so, we shall have to regard the beginning work in the department as serving majors and non-majors alike. In other words, practical considerations, and for many of us theoretical ones as well, force us to assume that general education in psychology is of equal value to all kinds of students who come to us and, equally, that this is a good way for the majoring student to begin his psychological studies.

Acceptance of such an idea will require revision of the concept of the major itself, as will be discussed later. This seems entirely likely because the simple fact of regarding a large block of elementary teaching in the psychology department as having only general purposes will have consequences such as the following. Methodological teaching would not be aimed at technical competence but rather at an understanding of the assumptions and the reasoning involved in the choice or the use of various methods, that is, at a search for principles of methodology and thought of use not only within psychology but elsewhere; our technical language presumably would be involved only to that degree thought essential for intelligent reading and discussion, and there would be more concern for the principles according to which definitions and concepts are formed than for mastery of an extensive new vocabulary; the total list of topics included in the elementary courses would be rather more representative of the needs of the student than of the profession of psychology, although it is agreed that an unrepresentative picture of the discipline would be a disservice to the student; to contribute to breadth of understanding, there would be rather more attention to the interrelationships of psychological ideas and those from other disciplines than would ordinarily be given in a psychology curriculum as such; and finally, there would be a continuing effort to search out what have been called the persisting problems of psychology, to deal forthrightly, but somewhere and to whatever degree we can, with problems concerning the relation of mind to body, or relativism and absolutism in thought, or faith, morality, and ethics, or the relation of the sciences to the humanities. Perhaps it should be said that the dual task of the teacher here would be to present the approach of science to scientific questions, yet be at least willing to regard as genuine certain problems interjected from outside the conventional scientific framework.

Curriculum and extracurriculum. It is usually desirable, in presenting ideas of the degree of abstraction represented above, to indicate concretely just what might be done to achieve what is recommended. In the present instance, then, it might be desirable to suggest exactly what kinds of courses and service facilities might best provide general education in psychology. However, in movements for educational reform, I am of the opinion that presenting a concrete solution prematurely is dangerous because reactions are likely to be to the particular program rather than to the principles it supposedly reflects. There is, furthermore, the very practical point that the implementation of teaching objectives accepted by a psychology faculty depends very much upon local circumstances, upon the staff available, and upon the college context within which the objectives are set and the arrangements made. Generalized statements of programs can never be entirely appropriate. Only moderately specific suggestions will be made, therefore, with the explicit understanding that they are inadequate to the final task of creating a concrete educational program, and with full realization that available information does not in any way suggest that reaching our stated educational goals is easy [118].

Since one of the aims of general education in psychology is to give the student a well-rounded and coherent picture of what the discipline is and has to offer to him, it would appear desirable to do away with the clutter of elementary courses we now offer and channel an equivalent amount of faculty manpower into perhaps a single, year-long, elementary course. This course would be taken in the context of general or distributional education and have that status in the eyes of both majoring and non-majoring students. It would integrate, and teach without duplication or needless repetition, the social and the biological approaches to behavior and experience and the theoretical and the empirical natures of the whole discipline of psychology. There would be concern throughout for methodological teaching or implications wherever appropriate. There would be attention to, discussion of, exemplification of, the various attitudinal questions of concern to either the professional or layman in psychological matters.

The kind of course just described would be the principal general educational activity of the department. It would be as clear-cut in the systematic sense as is possible in the present state of the development of our science, it would be given as much generality as possible, it would be linked to as many life experiences of the student as possible, it would wherever possible place the discipline in historical perspective, and it would be given the best pedagogical arrangements possible, with attention to experimentation, demonstration, discussion and other forms of enhanced intellectual stimulation. Only in a department willing to reconsider entirely its specialized functions will there be a chance of instituting such a course; and, of course, the text materials for it have not yet been provided. Indications that such a course is feasible can be found in Oeser's description [204].

Two further services in the interests of a general education in psychology should be given due consideration. One of these is the use of counseling, adjustment, or other services, outside the curriculum but aiding in the achievement of curricular objectives. The other is the possibility that within a general education context and within a psychology department there may be reason to create certain particular-interest courses. This kind of proposal was suggested by Wolfle *et al.* [288], and, as they point out, appears to be sound so long as the courses are consistent with college objectives generally, do not degenerate into vocational or fad courses, and are planned to seize upon and expand the range of interests of students rather than merely cater to special interests of a narrow sort. In this category of courses psychologists might well give more attention than they have in recent years to such topics as the arts, literature, or religion, as well as to the more conventional and partially applied courses. It is suggested here that this kind of work would only follow after a general introduction and that it would always remain in the status of an elective in general education, if such can be conceived.

It is of course immediately possible to find practical objections to the proposal that most of the teaching of a department, that is, the teaching planned for the largest proportion of the students, should not only have the general character just proposed, but should occur in a single year-long course. One must admit that the tendency toward chopped-up curriculums and rigidly required sequences or numbers of different courses is not peculiar to psychology, so that it will be difficult to persuade psychologists to reintroduce the year course and thus risk losing students who do not have that long a period to devote to psychology, or students who wish a narrow rather than a general knowledge of it. It must also be admitted that psychologists themselves will be loathe to give up their introductory courses in their own fields, such as social or educational psychology. It therefore can only be stated as an article of faith here that a prospect for educational gain should not be sacrificed before it gets a full trial. More specifically, compromise with the objectives indicated above for the longer and more generally oriented elementary course should be viewed as temporary and tactical rather than as final or obligatory. Perhaps the small colleges, where it is impossible for the faculty to be specialists, can lead the way.

SPECIAL EDUCATION IN PSYCHOLOGY

Special education, we have said, is dedicated to the same ends as general education, but the method is different. There is concentration upon the ideas and methods of a more narrowly selected field, so that the student not only has the opportunity to explore his special interests or prepare himself for graduate and professional training, but also gains the experience of high-level mastery which can occur only when the subject to be mastered is restricted in scope. There may be students who will wish to go part way but not completely into the field of concentration in psychology, but the working assumption is made here that their objectives are the same as those of the majoring student.

Objectives of instruction in the major. Because we are now on more familiar ground we can review quite briefly the aims of instruction for the student who majors with us. In the realm of methodology and tool-skills, we can list at once some of the more exacting or precise techniques in which we expect mastery: experimental and statistical design; experimental operations, as exhibited in carrying out independent research; understanding of and skill in measurement and quantitative operations; ability to formulate, analyze, or criticize theoretical ideas; ability to discuss and write psychology intelligently; familiarity (at least) with the problems of interviewing and testing. In the realm of knowledge objectives we might suggest: a broad awareness of the kinds of psychological theory, the reasons for the existence of differences in theories, and the methodology for resolving differences; high-level competence in some realms of psychological knowledge, up to the research margins there; a general knowledge of scientific vocabulary and symbolism; and balanced competence in both the social and the biological science aspects of psychology. In the realm of motivational developments we might expect movement toward such objectives as these: interest in and reasonableness toward the divergent activities encompassed within our total professional and scientific field; development of special topical or other interests in psychology; confirmation or strengthening of intellectual curiosity in the particular field of psychology and elsewhere; pleasure in exploring the relationships between psychological-scientific and other kinds of knowledge or activity. We should hope for continued progress toward any of the goals of general education in psychology which are not implied in the attempt here to single out what might be the particular contributions of the major.

I shall again resist the temptation to be overly concrete in stating the curriculum and extracurriculum procedures (such as journal or research clubs) by which the objectives of the major program might be reached. The problem of formulating the procedures and the problem of translating the objectives into teachable form are not so unfamiliar or so difficult here, for much of what is done now in the psychology major could easily be adapted to the proposals for change, provided only, as we have several times implied, that there is more concern with the development of the student than with the needs of the faculty or the discipline as a scientific and professional entity. Of particular importance would be the adoption of an introductory course like that described earlier in this chapter, for this would condition the kinds of concepts, the language, and the range of methods that would logically follow in courses in the major.

Perhaps the main change to be stressed here is essentially pedagogical. That is, to achieve high-level mastery of psychological matters efficiently, we must be much less eclectic in our assembly of materials for particular courses, more insistent upon utilization of small classes, firsthand experience, and free discussion as techniques of teaching, and more demanding with respect to standards of psychological analysis and systematic thought. We shall probably have to teach fewer courses more thoroughly, and with a sharp eye to sequences and interrelations among them. The core-course concept of Wolfle and his associates [288], as mentioned earlier, is an example of an effort to achieve some of these aims. Many other efforts to achieve systematic rigor, such as combining statistical and other methodologies in order to give them the fullest meaning, or organizing courses around a particular theoretical system, are likely to lead to more devoted teaching and more comprehensive understanding. And certainly, for the student who has made provision to develop this systematic framework and understanding, any accompanying opportunity to examine particular interest fields in courses devoted to this purpose could only be of value.

Perhaps the sense of teaching in the major could be summarized thus: It would place rather more emphasis upon methodology than upon content in the beginning (for example, in the junior year), but the reverse would be true in later stages; it would give attention, whether in separate courses or in each course, to problems of both analysis and synthesis; it would be concerned not only with an over-all view of man's nature, conduct, and society but also with an over-all view of the nature of psychology, as both science and profession; perhaps above all it would stress the possibilities and the rewards of high-level mastery and independent study.

The curriculum and recruitment. It should be clear now that the psychology major is not regarded as having a proselytizing function. Nevertheless it is a point of pride with faculty members that some of their students decide to enter the profession and we may ask whether there is anything about the curriculum which influences such decisions. It may be said, for example, that real respect for psychology is built only by rigorous teaching of substantial material, and only this kind of respect will ever lead a student into the field. But the kind of curriculum this implies (typically, experimental psychology, statistics, etc.) repels a good many students, and so it can also be said that the curriculum should emphasize materials illustrative of how psychology meets personal needs and deals with real human and social problems. Somewhere between these two extremes, we may suppose, lies the truth. Neither impersonal and cold scientific material by itself nor uncritical and overgeneralized material will attract the able but normally motivated student for long. There must be a sense of genuine human value in the material and acceptance of the student as a person, yet there must also be the impression that work in the discipline is intellectually respectable and self-enhancing. Then there may be some genuine recruiting value in the curriculum as such.

5

THE CAREER OF THE COLLEGE TEACHER

It is common for the beginning teacher to realize belatedly that he has not fully anticipated the complexities of a teaching career. This is in no way surprising, for he has passed through a career as student with no particular reason to learn about faculty life and tactics. My experience with this particular cause of concern in the beginning teacher suggests that there is a good deal that words can do to alleviate the problem, for straightforward information is often all that is necessary. There will remain a good deal of factual learning—for colleges and universities do indeed provide an instance of a complex culture, one full of necessities for fine discriminations. And a certain amount of emotional or attitudinal learning will be necessary—for the college teacher must sooner or later begin to identify with the field of education and with the teaching process in the way he identifies with his particular field of specialization, or he cannot remain motivated to teach. But the pooled experience of other teachers is often useful as a source of advice to the beginning faculty member. Two of the strongest arguments for capitalizing on such experience and shortening the adjustment or learning period are that the possibility of satisfactions in becoming a teacher is thereby increased, as is the probability that the new teacher will stabilize his program more rapidly and be able to start his research.

CHOOSING AND FINDING AN ACADEMIC POSITION

The job market. The criteria as to what constitutes an acceptable teaching position are, of course, largely personal. We find the usual blend of rational and irrational in the decision —so that one new Ph.D. is determined to return to the portion of the country he came from while his laboratory mate makes exactly the opposite decision. To increase the degree of rationality in the decision it may be helpful to consider some of the determiners of choice which originate not so much in the individual as in the impersonal job market.

What kind of position and salary one can expect to command is determined partly by factors in the national economy. One obvious point here has to do with the economic cycle. Colleges and universities almost always would like to have more faculty members than they have, or at least to replace all those they lose, and their ability to create or retain job "slots" depends upon income. But the demand for faculty does not fluctuate in an uncomplicated way with good times and bad in general, for student enrollment pressures also influence the need for teaching personnel. Certain types of institutions find themselves required to accept many more students in time of economic depression than in times when more jobs are available to attract college-age persons. In addition, in the college and university world there are other kinds of stresses, some of them produced by new administrations, by legislatures, or by boards of control, in which, periodically, budgets get tighter, overly rapid promotion of the existing faculty becomes a matter of concern, and so on. One can only try, then, as a prospective Ph.D. and prospective beginning teacher, to learn through conversation and reading what the probabilities are in the geographical area and in the particular kind of institution in which he would like to teach. Failure to be realistic about the number and kind of job openings can, it is quite clear, lead to failure to take the job one should have taken, or failure to wait until the most appropriate one is available.

Another determiner of the job market is found in the particular discipline one is in. In psychology, the discipline as both science and profession has undergone a great expansion, both during and since World War II. As a consequence, the number of teaching positions has inevitably increased rapidly, and young psychologists, through scarcity, have commanded higher salaries and ranks than ever before, somewhat to the embarrassment of institutions which attempt to ensure fair rewards for those who continue scholarship in the less spectacular fields such as the classics. This also happened after World War I. In that instance and, we may expect, in this, there has to be a leveling-off period in academic appointments such that, regardless of what the new Ph.D. can command in government service or industry, he may have to take a modest instructorship as his first academic post. On the other hand, another factor in the general economy of the nation suggests that this tightening of the job market, if it occurs, can only be temporary. This is the imminent increase in college enrollments as the World War II and postwar increases in birth rate begin to have their influence. All competent surveys suggest that colleges and universities must in the next years increase in size. There will presumably be some tendency to absorb the increase in student enrollments by increasing the size of faculty teaching load, at least in some institutions, but this will not be sufficient to solve the problem. Jobs must therefore become more numerous again.

At any specific moment of decision about a proferred job, various pressures of the times will have influenced many factors in that decision. The job applicant should have secured the relevant information not only about salary and rank available, but also about such things as kind and size of teaching load, amount and kind of research support, promotion prospects and procedures, accessibility of tenure status, living conditions for the faculty family in the given community, summer and other opportunities for extra compensation or research time, and number of extracurricular duties (special jobs within the department, committee service, etc.) expected of the new faculty member. (The book by Woodburne [289] contains much useful information on the personnel practices of colleges and universities.)

Self-evaluation in seeking a job. Although it would be unrealistic to attempt to divine in detail the complex personal factors involved in job decisions, it does appear possible to list some of the relevant considerations in the academic world. To begin with, the person planning to seek a job must in his own way size up his standing in the eyes of those who must recommend him. His aspirations as to kind of institution, rank, and salary in his first job will be largely influenced by the expectations of his graduate faculty concerning his productiveness as a scholar, his promise as a teacher, and the relevance of his prior experience to what he might be appointed to do in any specific job. It is clear that direct attempts to investigate the private judgments of the graduate faculty will be fruitless, but the student knows the marks given to him in various kinds of grading situations—courses, research, and so on—and should be able to sense fairly well the degree of enthusiasm or acceptance his work arouses in his faculty and his peers. More than this, talk with the faculty about kinds of possible jobs, and the kinds of posts they think him suited for, should fairly quickly make it possible to infer whether one may realistically hope for strong support, or must settle for something less than this.

It should be emphasized that the new Ph.D.'s view of the job situation is strongly influenced by the fact that he is just completing three or four years in a graduate school environment, an environment both highly specialized and usually chosen because of its unique advantages for him. We need not be concerned about the new Ph.D. who is eminently fitted for and able to command a position in the same sort of situation, but we do need to note that this background may lead to a lack of realism in the wishes or expectancies of a good many other prospective teachers. For example, the graduate school environment may lead to overly rosy expectations about the amount of research time one can expect to have, and about the size of classes one will teach. Sometimes the prospective teacher is frustrated to learn that at the undergraduate level there is no apparent teaching assignment corresponding to his graduate field of specialization. And, interestingly enough, it is common to find that the new Ph.D. feels a lack of confidence in his ability to take on undergraduate teaching assignments in areas which are somewhat unfamiliar to him—as though ability to "learn ahead of a sophomore" were beyond him, or as though not having had a graduate course meant that a certain realm was closed off to him. A different kind of a consequence of graduate school may in some instances be a loss of esteem for college-level or college-type jobs, perhaps as part of a pattern of upward social mobility in which the large or famous university setting is deemed to have more prestige. Be that as it may, it should be remembered that the total number of jobs in the colleges is very large and that many colleges offer faculty opportunities of the best kind [197]. It may be true, for example, that a good college permits more genuine opportunity for original scholarship than does a large and impersonal university where the youngest staff members have numerous repetitive sections of an elementary course to teach and little else to sustain or occupy them.

Locating an appropriate faculty position is one of those activities for which the academic culture has an unwritten but nevertheless enforced code [205]. The sense of it is that the person who wants a position is somewhat like the young lady who wants an opportunity to change from single to securely married status—she can do certain things to facilitate the change but there are other things she must at all odds not do. The prospective teacher must not attempt aggressively to advertise his virtues or buttonhole prospective employers and attempt to sell himself. Notices in the placement columns of professional journals should be only a factual statement about training and background. (For example, one should not utilize an advertisement like the following, which is adapted from one in a nationally circulated scientific journal: "Forward looking, aggressive young psychologist seeks contact with person or foundation interested in endowing a chair of behavior theory. Backward looking institutions need not reply. Write Box . . .")

The thing which one can do is to work through one's own faculty, especially one's adviser. Surprisingly enough, the new Ph.D. may not realize that it is part of the graduate department's pride, and felt obligation, to place as many of its graduates as it can in appropriate positions, and he should therefore feel no reluctance to seek aid from the faculty. It may sometimes be true that the graduate adviser does not know the teaching field intimately, or the undergraduate field very well, and it is therefore useful to consult with other faculty members, including the department head. The code involves heavy dependence upon such persons to inquire about positions from their friends, or to receive inquiries, and in due course to arrange for direct contact between prospective employer and job candidate.

It would be misleading here to give the impression that jobs in the academic world are not offered or found in other ways.

Certainly the placement services of the American Psychological Association, the American Association of University Professors, and university placement bureaus provide a kind of intermediary service. On the other hand, it appears to be true that the great majority of positions are still filled on the word of those who are in the best or most knowledgeable position to judge prospective candidates. This leads to a further suggestion: the prospective academic person will do well to make it easier for such judgments to be made. This can lead to sounder recommendations for him, or it might in some cases lead him to decide that he does not want to become a teacher at all, something best found out early. Accepted methods of making it possible for others to judge one's promise for an academic career include, in addition to the obvious devices of doing good course work and good independent research, such tactics as seizing opportunities to try a hand at lecturing or conducting a seminar, presenting papers at scientific meetings, publishing rather than hoarding one's papers, talking research and teaching with those from whom one can learn—either in one's own department or elsewhere, and visiting other laboratories or institutions as opportunities naturally present themselves. One cannot keep quietly to himself all through a graduate career and expect intelligent help, or much help at all, when the time comes to find an academic post. There are now a good many institutions providing more or less formalized preparation for teaching at the college level, and the person who knows himself to be academically oriented may well take advantage of such training opportunities. (For a discussion of this area of training, see [53, 54, 111, 131, 187, 273]; additional references and comments in [57, 74].)

In the larger graduate departments, there may be problems of communication between the job candidate and those who are supporting his candidacies. This means that when you accept a position it is important to let your endorsers know. Quite apart from simple courtesy you should prevent the embarrassing circumstance of having an adviser recommend you for a job when you have already taken one.

As we have so often had occasion to comment in other contexts, the problems of job-finding (and holding) are similar in fields related to psychology. The essays of Bogardus [39, 41] show that sociologists have many of the same concerns, and his discussion of the teaching problems of young sociologists is related to the section which follows [40].

REQUIRED LEARNING IN THE NEW JOB

Although it is not possible to predict the details which the new instructor must learn as fast as possible, experience suggests the *kinds* of knowledge he must acquire [see 20, 35, 50, 82, and especially 260 and the references provided there]. Whether or not the immediate need is apparent the new instructor will do well to fortify himself against demands for judgment or action that are likely to turn up early in his career. It is sound advice to the beginner to arrive at his new post well ahead of time, if he possibly can, not only to arrange for housing and other necessaries, but to permit advance preparations and subsidiary learning.

Academic routines and procedures. The intricacies of the academic situation are nowhere more confusing than in the simple business of learning routines in a new place. We can itemize, almost in check-list fashion, some of the bits of lore which are always somewhat different than in one's last institution and which, taken together, give a distinctive tone to each institution. To begin with, one needs to learn something about the administrative organization of the college or university—not because the details of administration are of direct importance to the beginning instructor but rather because one needs to learn about the kinds of communication channels there are to service agencies, and about the need for or mode of contact with the dean's office, registrar's office or, for that matter, the senior members of one's own department. One should also acquire the necessary information about registration rules and procedures and about requirements for the major or for the degrees granted by the particular institution. This kind of information is essential for participation in registration itself (perhaps before the first term opens!), and in counseling or advising students who will inevitably expect the new instructor to perform as though he had long experience on the job.

To continue this listing, the new instructor must learn about the grading system of the institution and of the liberties one takes with it or the conventions concerning it, since grading is after all arbitrary or conventional rather than sensible or predictable. Closely related to marking systems are systems for dealing with delinquent students, midterm information about course standing, and traditions or rules for dealing with disciplinary problems such as over-cuts or cheating. One also does well to inform himself, even before he starts to prepare for courses, about the academic calendar; he will learn eventually how seriously this is taken by students and faculty.

To plan fully for one's teaching procedures and one's own scholarly work it is desirable to become acquainted early with the way the library operates, and with the methods by which new materials are added to research collections or to reserve reading shelves. One needs to learn how to secure funds for research (if, lamentably, he failed to inquire about this before taking the job) and what are the accepted procedures for securing access to shop facilities or assistance. In addition it is highly desirable to learn about the possibilities for having teaching or research assistants (the latter being unlikely for the beginning instructor) and the expected methods of utilizing or dealing with assistants.

The new instructor also should not fail to learn about the business aspects of his activities and his own situation. These will include purchasing procedures for teaching materials or for research, the arrangements for insurance or annuity deductions, arrangements for personal purchases on institutional voucher and discount in some institutions, and subsidized travel to professional meetings. Although it may not be appropriate to raise the question in the earliest years as an instructor, it may be well to learn what the attitude of one's colleagues or institution would be toward procurement of outside funds for research, especially since a number of grantors now approve of payment of part of the instructor's salary (to enable him to carry a reduced teaching load) or his total summer salary. Of course such funds are granted only to those whose research meets the regular standards of the granting agencies; after all, such agencies do not take a direct interest in easing the life of the college teacher.

The most useful source of information about the academic aspects of a new job is likely to be, first of all, the bulletins and catalogues put out by the institution, and occasionally even reports of strategically placed committees, such as those on the curriculum. Programs of instruction, requirements, administrative organization, instructional objectives, and many other pertinent items of information are to be found in the pages of the bulletins the teacher so commonly passes over lightly. (It is well to note that one way of evaluating a possible job is to secure and study the catalogue of that institution.) A second source of information is obviously conversation—with one's new colleagues (short of exhausting their patience), with one's new department head, and with the operating personnel in such places as the library or business offices, for these people are usually happy to educate the new person and thereby reduce their own difficulties with him. Perhaps it is sufficient to say that the new instructor must keep his ears open and take considerable initiative to get over the great quantity of initial learning and ahead into the things which matter most to him.

The individual sphere of action. The new instructor begins, naturally, by learning what courses he is to teach, and might expect this to define his sphere of action. Such is not the case. In the first place, his students go on to other instructors. His teaching, including the choice of concepts or theory as well as the details of factual content, must therefore be adjusted in part to what goes on in other courses, or to what other faculty members expect to go on in his. Consultation with others is the obvious necessity here.

There are other factors determining one's freedom to act which are not so directly open to discussion. For one thing, academic tradition has long tolerated a kind of squatters' rights practice, in which the better established or more advanced faculty members have, or may feel they have, first priority for certain kinds of teaching, or certain research areas, or other kinds of departmental functions or prerogatives. The new instructor can learn a certain amount from talking to other members of his department, but for the rest he must observe and judge for himself.

Particularly is it wise for him to sense whether the departmental faculty has within it any smouldering or active volcanoes of dissension. Whenever such possibilities exist, he does well to conduct himself circumspectly, to avoid taking sides until or unless he wishes to do battle, and in general to pay attention to his own research and teaching while others dissipate their energies as they will.

The care and feeding of administrators. This hardly new heading is still a very necessary one in any discussion of what the new instructor encounters [see 45]. It is true that deans are sufficiently august and remote that they do not matter very much to the beginner in teaching, except that one may be taken to the dean's office for a courtesy call when being interviewed for a job or introduced to it, and one may in addition care to know such things as whether his dean backs his faculty, plays his disciplinary role with students straight or in a devious way, and has the courage to stand up to alumni or parents in matters of academic freedom. Rather more important than the dean, to the average new instructor, is the head of his department. Granting that there is exceedingly wide variation in the duties and prerogatives of a department head, it nevertheless seems desirable to make a few generalizations, in the hope that this will make easier the relationship between him and the beginning instructor.

The major responsibilities of a department head are typically as follows. He is concerned with all matters of departmental budget and expenditure, and is ordinarily the person through whom purchases, stipends, and salaries are arranged for all categories of departmental personnel. He also is typically the channel of communication to the administration and to other parts of the institution on all except record keeping or other aspects of the student-faculty relation, and for all except the members of the department who are well established in the local scene. In addition, the department head is likely to be responsible for the hiring and firing of nonacademic personnel on the departmental budget, and for the handling of library, registration, space, and equipment routines. A good many of these responsibilities are delegated, in the larger departments, but inquiry will usually indicate whether the department head is ego-involved in any of them.

It is perhaps well to suggest also what a department head should not take upon himself without due regard for the rights and feelings of others, particularly in those institutions where he is labeled *chairman* (the title *head* often indicating a more autocratic arrangement). It is of course not my purpose here to foment rebellion, but rather to remark on some more of the lore of academe which would otherwise have to be discovered slowly or, if a person has no experience of varied institutions, might not be discovered at all. The most important things which the chairman should not personally control are the making of appointments and promotions and the control of educational policy. It is normally assumed that these are faculty matters, not simply administrative matters, and it is to be expected that the administrative actions taken by the department head will reflect proper consultation with his group. It may well be, of course, that the proper departmental subgroup with whom he should consult on various matters may not include the youngest members of the department, but the operating principle is nevertheless clear. Another matter which is not the personal responsibility of the department head, except in a general way, is the choice of content for courses, or teaching methods in them. Here the instructor is the responsible individual, being governed only by general group considerations, such as the need for conforming to the role agreed upon for his course in the departmental curriculum. It is also true that the department head is not responsible for the private or extracurricular life of his faculty; he most certainly becomes interested when the actions of particular department members in any way jeopardize the rights or welfare of other department members, or, more importantly, the educational effectiveness of his department and discipline, but beyond this he is bound by the same considerations of academic and personal freedom as is anyone else in the administrative hierarchy or faculty. Every now and then, of course, a department head steps out of line, but this does not endow his office with any new liberties.

Perhaps it is wise to call attention to one further aspect of the department head's role. He is likely to take a friendly interest in getting the new member of his group off to a good start, professionally and socially. (He and his wife may come to call even before the new people are fully unpacked!) He will almost certainly take steps to ensure that the new staff members become acquainted with other members of the faculty. At the same time, he is in the position of being a judge, or at least of being the agent of reappointment or promotion even though decisions about such matters are made in consultation with others. This duality of interests is conducive to saying or doing things which the new or insecure person interprets differently than does the speaker. It is therefore not surprising that only the most experienced (or even wily) department heads are able to appear entirely consistent in their dealings with the new instructor. Just as it is necessary for the department administrator to be tolerant of the ways of the new staff member, so it may be necessary for the instructor to develop tolerance for the ways of the administrator. This in no way removes the responsibility from either to conduct himself in accordance with democratic standards.

STATUS, ROLE, AND ADVANCEMENT

The signs of status. Professors are people in the ordinary sense that they aspire, as their careers develop, to enhanced status. Conversely, those possessing certain status signs tend to be protective of them. There is therefore need to make clear to the beginning instructor just what status consists of in the academic world, and a need to indicate ways of enhancing status without trespassing on what others consider to be their rights. A thorough and interesting study of this is contained in Wilson's sociological work, *The Academic Man* [280].

There are surprisingly more signs of status than the beginner might expect. The list begins with rank (public information) and salary (private information, except in certain publicly supported institutions). In the way our western culture views such matters, these may be valued for the freedom of action they imply, for the power implications, or as signs that a certain competitive prize has been attained. In addition to rank and salary, however, there are many other and not necessarily lesser signs of advancement in status. For example, the form of the title may be significant—a person called Lecturer or Research Associate in one institution may be a part-time academic stray, while in another institution the titles may be honorific indeed; one will then observe avoidance and seeking behavior among appointees in the two institutions.

To depart from the realm of titles, we find that the size of teaching load tends to decrease as status advances, that the assigned classrooms become the preferable ones, and that the number of inconvenient class hours decreases (how often does a full professor teach a large eight o'clock section of a required elementary course in a poor lecture hall?). As has been remarked many times, the higher the status of the faculty member, on the average, the fewer introductory or elementary courses he teaches; conversely, at least some opportunity to teach at the graduate level is the goal of most new instructors. (This influence is strong enough in some independent colleges that on one pretext or another some M.A. work has been introduced into them.) We can also catalogue the amount of research space that people have, the amount of equipment, the extent to which they can call on teaching or research assistants, whether they have their own telephone and allotment of secretarial time, and whether they inhabit a comfortable and well-located office. All of these have status implications. One of the less desirable status indicators is the degree to which a given individual feels himself dominant in a research area, thus to have established pecking rights there and to claim the graduate students in it as his own advisees.

We would repeat that such status signs are expected to be significant in most academic settings, although varying weights may be attached to the particular signs in particular institutions. Their number or subtlety may perhaps be a reflection of the lack of thoroughly satisfying financial returns in this kind of career.

It must be remarked, however, that in a fair number of psychology departments (and in certain entire faculties) the effort has been made to reduce concerns for status. To lessen the competition and wasted effort involved in efforts to build and protect a private preserve within the department, opportunities and responsibilities for departmental members of all ages and degrees of experience have been equalized wherever this is at all possible. In such departments, newcomers are given an advanced course to teach, and professors take their turn at elementary courses; newcomers find that they have research time and support, which the professors help protect; newcomers are consulted on every departmental matter in which they are reasonably competent or entitled by institutional statutes to have an opinion on. There inevitably and properly remain some important signs of status, particularly as these center about the degree of respect accorded to the expression of opinions or interpretations and as they have to do with direct material rewards, but the pursuit of status becomes less complex and more closely correlated with effectiveness in the main tasks of an academic institution.

The nature of academic role. We may define academic role here as the composite pattern of the functions a particular person fills in his department or in his institution. Except at the lower levels of ranks in the mass departments of instruction, roles must be established, or at least do get established. There evidently must be specialization of function within a limited staff; there must be division of labor and responsibility; and there must be identifiable or distinctive assignments to clarify and justify budgetary demands for any particular department.

Roles, like status signs, may be defined in numerous ways, and the weights assigned to the defining characteristics will vary from one institution to another. Any or all of the following functions may serve to define role, at one time or another. The courses one teaches and the research area in which he functions are perhaps the most obvious signs of role; if the two are closely aligned the role is clearly perceived (and, it might be added, it is a status sign to be able to arrange this very satisfactory state of affairs). Teaching courses and directing or doing research are but two of the manifold functions within, especially, a larger department, and so it may be that accessory skills, such as those in apparatus design, electronics, equipment purchasing, statistics or mathematics, surgery, or the languages help define the uniqueness of certain individuals. Others have special success in educational subtasks, such as curriculum-committee work, lecturing to large classes, or dealing with or lecturing to nonacademic groups. Still other faculty members become known for their effectiveness with such special assignments as direction and stimulation of undergraduate research, or tutorials, advisement of premedical students, administering intradepartmental programs as in clinical psychology, or liaison with extradepartmental agencies or other departments, or even social skills, as in arranging for colloquia or lecture series. Whatever the circumstances, it is probable that the new instructor will very shortly acquire one or several of the tasks or responsibilities enumerated above, or others peculiar to his institution, and these, added to the teaching and research responsibilities, make it progressively clearer just what he is or does.

Increases and promotions. The foregoing discussions make two things clear. The first is that improved status comes not only by way of increased rank or salary but also by the acquisition of other status signs. As one is accepted into and promoted within the departmental group, he occasionally receives an obvious change in status such as an increase in rank, but he may merit and receive in a rather steady succession other signs of improved status. The other thing made obvious is that the improvement in status, especially at the higher levels, depends upon increasing clarification of role until finally, at the level of professor, it is almost essential that role within the department be unique, in order to justify the appointment. Perhaps the major point of these remarks for the newcomer to a faculty is that as he can, he will do well to create a distinctive role for himself, by willingly taking on those tasks best suited to his competence. He may also do well to be realistically perceptive about the available signs of status, particularly as this may be essential for support of his morale during the difficult initial years of his academic career when the obvious or outward signs of advancement may seem slow in coming.

The establishment of criteria for appointment and promotion is one of the most poorly handled aspects of educational administration. There always *are* criteria, clear or unclear, in some respects quite rigidly operative. There is rarely a clear justification of them, or an objective reason for their existence in a particular form or pattern. Nor is the evidence considered relevant to those criteria very often clearly defined, though it may be searchingly sought. The hard facts of life seem in general to be these: that appointments, at least beyond the barest beginning level, depend in most institutions (including many of the independent colleges) upon research output as a first criterion, upon teaching competence as a second criterion, upon general (role-defining) contributions to the department as a third, and in some institutions, upon contribution to the activities or the welfare of the institution generally or to the community at large. There are some colleges (and a very few college divisions of universities) in which effectiveness at teaching is ranked ahead of research output in importance as a basis for appointment or promotion. And there is some evidence from a survey [74] that among the humanities and the policy sciences many faculty members believe research and teaching are weighted about equally in considerations of advancement. Bearing in mind these possible or probable exceptions to the generally stated situation, the beginning teacher in choosing a job should try to make a realistic appraisal of whether the research emphasis does in truth characterize a particular institution and then decide whether to conduct himself accordingly.

There are a number of factors bearing upon the likelihood of receiving increases or promotions. One is the ease with which one's work can be assessed. In this context, it may be deemed advisable to secure student comment on one's teaching, to invite visits to one's classroom or to discuss course plans, operations, or objectives with other faculty members. It is definitely advisable not only to do research but to get it into print, or at least accepted for publication, so that the finished product is available for evaluation by others without overly embarrassing efforts for them to find out what has been going on. If these suggestions seem like an urging to overly virtuous or dangerous exposure to the judgments of one's colleagues, it may be well to remember that it is both desirable to be judged on bases other than rumor or hearsay and essential to learn as early in the game as practicable the probabilities for success in any given post.

Mention should be made of an open secret among academic persons: that opportunity to move elsewhere is one of the most potent influences in mobilizing sentiment to improve status at home. It is more than a joke that people in the lower ranks should not buy houses unless it is well known that they can afford to sell and move any time they feel like it. And it is quite a serious point that being willing to move if it is advantageous and being interested in learning new viewpoints and getting away from overspecialization or provincialism are ordinarily desirable traits. To be sure, moves every few years can be detrimental if they are interpreted as inability to be happy or effective in a given environment for very long. Without doubt, they hamper prosecution of a sustained research or teaching program. It is especially vexing if a resignation is received without due notice (several months at least) of the necessity for finding a replacement. The classic danger in using the competing offer to exert influence is, of course, that one overestimates his support at home, and thus puts himself out on a limb.

THE BALANCE BETWEEN RESEARCH AND TEACHING

One of the great American expectations, in the college and university, is that a faculty member is both scholar and teacher (see, for example, the rather eloquent statement by a member of the Committee of Fifteen [74, p. 17]). One of the great conflicts, however, is over the balance to be maintained between these two roles and the rewards to be attached to success in each. The remarks on appointment and promotion policy made above merely illustrate a common dilemma in American educational administration: a person is appointed (usually or primarily) because a teaching slot is open, but he is promoted (usually or primarily) on the basis of research output.

Origins of the greater stress on research. Although the analysis is scarcely open to objective check, it is somewhat illuminating to try to discern why, in psychology particularly but in many other disciplines as well, the research function receives greater emphasis than the teaching function. What follows is largely based on an earlier discussion of mine [55]. See also discussions by others [82, 152, 181, 206, 276].

One reason is probably historical. The German university, particularly in the era in which its scholarship and its trained scholars began to affect significantly the pattern of American education, was dedicated first of all to that scholarship. Teaching was done, of course, but oftentimes in the manner of providing a platform from which the eminent scholar could inform the public of his discoveries or his theories. The student was expected to be able to learn primarily from his own studies until, if he were going into the academic world himself, he reached the level of apprenticeships of various kinds. In this tradition, teaching as such is perceived as a distraction from the scholar's main job and is assigned a lower status. Such was probably the effect of our great adoption of the German academic tradition and German-trained scholars, of European or American origin, during the formative period of American higher education in the late nineteenth and early twentieth centuries (see the related discussion in Chap. 1).

We can enumerate other probable factors in the heavy stress conventionally placed on research and research output. One of these may be the tendency to value intelligence highly as a personal attribute and, together with this tendency, to regard evidence of original scholarship as evidence of great intelligence. That there is a cult of intelligence in this country is indicated by the vogue for intelligence testing, the sensitivity of many persons to comments about intelligence in themselves or their offspring, the great concern for whether intelligence is inborn, and so on. The cult has as one of its concerns the degree of productivity of abstract or creative ideas. Research, particularly in any very advanced field of study, more and more takes on such characteristics. Research therefore may take on high value, in part, because it is supposedly an indicator of a valued personal attribute, as well as an indicator of achievement of institutional objectives.

There is another clear possibility why research receives the heavy emphasis in determining appointments and promotions. A faculty cannot decide whom to appoint or promote without evidence; evidence of research promise or productivity is, to date at least, much easier and less embarrassing to secure than is evidence of competence as a teacher. One can even say, with a relatively clear conscience, that the arts of teaching have no standard or assessable pattern, or that there are no criteria against which to evaluate the results of teaching. A contributing force here may be the reaction of the candidates for promotion themselves. Being quite aware that competition for advancement in status depends upon availability of evidence, the younger faculty members, unable to marshal competitive evidence with respect to teaching, may naturally stress the laying up of evidence concerning their research competence whether or not this is wholly in accord with their preferred mode of life and function.

It must be observed also that while many of the important rewards for good teaching remain internal to that teaching in such forms as good student response, appreciation expressed by alumni and parents, or self-satisfaction with a job well done, the rewards of research may include not only some of these elements but also invitations to travel and lecture, bids to serve as consultant or adviser to important agencies, foundations, or groups, and royalties, or even profits from patents or inventions.

All of the above suggestions would probably apply equally well outside the field of psychology. We can make two more suggestions about the prestige value of research which are perhaps peculiar to disciplines in the same stage of their historical development as psychology is now. One is the possibility that our own unsureness about the firmness of psychological knowledge impels us more often than we realize to draw about us the socially acceptable mantle of modest ignorance combined with research intent. The other is that our discipline is so young that we have only recently lost most of the pioneers of the era of scientific psychology (see Chap. 1). Those pioneers were the persons who not only were affected markedly by the German tradition mentioned above, but were genuinely in the position of needing to develop the science more than to teach it; they, and the first generations of graduate students turned out by them, inevitably set the further tradition that the young person who devoted too much of his energy to teaching was less desirable than the beginner whose foot was set firmly on the path of research.

The problem of the beginning instructor is to live with this state of affairs, whether it be in accord with his own standards or something he will wish to change. Only a few suggestions can be made here, and the burden of these is: Be perceptive of the circumstances into which you go in order to secure information upon which to base personal choices of action. Certainly the new instructor should, through conversation or questioning, learn the existing balance between research and teaching emphases in his own department and institution. He should bear in mind, however, the possibility of hearing only a publicly statable version of the truth on this rather delicate question. It is almost certain that he should try very early to get a demonstrable research program under way (this presumably being one of the consequences of a lively Ph.D. training anyway). He may be as virtuous as he likes about his teaching responsibilities, but he will do well to keep them as restricted as he can (that is, as to the *number* of assignments) in order to ensure performing them well, especially if he is a person who cares greatly for teaching and refuses to do it badly. Beyond this it is only to be suggested here as elsewhere that knowing one's own mind, formulating one's own standards and being willing to abide by them, and forthrightly albeit courteously explaining one's own position are regarded as signs of maturity and good sense in even the youngest instructors. Within reasonable limits, then, individuality rather than conformity is both possible and desirable.

It is usually said that research is necessary and natural in the process of keeping intellectually alive and in being a good teacher, although as I have said [55], what is meant by research in this context is too often in a fact a required ritualistic production of printed pages, rather than feedback to teaching as intended in the claim. One interesting commentary on the whole problem is suggested in a quotation from William H. Cowley in Kelley's book [157]. Cowley suggests that the matter could be clarified by regarding research as having to do with primary data and the understanding thereof and then using some other term, such as scholarship, to refer to the processes by which the primary information is incorporated or interpreted within the larger body of knowledge in any area. It is Cowley's idea that teaching depends not so much upon the primary process as upon the second, and that we may therefore discriminate between the direct virtues of research for its own sake and research as supposedly contributory to the qualities of teaching. Accepting such a distinction, it might be feasible to reward good research directly, to reward good teaching (and the necessary scholarship) directly, and to give appropriately greater rewards to the rarer person who makes both contributions. Certainly, any policy change that would avoid the fiction that all faculty must be superb teachers *and* spectacular researchers is to be desired.

The conclusion reached after one reads the foregoing discussion may possibly be the cynical one that the rule really is "publish or perish," and that it does not matter what is published so long as the pages pile up. Such a conclusion would be unfortunate. Those who work within the current system and must evaluate younger staff members are usually aware of the weaknesses of the system and feel some responsibility to allow for them or compensate for them. Thus it is that genuine competence and integrity are still sought, and the young faculty member does well to make the subtle distinction between keeping his eye on good performance and on advancement for its own sake. There is usually an effort to discriminate between research of quality and that done for administrative-quantitative reasons. There is usually an effort to give credit for any available sign of good teaching. The recommended conclusion for the beginning teacher can only be, then, that he be a realist about what things are important but that at the same time he maintain personal standards of performance such that his basic chances of success and his self-respect are not lessened.

BEYOND THE FIRST YEAR

Because the effectiveness of both his teaching and his scholarship depend so directly on it, the academic man must maintain his freshness of approach, his drive, his liveliness of intellect. There are a number of steps which he can take to keep from getting into a rut, and it may be well to utilize some of these when the first excitement of being a full-fledged member of the academic profession wears off a bit.

One of the surest ways to keep one's teaching alive is to revise old courses. If necessary, he can bring this on by the hair-shirt technique of discarding old lecture notes or syllabi in the spring, so that in the fall he is forced to start anew. He can sometimes create new courses, or exchange teaching responsibilities with another member of the faculty. Many faculty members will testify that a great deal of their best scholarship has been related to the necessity for mastering or clarifying what is to be presented to or discussed with students.

For the good of both teaching and research, perhaps the best advice is get out; get out of the old environment, and encounter new ideas or minds in other environments. With varying degrees of difficulty, it is possible to make arrangements which ensure this. There are now available, for example, a number of kinds of postdoctoral fellowships, subsidized by foundations or granting agencies of the federal government, which will support a year's work (at no financial profit or loss to the fellowship holder). Study of these possibilities may be quite rewarding, but it should be said that they are not intended merely to provide vacations.

Rather, they are given to support specific projects or experiences which relate to established programs, and the grantors work on schedules with deadlines. Limited numbers of opportunities are now available for part-time support of the junior faculty member for research purposes (as through the Social Science Research Council), so that he can carry a reduced teaching load for, say, a three-year period. It is sometimes possible to arrange summer school or other special teaching assignments in a department other than one's own. And almost any young faculty member has the opportunity of participating in the meetings of scientific and professional societies in his field.

ACADEMIC FREEDOM

Much has been written in recent years of the freedom of the teacher to seek and discuss truth as he sees it from the point of view of his discipline. The beginner in college teaching would do well to familiarize himself with such excellent works as MacIver's *Academic Freedom in Our Time* [170] and Hofstadter and Metzger's *The Development of Academic Freedom in the United States* [138]. We shall not try to deal here with philosophical or political aspects of academic freedom, but limit ourselves to the significance of academic freedom for the beginning instructor.

Academic freedom is generally defined as freedom to seek the truth, to express it as one sees it, and to be free of persecution for doing so to the best of his ability. It is most carefully defined at intervals by the American Association of University Professors, and a perusal of recent volumes of the A.A.U.P. Bulletin will show how lively and detailed is the concern about the concept and about infringements of academic freedom. Academic freedom in practice is very closely related to problems of tenure.

We can in fact say that one of the chief reasons for having a tenure system is to protect the livelihood, in time of attack and crisis, of those who as teachers or researchers find themselves propelled by their work or their personal standards into a position unpopular with someone else [5]. Tenure is therefore precious to the scholar, decry as he may instances in which he sees tenure protecting sheer slothfulness.

The new Ph.D. in the field of psychology may think of academic freedom, particularly in the present era, as a political freedom and perhaps not of direct concern to him as a scientist. This is not so. Freedom to search out and express many kinds of psychological ideas or scientific ideas is both essential and, from time to time, capable of being threatened by attacks from students, alumni, the institutional administration, or other groups holding views challenged by the person seeking what he regards as an adequate scientific view or expression. It is notorious that discussions of sexual behavior or standards, in even the freest academic or scientific settings, may arouse anxiety or hostility which, under certain circumstances, may lead to a denunciation of the person expressing those views, or to attempts to prevent him from expressing them. Equally certain is it that discussions of causation in human behavior, involving as they do some comment upon free will and predestination, stand a chance of arousing enmity, as does any scientific analysis of religion or other emotionally loaded conceptual system. And in the realm of social-psychological or industrial analysis, the psychologist concerned with a liberal-scientific presentation will almost surely find himself in conflict with conservative or reactionary thought in the groups he addresses. (See the suggestive article by Landsman and deMartino [163].) Even psychologists, it must be remembered, have been objects of concern to elements of the American Legion and state or federal investigative committees. There is much at stake for all of us in maintenance of the concept of academic freedom, for here lies the only protection of the individual scholar's right to follow his bent to inquiry and his need to communicate, and herein exists the best chance of capitalizing fully upon his individual talents for the general good.

With freedom goes responsibility, and in this instance the responsibility is partly one of recognizing the limits of freedom. Specifically, the faculty member must be aware that the code of conduct includes such items as the following. One's academic freedom extends only to the boundaries of one's competence (which may go beyond or not as far as the boundaries of one's formally assigned discipline). In communicating ideas to other people, the methods of exposition are the acceptable ones; methods of propagandistic indoctrination, withholding of counterarguments, distorting the weight of arguments or evidence, and so forth, are not regarded as either ethical or scientific. The teacher is expected to exhibit ordinary concerns for decency and mode of presentation of his ideas. He is expected to speak for himself alone unless explicitly authorized to speak for a group or his institution. In fact, he ordinarily does his best to dissociate his own ideas from any implied acceptance by others, preferring to let the evidence or the ideas speak for themselves rather than through the authority of numbers or institutions accepting them. And finally, we may suggest, there is a responsibility to teach respect for the concept of freedom itself, if only because many lay and other groups do not appreciate as fully as the faculty member himself the degree to which such freedom is essential under a democratic political and educational system.

The teacher of psychology may have some unique problems of responsibility. Some of these are touched upon in the ethical code published by the American Psychological Association [7, pp. 89-112]. For example, although the teacher of psychology often discusses matters which relate to the personal and private affairs of his students, he cannot in his role as teacher lose sight of the right of the student to maintain his privacy. In his role as teacher-counselor, a role which is particularly common in the smaller institutions, the teacher must give thought to whether his teaching arouses anxieties about personal adjustment problems which he is not competent to cope with, and whether adequate facilities can be found to help students who need such help (see Chap. 13). Judgments about students, when these bear on their personal characteristics as distinguished from their publicly demonstrated intellectual characteristics, must be treated in a professional manner, and particularly must the temptation be resisted to psychologize about a student whose name happens to come up in casual faculty conversation. In research, whether his own or that of others, the instructor must ensure that legitimate educational ends are served by any use of students as subjects. Exploitation of students to maintain course enrollments or a research program is surely to be avoided. Other formulations in the ethical code from which these examples are taken are worth study, as are implications of the article by Landsman and deMartino [163] concerning the safeguards which may be necessary in teaching.

Only one general kind of remark will be directed here at the beginning faculty member's response to concepts such as those described above. It is this—that independence, courage, and thoughtful understanding of one's own position are regarded as desirable attributes in an academic person, whether young or old. Sensitivity to the circumstances of one's situation is essential, of course, but ability quickly to find a place and take a stand on matters of principle is both desirable from the viewpoint of the academic system itself and in the long run likely to be important to the career advancement and the feelings of personal integrity of the beginning instructor.

6
PLANNING THE INTRODUCTORY COURSE

The new instructor probably will begin earning his salary by planning how he will teach his assigned courses. This initial planning must often be done under considerable pressure, and simplifying or routinizing it is therefore of great aid. Furthermore, the initial course plan one lays out is important because it often influences all plans for that course for the next several years.

The one course which the new teacher is most likely to experience, and in which his specialized Ph.D. training is least likely to be directly applicable, is the introductory one in his department. We therefore can profitably use this course as a model in discussing planning problems, as was done by McKeachie and Kimble [192], although we should not, as Field's experience makes clear [106], assume that the model has widely standardized properties. It is widely believed among social scientists [e.g., 6, 261] that the introductory course is not only one of the most difficult to teach well, but the most important course in and to the department. It is the course where the sheer numbers of students and staff make important the time, money, and effort expended. It is the course with most obvious opportunities to contribute to the general objectives of the institution. It affords the initial opportunities to recruit students into the major and the profession and to affect public opinion by showing the layman, as it were, the nature of science. Under ordinary circumstances, therefore, instruction in the first course should be planned most thoroughly, in close consultation with instructors of the later courses and with careful consideration of the overall teaching objectives of the departmental curriculum.

Background information. One must learn the conditions under which a course is to be offered before one starts to plan it. Just as institutions vary widely in their characteristics, so do the circumstances, even within an institution, under which a given course must be offered. These variations inevitably determine in part the kinds of specific objectives one can adopt. They also very definitely affect the teaching methods one will intend to use, the kinds of reading materials and illustrative materials, the number and kind of examinations, and so on. Perhaps a general rule could be stated: Learn all you can about the conditions which might influence what you plan to do in your course.

One of these is simply the kind of student population to be dealt with. Those students may be entirely concerned, in the purest liberal arts tradition, only with extending their own liberal educations; they may come from pre-professional programs, or they may be taking some kind of terminal program. They may be intensely practical in their interests, highly competitive with respect to marks, or cultish in an intellectual sense. They may be altogether a resident population or they may be commuters, with consequent variations in degree of acquaintanceship and in-group feeling among students and in opportunities for extraclass activities or scheduling of special events.

Of particular importance is the level of maturity of the

students, most readily indexed (but not adequately) by their year level in college. Most introductory psychology courses are at the sophomore level but include a few freshmen, a few more juniors, and a sprinkling of misplaced seniors. It is probable that the lower the year level of one's students, in a given college, the more slowly must the course move, to allow for poorer backgrounds, poorer study, note taking, or listening habits, or the presence of not-as-yet-eliminated students of lower ability. One may infer from a number of the relevant studies [61, 107, 117, 227] that the critical factor is not the academic year level but rather those co-variables that happen to operate in a given situation.

In spite of all the possible variations among his students, the instructor may feel that his ultimate objectives in teaching must remain constant. It seems obvious, however, that he may to some extent need to cater to, and certainly he may capitalize upon, the characteristics of his students in shaping the way he will attempt to reach his ultimate objectives. Otherwise he runs the risk of getting little response from his students.

In a more routine way it is necessary to learn the characteristics of the course itself, as these are defined by the department or the college. There is the question of how many credit hours and how many terms are allotted to the course. The most typical elementary course at the present time is one which occupies three hours per week for a semester, or four or five hours per week for an academic quarter, totaling perhaps 45 class hours in all. As suggested in Chapter 4, there are conceivably very good reasons for changing to a year-long pattern, but the short course is now the one to be expected. One also needs to learn the functions served by his particular introductory course in the degree granting operations of his institution, in particular whether the course is classified as social science or biological science, or both, and whether it serves corresponding distributional or general education purposes. One must learn whether the course is required for either a particular degree or particular programs (such as pre-nursing, advertising in the business school, personnel management in the engineering school, pre-theology, etc.). We might add the hope that the beginning instructor will have as small a proportion as possible of students who take his course only because it fulfills a requirement, for this always carries with it the possibility of resentment and resistance or superficial motivation.

The tactics of course planning will also depend upon the accessory services available to the instructor. Directly relevant will be the existence of such facilities as an institution-wide personal counseling service (which can absorb the service load created or released if one teaches to personal adjustment objectives) or formal recognition that the instructor must do this work himself. It is important also to know whether there will be teaching assistants, adequate secretarial aid, and examination proctors to help absorb the routine loads, especially where the enrollment is likely to be very large. One needs, further, to check on the availability of teaching and demonstration equipment; on quantity, quality, and availability of materials in the library; and even upon the fittings of the classroom in order to judge what kinds of activities one can carry on there—whether films can be shown, discussions readily created, demonstrations made visible from all corners of the room, blackboard readily used, and so on. Just how all these considerations will bear on decisions about teaching plans cannot readily be said in a generalized way, but it is clear that in a given concrete situation the instructor will do well to look for non-subject-matter items significant for what he will attempt to accomplish and how he will attempt to accomplish it. He need not necessarily accept passively all the limitations of his environment, but until he knows a good deal about that teaching environment he can scarcely attempt to improve it or capitalize on it.

OPERATIONAL DECISIONS

Objectives. Although we discussed the matter at some length in Chapter 4, we again call attention to the necessity for the instructor to formulate as clearly as possible the objectives of any course, and especially in the case of the introductory course to discuss these objectives with his colleagues who will teach his students later on. Wolfle [285] made a detailed study of the objectives suggested for the first course by various teachers of psychology and found that three were most commonly accepted: teaching the facts, principles, and vocabulary of scientific psychology; training students in the scientific method and critical thinking; and developing the student's ability to understand and to cope with the personal adjustment problems of daily life. Interesting the students in psychology and preparing them for later work or reading in it was offered as an objective by a considerable body of psychologists, and, by a smaller group, training the student to distinguish between scientific psychology and psychological quackery. The first three, and most widely accepted, objectives were regarded as the common ones several years after the Wolfle paper [as in 52, 82]. They were modified and spelled out in some detail by Wolfle *et al.* [288] in 1952. Another formulation of objectives is provided by Marsh [177]. Perhaps the most detailed statement is that of the University of Michigan staff working with McKeachie [190]. Their effort is to specify almost the daily teaching goals of their course, together with background considerations leading them to choose these goals. Teaching aims related to the contemporary concern that psychology be a socially useful profession as well as a science have sometimes led to a different balance in the statement of objectives than that suggested by the authors mentioned above [13, 29, 129, 214, 215, 222]. We need to stress the necessity for choosing relatively limited and workable objectives and for reaching the best compromises possible in the face of certain other predictable dilemmas, such as whether to worry more about motivating the beginning student or informing him, and whether to stress breadth or depth in teaching. The decisions made in these respects will not only reflect what is known about the teaching environment, but will influence decisions of other kinds to be discussed below.

Reading materials. Although it is rarely possible to find a textbook which exactly suits a particular instructor (Dean Carl E. Seashore used to say the only way to get a really good textbook was to write your own), it is ordinarily desirable to use one in an introductory course because of its supportive and organizing values for students. Furthermore, if classes are large, it may be impracticable to use other types of materials, or materials to be found only in the library.

The tactics for selecting a text are highly varied, but experience suggests certain points to be kept in mind. One is that the student typically prefers to read through the text in the order in which the chapters are numbered by the author, rather than to skip about. Unfortunately, the commercial pressure seems to be toward the package chapter that can be put anywhere—which yields a certain flexibility and presumably leads to more adoptions of a text, but creates problems in the process. In my opinion the packaged chapter which permits mention of all the ideas related to the central theme tends to become sprawling and overly comprehensive. Also, when the book—and therefore the course—lacks an orderly sequence or development of concepts, it appears to be difficult for the student to retain a clear-cut idea of the over-all development of the subject matter. Rather, he ends the course with a thoroughly cluttered mind. The student also typically prefers to read all of a text and may resent purchasing or using a text from which the instructor seemingly feels obliged to omit certain assignments. Further, it does not sit well with students to be told that they should merely skim certain materials but study others carefully, since this too raises questions about the stature of the textbook. And finally, students do not care to have the instructor sniping at or differing with the text continually, whether to show his own superiority or to prove publicly that he made an unwise choice in the first place. For all these reasons, a textbook should be chosen carefully, so that the instructor can live with it with minimum pain and the students can feel that it is to be read with profit. Surprisingly enough, it is necessary to urge that the instructor read the text himself. It may be different from the earlier edition, or from what one expects! If so, it is better to know this in advance and not to learn it from the students.

Textbooks are often supplemented with books of readings, or mimeographed materials of private issue, or with reserve materials in the library. The choice of these also involves certain matters which the instructor can anticipate. One is that for beginning or lower level students, it is easy to assign too much reading or reading in sources of too many kinds or styles, so that students are taxed unduly, or give up, or have severe problems of integration. The use of reserve library shelves should be considered very carefully, for it is a rare library that can adequately handle books or other reading materials which large numbers of students demand to have instantly available, especially on the night before an examination. Another difficulty may arise if the textbooks (or lectures) and the supplementary materials cover much the same ground, but in somewhat different language, or with emphasis on somewhat different points. Moderate similarity between the two sets of material is a condition for maximum confusion, so that the student has difficulty in being sure of exactly what he does know. Perhaps the worst example of this is found when the reading for an introductory course consists of two textbooks, with approximately the same coverage but rarely exactly the same approach to any topic. (In parallel vein, I cannot help but recall a conversation with a well-known psychologist in which he jokingly remarked that perhaps he should not have taken a leave during the previous term, for while he was away his colleagues had decided to change textbooks in the introductory course—to the very one he had been using as his lecture material.)

It is important, whatever one's teaching objectives may be, to estimate as accurately as possible the level of difficulty of material in any prospective reading and then to attempt to match this with the ability of one's students. The standard beginning texts in psychology vary all the way from ones which are quite precise and technical, written by specialists in the various subfields and thus quite difficult for a beginning student, to the greater number which are written for the mass market at lower division levels and in junior colleges. Just as certain classes may be unable to cope with abstract or difficult materials, so may other classes feel let down or insulted by materials which they perceive as too elementary for their level of maturity. The attitude to take toward these latter reactions is not altogether clear, either, for students sometimes feel that a really worthwhile and substantial book has to be dull. A well-written and sprightly book which has good content may erroneously be regarded by students as unsuitably superficial.

In the beginning of one's teaching experience it may be wise to reserve the intention privately of being willing to change reading materials or at least some of the assignments after a course has started, if one's initial decisions prove unworkable. This may be justified, within limits at least, on the grounds that reading is after all one of the principal avenues to learning in the typical college course, and the student should not be made to suffer from an inadequate first decision by the instructor.

One more commentary on reading materials is perhaps worthwhile. This has to do with the attempt to extend the range of materials experienced, by the able students especially, by suggesting optional readings. Various kinds of checks upon how much of this optional reading is done show that in many institutions practically none of the students will bother with it. Whether this is to be regarded as a weakness of the institution or the students in it, or of the instructor's methods, one should in any event be realistic about the probably minor contribution of optional readings to his course, or make very special provisions to motivate students to take advantage of them. One concrete suggestion, not often adopted because it means extra work for the instructor, is to permit optional papers, or examinations for extra credit, so that the student who is able and willing to do extra work clearly gets extra credit if it is satisfactorily or well done. Another suggestion is to place on an optional reading shelf a collection of those materials which the instructor does not wish to cover in his course, particularly materials dealing with some of the more popular marginal subjects such as hypnotism, extrasensory perception, or with psychological quackery [e.g., Steiner, 258], and so on. Whether the availability of such materials is sufficient to lead the student to explore them has not, however, been demonstrated.

Choice of classroom procedures. In these days of crowded classrooms the instructor of the elementary course may find that circumstances dictate the procedures he may use in teaching, and that lecturing is about the only one available to him. Even so, variety is desirable, and one should plan for or seize upon any possible opportunities for creating demonstrations, showing motion-picture films, reviewing previous lectures or examinations, answering questions or stimulating discussion, and so on.

While variety is a great aid to the teacher, he must realize that different methods of teaching move toward different objectives, and at different rates. For example, discussion in class never appears to cover much ground, in comparison with a tightly organized lecture. It can be argued, however, that discussion accomplishes different things and that the smaller coverage of, for example, factual material, is for this reason irrelevant. As another example, a demonstration or a laboratory period typically may not teach as great a quantity of material, but teaches more vividly. The same perhaps may be said of role playing, or the buzz session, or other procedures which may be adapted to the large classroom (see Chap. 9). In any event, the choice of teaching procedures should be determined in part by the teaching objectives one has accepted, and in addition should be adapted carefully to the reading and other components of the course.

Examination and grading systems. In Chapters 10 and 11 we shall discuss evaluation problems in detail, but it is relevant here to say that examinations and grades are, after all, a focal point of student anxiety, as McKeachie and Kimble [192] have effectively pointed out. The instructor is therefore wise to learn the local attitudes toward examination types and toward various grading procedures, the expected ways of dealing with make-ups and delinquencies of various kinds, and so on, in order to be able to decide how far he will adapt himself and where he will deliberately create his own pattern. The importance of examinations and grades to students is such that not only should the instructor employ as clear and fair a system as he can, but he should plan to communicate this as fully as possible so that students will know what to expect. This communication may well include information about kinds and numbers of examinations, their assigned content, and the relative weights to be assigned to different kinds of questions or content, for as Ruja [230] suggests, we can use whatever texts or outlines we wish, but the students will study what they think will be sampled on the tests. Students should know what can be done about missed examinations or debated scoring. The instructor who anticipates these examination and grading procedures not only makes the machinery of his course run more smoothly, but takes the mystery out of his procedures so far as students are concerned and thus gains respect for his grasp of his job.

Content. Related to all the kinds of decisions discussed above, and dominating the planning, will be considerations as to what is to be taught. Through this content, perhaps more than through any other aspect of what the teacher does, he expects to move toward whatever objectives he has elected to teach to.

Like a suit of clothes, a plan for an introductory course cannot really be designed to fit any situation in general, but must rather be planned around a given situation and the instructor who will work in it. Generalized plans have been suggested, it is true [52, 288], but in one of these instances the generalized plan was intended to aid the postwar instructor who had not yet had time to do all of his own planning, and in the other case the generalized plans were meant to be illustrative of an argument for particular ways of constructing a curriculum. Perhaps the most useful remarks in the present context concern the ways content choices are influenced, for we cannot fill in for the individual instructor the substance of what he will choose to teach.

The backgrounds of student, for example, will obviously determine in part whether one can or will teach certain materials. If the instructor cannot count on any background in biology, he is likely to avoid stress on sensory processes or genetic factors in development, unless he can also allow for the time to teach the related biology as such. If, on the other hand, all students coming to the elementary course are known to have had either the calculus in freshman year or sufficient mathematics in school to exempt them from this requirement, it may be possible to utilize more technical materials in statistics, measurement, or scaling, in order to achieve certain objectives, than one would with some other kind of group. Perhaps the point should be stressed that tactically the instructor needs to be adaptive, electing whatever content he can best use with a particular group in order to achieve the objectives he has set for himself. This approach is different from the perhaps more common one of accepting the necessity for coverage of certain content without full care for the implied objectives and kind of group, and then teaching only that content.

It is also clear that the content of a course depends in part upon the personal competences and enthusiasms of the instructor. This comes about naturally and may be defended as appropriate, on the grounds that we teach best what we know best and are interested in—assuming only that this is not carried to such an extreme that it distorts the over-all plan of the course. It is clear that different individuals, teaching the same course, will present the subject matter in quite different ways. I myself have found that an introduction to psychology through the analysis of experimental procedures and the nature of scientific method has achieved good results. But I once had a colleague in another section of the same introductory course who began with the mind-body problem and, in some way I never could fathom, managed to make this equally plausible as a way to approach psychology. In both instances we were headed in the direction of a discussion of the causation of behavior, but had we been forced to exchange the approaches used, we should probably both have been dismal failures. Adapting the choice of content to one's own interests can of course be carried too far, as with the new Ph.D. who finds his dissertation ready and fascinating material for a goodly portion of the time in the first course he teaches. In such an instance the content of the course becomes overly idiosyncratic, and the chances are great that the student will in the long run suffer.

Depending on both content and the instructor's enthusiasms, there is a value in having the order of topics in a course encourage interest in addition to satisfying sheerly structural or intellectual demands. Specifically, one should always seek an interesting beginning and a resounding conclusion. Dull topics, however essential, should not be bunched. And certainly no one course in the curriculum should be given the burden of covering essential topics which are avoided as dull in all the other courses. Ruja [231] surveyed the attitudes of 27 elementary textbook authors, and found that they agreed only that the order of topics should promote understanding and interest, although it is clear that at times these may be incompatible (as when a rather dull topic has to be mastered early, to lay the groundwork for interesting materials to follow). Ruja himself believes that it is desirable to order the content of the topics of the first course from practical to theoretical, from familiar to strange, from concrete to abstract, and from larger context to detail. He feels the order of topics is to be thought of as determined by pedagogical considerations rather than by systematic considerations of the theoretical-scientific sort.

So far as the first course is concerned, if not also the whole undergraduate curriculum, it is possible to discern one other kind of influence upon the choice of content. This factor, illustrated readily by a study of past and present introductory textbooks, is a shift in the popularity of various topics, a change in the degree to which they are considered fundamental for a beginning course, or a shift in the way they are treated. For example, there probably has been a decreasing concern over the last decade or so for physiological and anatomical materials, or they have been removed to the appendix of the introductory text, but some of the exciting new developments in neurophysiology may bring this material to the forefront again. There probably has been an increasing concern for statistical or quantitative thought in general, but a decreasing interest in the strictly normative. There probably has been an increased emphasis upon environmentalism and with it more attention to such topics as motivation, emotion, personality, and adjustment, which can be both more useful and more threatening. There is probably much more social psychological material, as in attitude formation and group dynamics, and more concerning society and culture, and much of this material is pointed in the direction of an understanding of major social phenomena. Finally, we may note that the higher mental processes, once respectable, then disregarded, are again assuming importance in such realms as cognition, problem solving, and concept formation.

Whether the particular statements just made are exactly correct is not so important as the point they are intended to illustrate: The course one plans to teach upon leaving graduate school cannot very well be the same one the instructor experienced when he was a student, because the world and the discipline have moved on. Nor should the course taught five years later be the same as the first one taught. Fresh material or topics must almost certainly replace the initial ones.

Laboratory teaching in the first course. A major tactical decision is involved in the question of whether to utilize a laboratory as part of the introductory course. In a good many institutions, even now, this is out of the question because the physical facilities and equipment are simply not available. But assuming that the matter can at least be considered, some of the points that come up immediately are as follows (a more detailed discussion of laboratory teaching problems will be found in the Appendix). Laboratory teaching demands time and energy from the instructor, even with graduate teaching assistants available, for there are simply more arrangements and more small classes to be kept going. Also, the conventional notion of laboratory work may not be applicable to much of what the instructor wishes to accomplish; he can, however, stretch the notion considerably. It must be admitted that there appears to be no good research evidence that laboratory experience is essential for an initial course in a science. This presumably is especially applicable where demonstrations, films, and other active-response instigators [11] are utilized. On the other hand, many of those who have tried using the laboratory alongside a lecture series in the introductory course feel warmly, as do Schlosberg [240], Keller and Schoenfeld [154], and Bousfield [42] that, evidence or not, there is simply no other good way to introduce the student to the concrete experience of science and science building. For those who hold this as one of their most important objectives, some version of a laboratory is likely to become almost an essential.

COMMUNICATION OF PLANS

In all except the most informal settings and those with closest contact between teacher and student, it is likely to be highly desirable to print and distribute to students a one- or two-page plan for the course (with a generous overrun in reserve, to allow for losses). This plan sheet may include such things as the following: statements of objectives; the calendar for the course, with examinations and readings indicated in exact detail (and general classroom topics blocked out as proposed below); ground rules for conduct of the course, including regulations governing seating, attendance, make-ups, use of special materials or library facilities, service as subject in experiments, attendance at laboratories, or payment of special fees. Not only does such a compact source of information provide an efficient way to present materials essential to conduct of the course, but it also clarifies for the student what is expected of him and in this way eases his concerns about the unknowns ahead of him. Perhaps the lowest level but nevertheless realistic argument for the use of a printed plan sheet is that it saves endless repetitions about such matters as assignments and examination dates and protects the instructor by having on the open record the requirements to which he holds his students.

Here are some things one should keep in mind in establishing the exact schedule he will try to follow in his course calendar. After the total number of class hours available is known (be sure to subtract the days missed on school holidays), one must allow for the time necessary for examinations, for reviews of these examinations, for the showing of films or other demonstrational materials, for review discussions, or other special sessions. Like a family budget in which no allowance was made for payment of income taxes, a course schedule in which no allowance was made for such things as questions about examinations or about suitable next courses, is likely to be found somewhat restrictive. Within the available hours for coverage of the content one must choose how many hours to allot to each topic; it is at this point that many questions of relative emphasis (as defined by allotted time) arise, and the temptation to disregard the necessities of preparing the student for later courses becomes almost overwhelmingly strong. It will also appear that time or timing is of importance in other ways. For example, to be realistic, one should not schedule examinations the day before or after important holidays; nor should a major examination be scheduled very near the end of a term when preparations for a final examination would have to go forward simultaneously with processing of an examination just given. (Part of the final examination may, if necessary, be given over to testing on the last materials of the term, providing the students know this is the plan.) In multisection courses, especially those meeting on different day-of-the-week cycles, the examination calendar should be constructed so that there are not some students who have tests before, some after, the weekend, and so on. If possible, all students in such a course should have major examinations at the same (some specially arranged) time, if the content is to be the same in the various sections. And for the benefit of the beginning instructor, or even the experienced one, one other matter of timing may be mentioned: it is desirable to plan and schedule the work of the course in relatively large blocks or units (only), not merely because in the beginning it may be difficult to anticipate what the schedule ought to be, but because this permits of adaptability as one goes along in the classroom. Under a block system of scheduling, that is, one can introduce materials or eliminate them as good judgment—or necessity—dictates. (For another discussion of planning, see McKeachie and Kimble [192].

7

LECTURING

Conant [76] has pointed out effectively that scientific knowledge in areas such as physics and biology has typically developed after empirical knowledge, such as that of the artisan or the craftsman, had first grown to the stage of usefulness. We may expect this to be true of teaching methods. There is no *a priori* reason why it should not be possible to make lawful statements about the teaching process and the limits within which these laws hold true. Yet we are well aware that while there have been many great artisans of teaching, the real science has lagged far behind. We may further expect that teaching can be done better wherever tested information is available about it. In this book, therefore, wherever it is possible to do so, we look into the available studies pertinent to the topic being discussed, to learn whether, in Conant's phrase, the degree of sheer empiricism has been reduced in a scientific way.

Most of the studies of the effectiveness of the lecture technique originated in practical concerns of administrators about costs of instruction. They have wanted to know whether it is *essential* to have small classes, which are more expensive of faculty time, at the college level. The researches therefore have been bent on learning whether the objectives accepted as standard in small class teaching, or quiz-discussion teaching, could equally well be achieved in a large class where by definition lecturing was the only usable method.

One of the major studies of this kind was done by Longstaff [166] in the general psychology course at Minnesota. The two conditions of instruction compared were straight lecture (three hours per week) and lecture-quiz (two lectures per week; third meeting in one of a large number of quiz-discussion groups in a class of about 40). Performance on objective examinations was the criterion of effectiveness of instruction. A total of 255 students taught under each condition were matched on measures of ability and previous grades earned, these 255 pairs being selected for matching purposes out of nearly twice that number who took the course. The findings were uniform: the lecture method was not different from the lecture-quiz method as used here, so far as examination performance was concerned. Furthermore, on the assumption that greater motivational effectiveness of either method would make each student perform closer to his ability level, correlations between examination achievement and the available scholastic ability measures were computed. Again, lecture and lecture-quiz methods did not differ. When students were asked for their reactions to the possible instructional methods, no important differences between methods of instruction occurred, except that there was some preference for the lecture-quiz method by those who had had it in psychology; interestingly enough, the students in this study did not rate small classes as desirable. In a second study, 60 superior students were identified in each of two large lecture sections. One group was pulled out for one quiz-discussion meeting per week, while its matched group of 60 was left in the regular lecture. It was found that the latter group actually achieved more on course examinations, so that in this second study, segregation of superior students into a class where there was opportunity to discuss or raise questions did not lead to superior achievement and, indeed, the students themselves indicated a preference for being in the (larger) heterogeneous group.

In three successive studies which were carefully done, Remmers [221] compared lecture and lecture-quiz methods of instruction in general psychology at Purdue. In the first of these studies, one group of students was given two weekly lectures and one quiz-discussion period, while another group had all three weekly meetings in the smaller class. Care was taken to equalize the parts played by the instructors of the consistently small classes in the larger lecture-quiz course. As measured by objective course examinations, the two techniques achieved about equal results, with a suggestion in the data that students of high ability profited somewhat more from the small group, whereas students of low ability did better under the lecture-recitation condition. In a repetition of this study only one difference occurred in the results; the high-ability students also profited somewhat more from the lecture-recitation procedure than from the small group procedure. In a third study, comparisons were made between students who had only three lectures per week and students who had only three quiz-discussion periods per week. There were 94 matched pairs of students (matched for grades, ability measures, etc.) in the groups, so that the slightly superior performance found in the lecture condition appears to be a reasonably stable (but not quantitatively impressive) result. In all of Remmers' studies the students liked their instructors better in small groups, a sort of halo effect from better acquaintance, in Remmers' view.

From studies like these, from the review by Cole [71] and from other empirical studies by Spence [255] and Husband [147], one is forced to draw the conclusion that there is no general superiority or inferiority of the lecture method within the limits of the research procedures used to date. However, it would be unfortunate to overlook some of the characteristics and the limitations of these procedures, for an examination of them suggests, not that lecturing is like other teaching techniques in all respects, but rather that more definitive research is yet to be done and that we may then expect to find specific and repeatable differences among techniques. For example, in the research done to date [147, 166, 176, 221, 253, 255], there is no convincing evidence that optimum use was made of the smaller group which has been termed a quiz group or a discussion group by several of the researchers. Therefore only a size difference may have existed between groups known to have received lectures and groups labeled as being of some other kind. Research on the size-of-class variable [139, 145] has shown that size as such has not been a significant determiner of achievement as measured. We may infer that size of class, like time as a variable in physical processes such as the rusting of a wire, is important only insofar as it allows other variables to have a greater or a lesser effect. To complete the analogy, it is necessary that researchers comparing lecture and quiz or discussion techniques specify what is done, other than to vary the size of classes. They will need to specify the objectives sought and the means to be used to measure achievement of these objectives.

This latter point leads to another one. The measures of achievement of instruction to date have been limited primarily to conventional measures of mastery of information, principles, and vocabulary, as these are presented in standard texts. As Birney and McKeachie [34] have very well shown, the development of other kinds of measures, to assess other kinds of achievement, must precede research comparing kinds of teaching techniques; and a rather wide variety of measures is now beginning to be available.

There are also numerous troublesome co-variables in studies of the kind we have cited here (this is not to imply these investigators are unaware of this point). For example, lecturers are likely to prepare more thoroughly or systematically than quiz leaders, under pressure of the need to put on a performance for a large audience. They are also more likely to be chosen for their supposed talents and to be somewhat more experienced before being entrusted with a large lecture course. The instructors of smaller classes, particularly the quizzes associated with large lectures, are often either not comparable in ability to the lecturer or to judge by their descriptive features (age, years of experience, amount of training) are less well qualified. Another co-variable always is what the students are used to. To create a difference between lecturing and some other method, for experimental purposes, is almost always to change also the similarity between treatment actually received and the student's aspirations or expectations; we ordinarily do not know what differential effects this has on performance in the various experimental conditions. Finally, there are interactions of various variables. Remmers [221] shows, for example, and Holland's data [140] suggest, that the ratings students make of an instructor depend *partly* on whether he is handling lectures only or discussions only for them. We may interpret this as an effect of instructor personality such that it differentially influences the operation of another variable, class size or teaching technique.

So the situation is this. Lecturing is still being done; its strengths and weaknesses, if we believe these to exist, have not yet been specified through research studies; and the college teacher is likely to have to use the method and might as well learn to use it effectively. In anticipation of the outcomes of future research as well as individual experience, each instructor will do well to be as analytical as he can about the usefulness of lecturing for him personally, in different kinds of situations (including small classes and large), with different kinds of materials and students. The advice that can be given to him at present is mainly not rooted in science but rather in the experiences of those who have previously gone through the same trial-and-error learning process.

It should be perfectly clear that when we now discuss lecturing skills we are assuming that the particular circumstances have not made the technique altogether and obviously inappropriate. There is simply no defense for lecturing which is bad because the technique should not have been used, for example, when the lecturer merely repeats closely what the textbook says, or when the need is for students to try formulating a difficult or personally involving idea for themselves. There is also no defense for lecturing that is ineffective because, as the page boy remarked about the Senator who had held forth on the floor of the Senate for four hours, the speaker hasn't said what he is talking about. It is presumed here that the lecturer does indeed have a content to communicate, and that he constantly enlarges and refreshes this content through his reading, his research, and discussion with his professional colleagues.

The objectives of lecture teaching. Assuming that text materials are used, as they commonly are in the kind of course where there is lecturing, perhaps the very first consideration is: What does the instructor try to achieve by lecturing that is not achieved by the readings? Evidently, by sheer word count, a lecturer cannot achieve the coverage that his texts do. We can be sure that his students will not like a re-presentation of selections from the readings, especially if this re-presentation is only somewhat different from, and therefore maximally to be confused with, the reading material. And they will not want a set of lectures totally unrelated to the readings, for this leaves them with a feeling of taking two part courses simultaneously and makes the discipline itself appear to be compartmentalized or unintegrated.

Although it is easier to say than do, it seems likely that the lectures in a so-called lecture course should try to teach the same ideas as do the reading materials and other components of the course, but to do so in ways which do not repeat, but rather reinforce, supplement, and illuminate. A number of somewhat more specific suggestions can be made to show what is meant.

First, lectures may provide material not found in the readings but nevertheless considered essential by the instructor. However, factual material which merely repeats the sense of what is found in readings is not necessarily useful to the student, for while it may give him a feeling that a shaky point has been nailed down, it may also make him feel that he knows nothing more or better than he knew after reading the illustrative evidence given in his text. A particular form of supplementation which is useful and interesting, because it gives the student the feeling of being closer to the growing edge of knowledge in a field, is to introduce factual materials which have become available since the text materials were published. Another form of supplementation is in a sense demanded by the kind of undergraduate textbooks now being published in psychology—very few of them give the student a theoretical framework upon which to hang his ideas and thoughts. The instructor in his lectures may give exactly this framework by showing how he encompasses factual materials in his theoretical view.

Lectures can provide illustrative material. This may take the form of concrete examples, or applications, differing from the ones in the reading material. They are more likely to be useful if they are drawn from situations more fitted to the specific audience than the situations utilized in a text can readily be, or if they are drawn from the lecturer's personal experience. Concepts, it may be suggested, are built from specific experiences; we aid our students to build abstract ideas by giving them a wealth of specific or concrete instances as a beginning point for the induction process. Where new experimental data make an already established law clearer by showing its operation in a new context, they may be regarded as helping form a concept and are not likely to be regarded as just a duplication.

Several comments can be made about possible illustrative materials for use in psychology lectures. One is that the instructor can train himself to observe daily events in the neighborhood, home, or elsewhere, with the intent of remembering specific illustrative incidents, perhaps keeping a notebook of such items. Another is that illustrative materials always have to come to a point, and not too many points lest they become confusing. A story which could serve to illustrative several different psychological ideas teaches less, we may presume, than stories of the kind told by Guthrie [124], a master of the story with a point. This remark applies equally to scientific data introduced for illustrative purposes—they are most effective when germane and reasonably limited to the point under discussion. Additionally, concreteness in the illustration is usually a virtue; abstract analogies, illustrations from related disciplines, or even samples from the animal world, tend to be less concrete, less real to the student listening to a psychological lecture than are examples from his own world. Yet it must be said that there is also virtue in extending the range of examples to which one's subject matter is shown to apply, provided only that this is not overdone.

Lecturers, better than reading material, or at least more forcefully, can have an organizing or integrating function. The lecturer can, for example, make cross references which relate his materials to those of the reading, so that the student can note these and compare or relate materials from the two sources. Or the lecturer can deliberately introduce organizational schemes or efforts into his presentation. These might be attempts at formulation of laws which summarize what is known on a given topic. This device I have used many times and found stimulating both to myself and the students, for it is obviously subject to analysis and revision, and students typically become personally involved in helping the instructor formulate the laws adequate for stating the simple structure of a topic or area. Another device, already referred to, is to create a framework of theory for a course, so as to be able to relate each new topic or process to the framework and within it to other topics or ideas studied. Finally, it may be suggested that formal organizational devices may be introduced, such as schematic outlines (printed, written on the board, or spoken in context), summaries, or previews. Each in its way can help the student relate what he learns now to other things learned or yet to come.

There is another very useful feature of lectures. This is to exemplify to the student, or to involve him in, the techniques of analysis in the field. Sometimes this is done by way of detailed consideration of case materials, or of an experiment, more detailed than can be afforded by printed materials. Sometimes it is done in the presentation of an application, especially in the determination of what is a legitimate application of a psychological principle. It is very effectively done in the context of concerns for method, including statistical analysis. Analysis as we are discussing it is of course by all means critical as well as expository. In the bit-by-bit understanding of a procedure or a set of data, in the back-and-forth detection of flaws of procedure or reasoning, the student is led to a more mature level of thinking about the subject matter. Topics such as the nature-nurture controversy in the realm of intelligence, or the determination of the nature of cochlear microphonics, or latent learning, or the validity of personnel selection methods or a dozen others, lend themselves to an exposition of methods of analysis which can be made quite as interesting as a good story. Particularly is this possible if the presentation is staged as a search for problem solutions [see 191, 192].

The sense of the above suggestions is perhaps that a lecture should attempt to make the total presentation of material (including what is read) more vivid, more forceful, more readily related to the realities the student knows. This leads to a final point about what a lecture may contribute. The impact of a lecture, if well done, is likely to be greater than the impact of most reading materials, merely because person-to-person communication is likely to be more arousing than impersonal communication. Properly used, therefore, the lecture may achieve another kind of objective which is perhaps implicit in what has been said; by means of his manner, his mode of presentation and his material, the lecturer may communicate such relative intangibles as enthusiasm for the subject matter, belief and disbelief in what is discussed, tolerance or respect for ideas, and the worthwhileness of intellectual values in general.

PREPARING FOR LECTURING

Outlines and notes. It is likely that the beginning instructor will wish to lecture from some form of notes, or an outline made into note form. Just how detailed these should be is a matter for individual judgment. Obviously, notes can be overly scanty, like the four or five key words one of my colleagues used to jot on a card before entering the lecture hall. They can be overly detailed, so that the lecturer is really a reader rather than a thinker expounding his ideas. But except for mention of these extremes there seems to be little wisdom in discussing the format of whatever notes are used. There may instead be real point to indicating other kinds of ideas that beginning lecturers have found useful.

Initially, it may be suggested, the goal of lecturing is after all communication, and it is likely to be the more effective if there is an evident order or sequence; the first concern of the lecturer may be, therefore, for the natural order of his material. It is usually desirable to plan, not simply a single lecture, but a block or unit of lectures, at least in skeletal form, at a time. This plan has the important advantage of enabling one to weigh proper time distributions for various subtopics and to make sure that no essential topic gets squeezed out for lack of planned time. Next, since the lecture plan, i.e., the sequence of ideas, is most useful to students when they are aware of what it is, it should be kept relatively simple, without subtle subheads and subsubheads. Thus, with relative ease the student can know where he is within an organization of ideas, and so listen and understand easily. A quite different kind of suggestion may be made to the beginning lecturer—all illustrative materials that can be anticipated should be allowed for and indicated in the notes. Despite the desirability of spontaneous illustrations and comments, to give life to a lecture, the probability is that the most completely apt illustrations do not come into being that way. Careful thought ought to be expended on illustrative materials, just as on any other aspect of a lecture, and due time allowance made for them. A notable profit from this is avoidance of the somewhat catastrophic experience of starting spontaneously on a lengthy illustration, only to realize partway through that it is not really relevant after all.

Another technique in lecture planning, useful to many instructors, is to include exact (literal) statements of all critical points and to develop the habit of reading these to the class in such a manner that they are flagged for the student—so that he is aware of their importance. Quite apart from the virtue of being exactly correct in stating important ideas, there is here the added profit that such ideas, commonly being the ones employed in examination questions, are both made to stand out in the notes by this device, to be sure to be noticed for lecturing and for examination construction purposes, and also to be put down and uttered in such a way that there is no argument, at examination review time, about just what it was that the instructor said.

Next, and this is really a special aspect of the general intention to give students a framework around which to organize and understand the lecture, there are several other specifically planned items which can go into the notes, or at least receive such careful thought that they are available to the lecturer in exactly the form he wants. One of these is an introduction to the specific lecture (or block of lectures) which includes a preview of the main topics to be covered, and their sequence, so that the student knows what is ahead of him. It need take only a few minutes, but it will be found to yield rather great returns for the time spent. As will be mentioned in other contexts, the planned introduction, especially if done systematically at each lecture as part of the style of the lecturer, has two other virtues: as something planned and ready to tongue, it helps the beginning instructor through the first and more difficult moments as he gets into the swing of his lecture and begins to relax and settle down; also, when expected regularly, it becomes a good device for getting a class to come to order and begin useful listening promptly. Another of the to-be planned items, and this is surprisingly important yet surprisingly seldom thought of, especially by the instructor who thinks in a rigid outline with its compartmentalizing characteristics, is that the lecturer needs to think through the transitions which are needed from one topic to the next. This certainly is an aspect of making the sequence of ideas apparent, and in its absence the lecture appears to be a series of unrelated oral jottings. It will be found that the attempt to say neatly just why one moves from a given idea to the next one will sometimes show exactly why that should not be done; better to find this out in the preparation stage than before one's audience.

It is desirable to close a lecture firmly and have done with it. An orderly summary is, of course, impressive and helpful, and one might expect to incorporate it into his notes. It is more likely, however, that the beginning instructor cannot tell exactly where he will be at the end of the period, and therefore cannot, except entirely on the spur of the moment, plan what to put into a summary. One of the most useful devices for meeting this problem, again assuming that lectures are planned in blocks, is to plan carefully a major ending and summary point only at the end of the whole block and to make this not a matter of a few hurried minutes but a generous portion of a period or even a whole period. In this way, the problem of closing a daily lecture is reduced to merely one of leaving the student clearly aware of just where he pauses for a day in the sequence of ideas being discussed. Some possibilities of time adjustment can be arranged by the instructor by having in his notes alternative materials or alternative treatments to be used for that part of his lecture where he expects to be at the end of the hour.

Planning beyond the notes. Certain supplementary suggestions can be made here. One is that, students and schedules being what they are, running over the allotted time for a lecture, if done very often, or because of incomplete planning or indecisiveness about handling of the lecture, is one of the things leading to an impression of incompetence. By contrast, the habit of stopping when one has finished a suitable quantity of material for the day, even though this may happen to be a good many minutes short of the end of the period, may surprise the students agreeably, and will build up one's credit with them so that on any occasion where it is truly important to hold them five minutes overtime to finish something, they will perceive this as unusual and regard it as probably essential. Certainly one of the least effective procedures is to finish five minutes early, look surprised, and without build-up or preparation announce that the remaining time is available for questions from the audience. Most of the students are present thereafter only in body. In this same train of thought it may be noted that because some students in a class are likely to be thinking of their post-class activity and are ready to leave at the drop of a clue, the lecturer should not give them any leaving clues until he is ready to do so. Specifically, he should avoid saying such things as "Just one more thought, and then we'll be finished," or "Although the hour is nearly over, I'd like to report another, similar study," and he should be capable of saying, as a final and routine signal, something like "That's all for today," so that students develop the habit of paying attention to him until that particular signal occurs.

Other miscellaneous observations which apply to planning for lectures can be mentioned. One is that in preparing a lecture, any accessory materials should be assembled and tried out and demonstration procedures practiced well in advance of the class meeting. The danger of assuming that apparatus, slides, or other demonstration material will surely be available and in working order in the lecture room cabinet is that when the assumption proves incorrect, last-minute stressful efforts to replan what one will do, or substitute other arrangements, are likely to be somewhat inadequate. Then there is the necessity for a good place for one's notes, with illumination suitable to the quick glance. The height of lecture benches or stands contributes a good deal not merely to the comfort of the lecturer but also to the impression he makes on his audience. Well-placed and legible notes enable him to avoid the impression some lecturers give, of a hen alternatively ducking her head into the food pan and coming up erect to survey the world about. One can scan well-placed notes easily while finishing his sentences on the last point, and so be ready for the next point or topic without a long pause given over to a frantic search for the next cue.

Another observation has to do with planning how much time to allow for any particular discussion. Here it has been noted that material taught for the first time, even assuming the instructor has thorough mastery of it, can cheerfully be expected to give trouble, and probably to take longer than material which can be presented in smoothly practiced ways. Also the less well the instructor knows a topic himself, the more rapidly his ideas on it disappear before a class. Perhaps the moral here is that except in desperation one should avoid trying to teach what he has not yet mastered so well that accessory ideas, alternative formulations, clarifying statements, etc., come to him in a steady flow when he needs them.

One should protect lecture periods by keeping out of them as many of the accessory aspects of teaching as possible. Announcements about examinations, requests for experimental subjects, distribution of printed materials with the consequent rustle and distraction, and so on, should be held to a minimum or bunched into time deliberately reserved for them on a particular day. This will avoid the appearance of beginning each lecture with a number of events irrelevant to it, which in effect trains students not to pay close attention.

Finally, and this point is important, it must be remembered in preparing a lecture that notes or outlines are skeletons only, and in the written mode at that. The most important polish one can give to a lecture plan is to think through how he is going to *say* it. This he can do by adopting the special set, in the quiet of his office or study, of addressing the at-that-moment nonexistent audience, while he practices expressing his thoughts to them.

DELIVERING A LECTURE

In an earlier day the teaching of speech technique, elocution as it was so often called, gave considerable attention to the mechanics of movement and gesture, and to other matters which were essentially form. In recent decades the emphasis in teaching speech techniques has much more often been upon having something to say, or upon the thought processes which are basic to effective public speaking. Once those processes are in reasonable order there can be attention to matters of effective delivery.

It should be evident from what has been said earlier that we here, in discussing the delivery of a lecture, do not presume, any more than the contemporary speech teacher, that form can make up for an absence of content. Rather, for purposes of discussion we assume that plans have been laid for adequate substance, so that now the question is how best to make its meaning apparent to others. It may be remarked, possibly as reassurance, that as Reid [220] found in interviews with students they are relatively tolerant of various peculiarities or inadequacies of form, at least many of the minor ones. I would add that students have the tendency to regard such matters as part of the to-be-expected and normal variations in personality or style of their instructors, within the natural bounds of what can be expected of a human being who happens also to be a teacher. Overconcern about form is therefore simply not necessary. Only those matters which seem most essential, or which are most capable of being acted upon without professional coaching or guidance, will be mentioned.

Getting and holding attention. Perhaps the first principle governing learning from a lecture is that, as a listener, one must be aroused to respond to it. But this response by definition must be one directed toward what the speaker is talking about, not something else altogether. A lecture therefore cannot effectively begin, continue, or terminate without holding attention—a truism which it should not be necessary to formulate for college instructors but which somehow gets overlooked far too often, perhaps because the lecturer assumes that every hearer has the same intense interest in the subject that he does, at the very same moment . . . though he ought to know better than this.

Mention has been made of using some recognizable procedure for closing a class meeting, and of avoiding using this sign until ready to close. We can now apply the same reasoning to the beginning of a lecture, where there is the problem of calling everyone together, as it were, from all the various conversations and other activities, and getting them all into the same line of thought. Suggestions by various commentators on this problem, seem to me to fall into three schools. One suggestion is that to get attention one should always start with something a little spectacular, or at least almost certain to be interesting: a well-chosen remark, an action or a bit of content (like a reference to something of current interest to students), whether these are directly relevant to the lecture content or not. The intention with such an opening is to get control of attention, then divert it into the subject matter of the day. Another suggestion is that one might as well be realistic and count the first five minutes lost anyway, while the notebooks get straightened out, the postures made comfortable, knitting put in order, the ears attuned to the speaker, and so on. He will therefore simply start talking to draw attention to the fact that the five (or other number of) minutes have begun, taking care to say nothing important while his audience is getting set to listen attentively to him. The third school, and this is my preference, believes in training students to expect something useful in the first few minutes (e.g., brief review of the previous lecture, preview, introduction). They will therefore learn to settle down before time for class to start, and should be rewarded for this by a clear and forceful beginning to the lecture itself. This beginning can be signalized in certain ways which the students come to identify as part of the particular instructor's style. For example, he may do well to stay away from the lecture bench until ready to begin the lecture, then stride purposefully to it (choosing to do so promptly but not compulsively). He thereby reinforces the notion of attending when "the preacher's in the pulpit" and avoids training the students to disregard his (silent) presence before them until another signal is added. He may also use some formal sign that it is time for silence and attention. It is possible to do this firmly and clearly, yet without a disciplinary overtone. A gesture or some accustomed words will come to do the trick if used consistently and for a clear purpose. I know one person who for years has waited until he is ready to begin, then has said, "Time for the meeting to come to order," waited 30 seconds, then started in with an important sentence. Campus lore describes him as a man whose classes begin on time and with something worth paying attention to. Once, in a class of more than 500 students, where it was sometimes difficult to be heard in order to call the class to order, I by lucky chance found at my command at the lecture bench a master switch which simultaneously darkened all the lights in the auditorium; a brief flick of this switch, and the unfailingly perceived change in illumination level was within a few class meetings sufficient to bring the class to instant responsiveness. Any other device which lets the audience know that business is beginning can serve equally successfully to get their attention.

In the same general vein of thought we note that often during a lecture it becomes necessary to re-engage the attention of the audience. If a diversion has been created by questions or discussion, or a demonstration, by some stimulus outside the classroom, or even by the conclusion of a well-told story, there will be a few moments in which the group is somewhat scattered in its thoughts, as it was just before the lecture began. Before proceeding the lecturer must make sure everyone is with him. This is likely to be easier than at the beginning of the period, simply because the diversity of audience response has not been so great. If only the lecturer remembers that he wastes his breath talking into a buzz of conversation, or to people who are all looking out the window at the low-flying airplane, or chuckling over the last punch line, and that he must get his audience with him, the matter is usually easily enough accomplished. (We should perhaps note that if it is one's practice to accept and answer questions from the floor, one should be sure the question is heard and attended to by repeating it or rephrasing it before answering.)

As to holding attention during the main body of the lecture, certain predictable suggestions can be made. Some of these have their roots in what has been learned scientifically about attention getting and holding. More are suggestions by the artisans of speech, with probable support from the scientific evidence were it directly pertinent (see, for example, Bane [18]). In the first place, stimuli have to be distinctive in order to produce predictable responses. Translated, this suggests that speech has to be intelligible, that the plan of a presentation has to be discriminable, and that, as previously suggested, it helps to know where you, as listener, are in a discussion. Conversely, slurred or overly soft speech, or a fuzzy plan of organization, are almost sure to lose the audience. We should further expect that to hold attention the lecturer must exhibit change and variety. Whether this is achieved through what he does with gesture or voice, or by the content of what he says, or by the introduction of demonstrational or illustrative materials, it is obvious that the effective lecturer avoids monotony by keeping something new or different coming along. One can deliberately think about this aspect of his lecturing, and plan for changes of style or material so that his hearers will be compelled to notice what goes on.

Humor, as variety, is of course most desirable, but a number of remarks need to be made about it. For one thing, forced or unskillful attempts to be humorous are probably worse than a perfectly sober treatment which leans on other devices to maintain interest. Being funny, especially in a way that moves a discussion forward rather than diverting it, simply does not come easily to many of us. And there is no point in straining at it, for this is pretense, and pretense is likely to be regarded as worse than a lack of comicality. Furthermore, the faculty is not always up to date on what is amusing to students; certainly, the styles and intricacies of humorous discourse are quite different on different campuses. We probably do well, therefore, to suggest that humor is good but should not be regarded as a prime necessity; that it may best come out in spontaneous ways, growing from the thought of the moment and being an aspect of animation rather than planned stage craft; that if not overdone it can reasonably safely be humor at one's own expense, a form of humor which seems to serve as an equalizer of egos; and that a cultivated wit is nevertheless a very precious and desirable human trait.

The lecturer can also adopt certain other patterns of expression with the intent of commanding attention. One of these is the deliberate repetition rendered in exactly the same intonation and phraseology; another is the repetition which is a deliberate variant of the form of the first statement. Either way the doubled presentation gives an important idea an extra chance of being caught by the hearer. Sometimes the obvious topical sentence may be utilized to draw attention to a shift in the subject under discussion. The simple matter of declaring that what comes next is important helps cue the student; after all, not everything can be equally important, so we might well be honest and help him know what should be central in memory. One can introduce climaxes and subclimaxes by noting and using the natural pattern of the material—even the description of an experiment can be put as a quest with a discovery. Finally, we might suggest, there is the general matter of timing. Talking into a hush created by a significant pause is one of the most useful skills for making sure that attention is effectively riveted on a significant statement. Such devices are not, however, perfectly carried off without practice.

On the speaking voice. Comments about the speaking voice will be made only briefly here, partly because genuine changes in the use of the voice require considerable expertness of treatment, and partly because it seems to be true that if a voice is readily discriminable its other qualities tend not to be so very critical to the success of the classroom lecturer. Reid [220], Hannay [128] and many others, however, have stressed the importance of the simple matter of being heard. Hannay, for example, suggests that a resonant tone (what some teachers of singing call a hard tone, as distinguished from a soft or breathy tone) is superior for the lecture hall because it provides a more readily discriminated voice line. Sheer loudness, according to the students Reid interviewed, is definitely a variable in whether they could understand a lecturer. We can further expect that talking directly at an audience, rather than to one side or at the blackboard or in some other direction, should make it easier for that audience to hear what is said. In any event the instructor will do well to ask students in the back row whether they can hear him satisfactorily, or may even ask them to give him a signal whenever audibility becomes a problem. (This overlooks the possibility that in some of the acoustically queer places we teach in, the back row may hear perfectly well while there are dead spots in other places in the room closer to the lecturer.) Sometimes it is possible to remedy an unsatisfactory situation only by means of amplifying equipment, which we should not be reluctant to use whenever necessary.

It should be remembered that much can be done with the voice to achieve the variety we have spoken of as so desirable for lecturing. One device which the beginning lecturer can utilize is deliberately to plan various major blocks of material, or units of discussion within a lecture, to be done in different manners appropriate to their content. For example, one can lead through an analysis of data or experiments into something of a climax at the generalization to which they lead, then drop back naturally to a quieter, lower pitched consideration of the significance of this generalization, or of its applications, or of its relationship to other generalizations. ("Now, what does all this mean . . . ?") Perhaps the chief point to be made about variety in the use of the voice is that the lecturer, if he possibly can, ought to avoid what I have come to call the patient monotone. This pattern of recitation of successive sentences and paragraphs in the same repetitive pitch and loudness pattern can become thoroughly boring or even exasperating. It seems to occur when the speaker is not relaxed and in his concern for himself does not perceive the way he is addressing himself to others, or, more rarely, when he is so wrapped up in his thoughts about subject matter that again he does not notice what impact he is having on others. An attempt to use a more ordinary and relaxed and conversational style usually makes for a reduction in the monotonous performance and, certainly, becoming involved in something interesting to the speaker is in most cases conducive to variety and spontaneity rather than sameness of speech.

Another consideration which seems appropriate for this lay discussion of voice usage problems has to do with securing emphasis at appropriate points in the subject matter. This can be regarded as an aspect of securing variety, but deserves special mention. As stated previously, in relation to the uses of outlines or other aids to definite organization of material, and in relation to attempts to achieve variety in presentation, it is helpful to the listener to make organization and relative importance of the material clear to him. Any instructor knows this, if he stops to think about it, and constantly tries to help his students discriminate the pattern of ideas and the high points. We can therefore merely declare here that variation in pitch, in loudness, and in rate of speech are among the aids available to the lecturer, and he need only let his speech be naturally emphatic, rather than monotonous or stilted, to secure these advantages.

Some analysts of classroom lectures have felt that a speaker could talk either too slowly or too rapidly for comfort or for understanding on the part of the listeners. The range of tolerance is evidently very wide, however. A good many hours spent listening to beginning lecturers have led me to think that the rate-of-speech variable is not directly critical (except, I suppose, at the very extremes). Instead, the more critical variable may be the rate-of-ideas. By this I refer to the fact that one man can use a relatively economical number of words per minute, well organized, distinctly presented, repeating very little and saying a good deal; students have to keep alert to stay with him but can readily do so. Another man may talk twice as fast, repeat often, and even speak less distinctly; again, students who keep alert may stay right with him, make just the same number of notes as those listening to the first man, and so on. Such variations have led me to think that rate of speech, as such, tends to be a sort of personal-style variable through which most of us as adults have already learned to penetrate to the basic meanings behind the words. It is the basic meanings which can come too fast, or not seem to come fast enough, to be rewarding. I feel sure it is meanings which cause trouble to the beginning lecturer who is overly tense or insufficiently prepared and therefore presents a little about each of many concepts rather than developing the import of each at enough length that his students know what he is talking about before he goes on to the next idea.

A final consideration about voice usage, and again we are reminded of the matter by Reid's interviewees, is that distinctness of enunciation is a very critical variable. It can be demonstrated that most of us have certain slovenly habits of tongue and lip. We swallow and muffle certain sounds, so that we put forth speech that we ought not to expect to be understood at any very great distance. It is also clear that for most of us deliberate effort to speak distinctly makes much difference in the distinctness of the result. The lecturer should have it within his ordinary powers, then, to attend to this matter and improve his enunciation as needed.

Gestures. Evidently the first requirement of gesture and movement by a lecturer is that it be a natural part of the total expression of what he is communicating. If the ideas are coming as they should, and the speaker is genuinely trying to communicate them to other people of whom he is fully aware, his actions tend to blend with his speech in the easy way, that is, they will be spontaneous and animated. Advising that the beginning lecturer attempt to do specific things with his body is very likely to make him wooden or artificial in his movements and self-conscious to the point where he feels like a fool. In reassurance to the learner we can go one step further, though, and suggest that the kind and amount of action a lecturer shows is perceived by others as some aspect of his personal style and not likely to be central to his success as a communicator of ideas. He need only be sure, therefore, that this aspect of his performance does not somehow interfere with communication. The rest is likely to take care of itself.

To be sure, learning is possible here too, especially with professionally competent help. I cannot help but recall, however, a young instructor whose classes I systematically visited. At that time it seemed important to me that he not remain so fixed in one position, feet unmoving for 50 minutes, and hands firmly anchored to the little lecture stand placed on the table top. We discussed this point, and he too felt that he was riveted to the spot unnaturally. He therefore hit upon a determination to move, a few times during the lecture and casually, from the center of the table around to one end or the other. During the next lecture that I observed I was somewhat startled to see him pace about in a reasonably relaxed way, but all unaware hugging to his chest the little lecture stand from which his hands were not yet separated. There is the danger then that piecemeal attempts to deal with such a problem may yield, not changes in the whole fundamental pattern, as might come with simple reduction of anxiety through experience, but rather strange, disjointed changes in the lecturer's pattern.

Mannerisms. The foregoing examples lead naturally into mention of what is probably an overdone bugaboo of the beginning lecturer, mannerisms. By the expression is meant tendencies to fall into unconscious actions which are objectionable to the audience. In this category may be pacing and fidgeting with the cord from window blinds, or half lying on the lecture bench. I once had an instructor who would take time off in the middle of a sentence, in early fall and hay-fever season, to use the flat of his palm in a lengthy and obviously rewarding massage of the end of his nose; after the first few occurrences, which I regarded as amusing, I began to wish he could find some other solution to his problem. There can be slumped or queer postures, or manners of dress which attract unfavorable attention. There can be peculiarities of speech, whether inappropriate choice of words, ill-chosen or overdone vulgarity, or odd uses of the voice. One of the most exasperating mannerisms can be the "ah-pause" or the "er-pause," a device well recognized for covering a blank in thought. In a department where I once taught the students used to keep a tally of the number of such pauses a certain lecturer made in each of three five-minute samples during the period (second five minutes, sixth, and ninth). Their motivation had become that of getting up a betting pool, the winner of the jackpot being the person who predicted most accurately the total number of pauses in the samples taken on a given day. Other objectionables in lecture-room behavior can include harping on a pet subject, or repeatedly using a certain line of joking-aggressive remarks, as about women, a particular political party, or rival universities, or telling shaggy-dog stories. Evidently what is involved in all of these will not always be modified by specific advice. Instead, what is needed is an increase in general social perceptiveness or responsiveness. Then the objectionable elements will presumably tend to be dealt with as recognized.

For two reasons it was intially remarked that mannerisms have perhaps been made into an overdone bugaboo of the beginning lecturer. One of these reasons is that, like any other aspect of classroom behavior, mannerisms tend to be regarded, as part of the to-be-expected variation among human beings. There exists a considerable tolerance for the peculiarities of other people, and students are likely to show this tolerance up to the point where factors other than simple mannerisms as such lead them to react negatively to a lecturer. The other reason that talk about mannerisms may have been overdone is that, after all, an important aspect of lecturer effectiveness is precisely his uniqueness. Manners of dress and conduct contribute much to this. One might say that mannerisms, like the way a lecturer organizes his lectures, are part of his trademark. Certainly the successful lecturer tends to be perceived by his students as distinctive in what he does and says; it would not make sense to attempt to level all college instructors to some entirely innocuous lack of variation in personal conduct. It may hardly be necessary to add that pushing too hard to claim a trademark may merely earn one a demerit.

The atmosphere of communication. Perhaps the most general and most important thing to remind a beginning lecturer of is that unless he is talking *with* people, not at them or over their heads, he will not teach well. Using forms of speech that would be used in talking with another individual; just looking at people, and making eye-to-eye contact with different members of the audience in turn; reacting to the reactions of the audience (perhaps even when these are irrelevancies); all of these and many more modes of behavior lead to the impression that the lecturer actually wants someone to listen to him and understand what he is saying. Too often, it has seemed to me, the beginning teacher is not merely tense and somewhat stiff in his approach, but in addition is so involved in the formulation of his ideas that he does not have time to look for and respond to audience reaction, or even to analyze other aspects of his performance. Fortunately, this is one of the things most clearly remedied by experience, for as the ideas are expressed or practiced more often, they roll themselves out more easily and leave a margin of attention for audience response. I have found it meaningful to say that some beginning lecturers work as though they were behind a cellophane curtain, through which they could see the audience indistinctly and hear it if it became noisy enough. Until this atmosphere or effect is removed, so that a feeling of person-to-person communication governs the lecture situation, it cannot be fully stimulating. As a caution it may be well to remark that this atmosphere of communication does not depend altogether on looking the audience in the eye. For example, a student of John Dewey has told me how in Dewey's days at Columbia he might slouch at a desk at the front of a lecture room, usually looking out the window, never appearing to study notes, hesitant in speech, but giving an impression of trying to get ideas in order and to get them out where others could understand and examine them. To this student, at least, the effect was that Dewey was striving in a personal way to communicate, that the very least one could do was to respond by trying to get the ideas straight. The result was that his audience could become completely involved in thinking with him, often having the satisfaction of getting something straight with him or ahead of him, and in the process being tremendously active and motivated learners. How we get the effect of personal communication, then, is partly personal style, to be learned through experience and deliberate exploration of methods.

ADJUSTING TO THE LECTURE SITUATION

For some who lecture for the first time the situation is an exciting and challenging one. In it they are likely to find its own rewards, which will support learning how to accomplish just what should be accomplished there. Most of us have to admit, however, that while we expect excitement, challenge, and satisfaction from learning to lecture, we are at least a little concerned about exposing our initial inadequacies in that situation. Some of us are downright scared of it, and probably will not learn to lecture well without being perfectly honest with ourselves and taking steps to overcome or reduce the fears. The remarks I make here are addressed more to the second and third groups than to the first, if only for the reason that there are more of us.

Correlates of high tension in a lecture are well known; as said in several contexts earlier in this chapter, they are such things as a failure of supporting or clarifying ideas to come to mind, failure to observe reactions of the audience or react appropriately to them, tendencies toward stereotyped behavior or mannerisms, and a certain kind of insistent rigidity or unthinking inflexibility. Evidently there is little point in discussing how to make ideas come to mind, or how to be flexible though tense. But there are some suggestions which bear upon relaxation.

First, it must be remembered that even undergraduates are people, and that as such they possess considerable tolerance for other people. Therefore the lecturer has a bank credit of learning time before any class will give him trouble over his lecturing inadequacies, and even then they are not likely to do so if his motivation is obviously sincere and other aspects of his conduct are not downright objectionable to them. Conversely, aggressive or arrogant methods of covering tension are likely to arouse active rebellion in students. A second suggestion is that confidence comes partly from being as thoroughly and broadly prepared as one can realistically expect himself to be at his stage of professional development. If he in truth feels that way, he is better able to shrug his shoulders and take his class meeting in stride. He will hardly be surprised or shocked if everything does not run itself off perfectly. Perhaps another way of saying this is to emphasize the importance of not setting one's standards too high—of not expecting to be perfect first time around. A third suggestion is that one must always be himself. He does not do well to imitate blindly some favored lecturer he once sat under. What made that man effective may merely make the imitator peculiar, like the imitators of Titchener who were able to dribble cigar ashes down their vests all right, but could not produce brilliant ideas as the master did. The basic personal style one has by the time he starts college teaching is not likely to be changeable within a few months, so one might as well assume that getting on with the job and the content is more likely to be useful than fretting overmuch about forms. A fourth suggestion is that at the very beginning it is possible to follow certain procedures which do not immediately focus full critical attention on the lecturer. Plans for demonstrations and other moderately diverting uses of class time take some of the pressure off, yet are useful to students while the lecturer is still getting the feel of the classroom situation.

Fifth, it is well always to remember that the beginning of any course is a little rough, if only because the students have not yet learned how to live with the particular lecturer, skilled though he may be. Therefore, while learning to lecture one must expect that it will take a while to bring his students to an understanding of how he thinks, organizes, and operates. One should not be surprised if, with insufficient attention to this point, he and his students seem to be working at cross purposes. Talking out how one plans to teach the course is the most straightforward procedure, but a word of caution is perhaps necessary; students may be inclined to be unhappy at drawing the newest instructor, and certainly will not care to have one who reiterates that he is inexperienced, regardless of how he does this. It is therefore desirable to make a general plan of action clear to one's self, and then to students, and during that particular course or with that particular group change this only for strong cause and then to make few alibis about it. Sixth, since one of the chronic concerns of the beginning lecturer is that he will run out of ammunition, one can simply take steps to feel assured that he has a sufficient supply of alternative topics prepared so that this cannot be a source of difficulty. Parenthetically, if this is read by an instructor who has taught long enough that he has trouble getting in everything he wants to include, and who has forgotten the fear of not having enough to say, let me refresh his memory by mentioning two men I know. One of them began to teach for the first time in summer school, having just taken his degree in June. At the end of the first week of lectures he was invited for the weekend to a neighboring city to a house party. He insisted on returning to his work early Sunday morning, and upon being pressured for an explanation remarked flatly that he thought he had prepared enough material, before the course started, for the first three weeks, but had shot his bolt in the first three lectures. Another man gave his initial lecture and afterward found it had last only 20 minutes. In something of a panic he burst in upon his department chairman saying, "I don't think I can last it out; I don't have enough to say to go on for 50 minutes." The chairman told him (this gets a little hard to believe, but he told it to me himself), "All right, next time tell them that you are rushed to catch a train; just don't tell them exactly what you mean, or what train you want to catch. You know then that if you run out of material, you can explain it's nearing train time and leave in a dignified manner." The suggestion was taken literally, and with the pressure off no difficulties developed in the next lecture. The point is that in this case, as in the first one, a perfectly capable man had not yet started to think in his normally competent way in the classroom. The one reassured himself by added work, the other was reassured by the rather unbelievable device which he accepted from his chairman. Both, to my certain knowledge, now fill a 50-minute period with ease and would be good for much more if the students would hold still.

We can conclude this discussion of how to be reassured though anxious by remarking that nothing succeeds like success. Or, nothing extinguishes concerns about lecturing like living through the first one, then the first week, then the first term, while occasionally, then increasingly more often, being rewarded by the obviously effective responses one has made in teaching.

The mere business of having taught seems to do more for confidence about being able to teach than does any other single factor.

OF STUDENTS AND NOTES

We have implied that a lecture should be planned partly to permit taking meaningful notes and that students evaluate a lecture partly according to how readily this can be done. Since notes are obviously intended to enhance review and retention, it may be worth asking whether these values can be increased by any action of the instructor over and above lecturing well.

It seems to be uniformly agreed that writing up lecture notes as soon as possible after hearing the lecture, so as to clarify one's understanding and rehearse it, as well as getting it into form so that it will be meaningful when cold, is an exceedingly valuable habit. One can point this out in detail to his students. He can go further and require that notebooks be prepared and handed in for inspection or grading. This involves additional work for the lecturer, and unless the student is forewarned about this aspect of the course, may arouse resentment in him. Nevertheless, some sort of sampling of notes, and attention to the manner in which they are taken or written up, can be very valuable to spur students to make more of the note taking technique.

There is another question: What concrete aids to better notes can be supplied by the lecturer? In passing we have mentioned putting at least a general outline on the board, to aid in clarifying the lecture organization. We can now emphasize the importance of this or any other device which ensures that the student is seeing the material the way the lecturer is trying to get him to see it (this has nothing to do with personal acceptance or persuasion). Some instructors have distributed outlines in advance, perhaps with the entries widely spaced so that the page also offers note taking space. Outlines have been printed in such form that only major headings are provided, with indications of the number of subheadings the lecturer intends to file under each one. And some instructors (including me) have objected to giving the student any such printed aid because of the likelihood that he will relax, become passive, not exert himself to stay with the lecturer ("It's all down on this printed sheet anyway, and I can read it better at home"). The outline formed or filled in on the board as the lecturer moves along has the double advantage of putting variety (even if it is a rather dull kind) into the lecturer's performance and, more importantly, forcing the student to sit up and pay attention at least often enough to make sure his notes correspond to what is presented visually before him.

8

DISCUSSION METHODS

Lecturing is usually thought of as a suitable technique for use with large groups of listeners, although of course it may be used with small groups, and can be entirely appropriate there. Equally, other kinds of teaching techniques may be thought suitable only for small groups, but may in fact be used in modified form in larger groups. Ideally, the instructor should be able to adapt a variety of techniques in his teaching situations so that he can use whatever procedure is most appropriate to the material, the students, or the need to relieve boredom. The instructor who is accustomed only to lecturing, or who begins conservatively by practicing that tried and honorable technique first, should know that the results achieved by introducing variations are likely to be surprisingly good.

It is commonly said that the lecture technique is inflexible, impersonal, and most efficient when used to present information or factual material. It does not fit any particular student exactly, because his interests or educational needs will not be those of the instructor, nor does the latter have any method for sensing what the individual student needs next. Furthermore, we know that the lecture permits the student to be quite thoroughly passive, a poor condition for learning. The small group techniques, by contrast, derive their appropriateness and strength from the fact that they arouse the student and secure participation, if only from threat of being found passive or ignorant. They are less efficient for imparting information but may be directly oriented toward clarification. Because the student is active, the instructor is better informed about what should be done next, and the learning situation is likely to be more real and vivid than when the student can sit idly on the base of his spine with never a fear that learning will invade him.

We should perhaps say flatly here that lecturing can be the best method under certain circumstances. We must say also that the small group techniques, badly used, may infuriate or confuse students. We therefore must discriminate which methods are best at any given moment. And we must further expect that our students will have to be trained to respond appropriately to them.

QUESTION-AND-ANSWER TEACHING

Modes of variation. Question-and-answer teaching is a time-honored classroom procedure, and many varieties of it have been practiced. We may note, for example, that the degree of control over what is supposed to occur in the teaching process has varied all the way from one extreme of a classical recitation-drill type of question (and implied teacher control), through more general discussion provoked by leading questions proposed by the teacher, to the other extreme of questions or commentary by the students themselves as the dominant theme of a class meeting. We may also note that the objectives sought in teaching have varied correspondingly. At one extreme such relatively precise and literal objectives as review of information or clarification of meanings in specific reading assignments may be sought, while at the opposite extreme, the objective of teaching may be to explore personal attitudes or to engage in joint problem solving. Perhaps the least recognized mode of variation, least recognized until one actually tries question-and-answer teaching, that is, is in the degree of exactness or predictability of what will happen next in the classroom, and in the degree of classroom formality. With recitation-drill questions, a formal and predictable state of affairs tends to be maintained. But the more students take over and guide the development of the class meeting through their questions, reactions, or commentaries, the less predictable and less formal the situation is. We may also add immediately, the greater are the demands for general wisdom, poise, and social perceptiveness on the part of the instructor.

We shall not pay direct attention here to the recitation-drill type of teaching. At the college level there are few settings in which it is appropriate for the classroom, if only because the classroom is not the best place for the factual or rote learning for which it is the best check or clarifier. Furthermore, the context of this kind of teaching is one in which good results from controlled and precise review tend in practice, whether necessarily so or not, to be masked by the undesirable results of making the instructor a drill master or authoritarian figure whose anxiety-arousing propensities may well generalize for the student into a dislike of the subject matter. Anyone who has ever sat under such a drill master is likely to recall the tendency to be more concerned about how he would select his next victim (no matter how kindly a drill master he was) than about mastering the material at hand.

The leading-question technique. Leading questions may be regarded as confusing, even dangerous, in certain contexts. In the classroom, however, they lend themselves to some of the most useful teaching processes. By the label of leading question we mean the use of perhaps three to six carefully planned questions which the instructor uses as organizers of a whole class meeting or a major portion of it. Such questions must adequately reflect the whole of the material the instructor feels should be discussed. The process of working over and understanding each question, then formulating various relevant answers to it and evaluating them, I have found for a good many years to be an effective teaching device in undergraduate courses from the introductory to the most advanced levels. The success of the device, of course, most certainly depends upon the choice of the situation in which to use it, and upon a good many other considerations which will be discussed below.

To begin with, the questions must be leading in the sense of drawing out connected and relevant discussion of a topic, rather than in the sense of obscuring or confusing. Considerable practice is therefore useful in aiding the instructor to avoid preparing merely nebulous questions and yet to create questions which provoke thought and demand that the student bring relevant factual information to bear upon the evaluation of answers. By definition, of course, the questions should not shut off discussion by the very nature of the answers they will provoke. For example, one would not ask, in this context, "Is the IQ constant?" Rather, he might ask, "To what extent do studies of foster children support the idea that the IQ is markedly influenced by environment?" The first form of the question tends to lead to a yes or no answer and encourages the whole attitude of seeking the authoritatively given truth. But the second version of the question cannot be adequately answered without considering the logic implied by the question, as well as which studies of foster children are relevant or most adequate to it, and why, and then presenting the evidence they have to offer and evaluating its significance. It should be remarked that although this example tends to be typical in that it shows how a number of kinds of materials (here, in experimental design, statistics, measurement, testing, and social class) can all be drawn upon to formulate a reasonable answer to a single discussion question, other kinds of questions can have quite different objectives in view. For example, a question may not have a clear answer in fact, but may lead to an exploration of attitudes, as when a discussion is oriented around the problem of desegregation, or around the relation between religion and science. It should be evident, then, that this method of teaching is intended to produce basic learning *during* the process of discussion, that this is likely to have integrative or organizational or evaluational aspects, and that it is best used in a group small enough that the give-and-take between instructor and students permits keeping track of individual modes of thought and reaction. (I have used the method with groups as large as 100, but must admit it was one of the most exhausting methods of teaching I have ever used and not really adequate to the situation.)

Leading questions produce more questions, as well as other kinds of reactions. The key to the success of the technique lies in how the instructor deals with these student reactions, and we shall consider next some suggestions about this. One of the basic problems resides in the fact that when a question of general and leading character is presented to a group they will not all have the same set toward it as does the instructor. Indeed, they quite commonly do not see at once where to get hold of it. The instructor therefore must assume responsibility not merely for presenting his first question, but for restating and reworking it as required either to meet student demands for clarity or to begin to get responses at all. Because the procedure is likely to be a strange one to students, it is desirable to discuss problems of this kind with them in advance, so that there is not an uneasy period of silence while the students are trying to figure out what the instructor is up to now. Happily, it will usually be found that once the students understand not only that the content of the responses to questions is their responsibility, but also that the questions themselves are subject to investigation or criticism, they will respond actively indeed to the topical bait offered by the instructor.

In eliciting and dealing constructively with student responses to leading questions a number of specific problems are encountered. There is, for instance, the problem of securing useful and wide participation by the members of the group. One can always expect some students to be dependent upon the instructor to evaluate their remarks or tell them whether truth has been achieved, while others are content to let the instructor or other students do all the talking. The instructor not only can discuss these problems with the class, if his relationship with them has had time to become sufficiently secure, but can use the opinions or replies of one student as a basis for asking the reactions of other students ("I wonder what others think of that suggestion . . ."), and so get them all involved sooner or later in working out an adequate answer to the original question. This may now and then require an occasional steering remark by the instructor, to remind the group of the original question. It may also require considerable faith on his part that, sooner or later, inadequate or inaccurate responses by students will be remedied by them or by other students so that the final product is reasonably satisfactory from his point of view. Perhaps this latter problem could be reformulated slightly. The instructor is typically so full of correct responses to his question that only with difficulty can he restrain himself from giving them, rather than waiting for students to puzzle them out. Perhaps the most useful antidote for this tendency is for the teacher to remember (if indeed he believes it) that the process of thinking their way through to adequate answers may be for his students the most valuable aspect of what goes on in his classroom, rather than the content of their answers as such. He himself should therefore become involved in guiding or eliciting thought processes, rather than trying merely to cover certain informational ground.

Another consideration about securing participation by all students is this. Participation is a new social venture for some students, and a risky one at that, so that the initially silent ones may sometimes begin to break their silence by blurting, or by talking at a tangent, in order to have something to say, or by formulating an otherwise inadequate or loose response to the question at hand. The instructor will do well, where he perceives that a student is beginning to learn to participate, to avoid all sarcasm or rebuke, and to accept the responses as given. Since reality must nevertheless be practiced in the classroom, he is not likely to wish to take an inadequate or incorrect answer as final, merely to avoid making a negative response to a tentative try, so he may need to comment upon it in an accepting even if critical way ("That's a good suggestion but we may need to work on it a bit . . ."), or pass it along to other students for comment. Nevertheless, he can control the spirit in which this is done so that the new participant is made to feel that his opinions are listened to, that he too can participate, and that he need not expect to be punished for opening his mouth. Furthermore, if it occasionally happens that an aggressive student leaps to attack the initial expressions of opinion by a less skillful participant, the instructor may need to intervene and see to it that the beginner is to some extent protected while he learns.

This last remark leads us to a somewhat related matter, that of problem personalities in the class. For example, certain students may be unusually sensitive to, or aggressive about, certain topics. They may be undiscriminatingly responsive and by their reactions confuse the line of thought of a whole group. I well remember here an instance in which I was discussing simple product-moment correlation in the introductory course. For some unhappy reason which I could never afterward recall, I decided to use as the two variables in an illustrative correlation, measured belief in God and measured attitude toward communism. Midway in my concern for co-variation in pairs of scores I was firmly interrupted by a student whose strongly sectarian religious views I had sensed previously: "Do you really believe in God?" It was difficult to get myself and the class back on the track of the little numbers we had been discussing (although I did have the minimum presence of mind to say, "You show me how the question is relevant to what I'm trying to teach here and I'll answer it"). One can learn from experience, it is true, that there are such sensitive topical areas, or that particular individuals have their sensitive areas, but perhaps the only general suggestion that can be made for dealing with overreactions to one's questions is that a head-on clash with the student is not likely to settle much. Quite possibly, instead, a restatement of the question, or redirecting the comment to the class and away from one's self, or to some extent merely repeating and thus reflecting the feelings expressed, may let the discussion get back on the track, let the student relieve his feelings somewhat, and achieve a constructive consequence in spite of the distracting character of the earlier response. Discussion outside class may be necessary to deal with the most insistently distracting individuals before they have seriously hampered the work of the remainder of the class.

Another and related problem in the leading-question method is what to do about the persons who dominate the discussion merely because they are overly eager to participate, or are superior in preparation. Because it is evident to all that their motives are relevant to what is being done and are, generally speaking, socially acceptable, it is easier to deal with these people than it is with some of the kinds of individuals we have just discussed. (Smith and Dunbar [253] found that participators in classroom discussions exceeded nonparticipators on such measures as intelligence, quality of adjustment, and critical thinking.) It is possible, for example, to discuss this problem in advance of utilizing the method, and it is possible to remind the group of the need for wide participation at any time when it appears that a few individuals or one have become overly dominant. A simple remark of the general intent, "Let's see what others have to say on this . . ." is often sufficient to remind the eager and stimulate the slow. Particularly is the instructor likely to note that if he has been effective in getting rapport with his students, so that they feel secure in the classroom and in what is permitted to go on there, they themselves will control the unduly talkative or domineering person to a surprising degree. On one occasion the chosen representatives of an 11-man seminar warned me outside of class that at the next meeting they were going to help me regulate an overly domineering member of their group. And then, by taking apart his every statement about subject matter, they put him in his place more effectively and forcefully than a faculty member could ever have done it. Yet they did it in a reasonably pleasant way, so that he simply had to modify his conduct in order to remain a good member of the group. (I must admit to a good deal of empathizing on this occasion.)

Certain other precautions, or possibly changes in personality structure, are necessary for the instructor. One of them has been implied previously: when a student reacts to a question with comment or with a question of his own, the instructor must be sure that he does not respond by drowning the student in the boundless sea of words he himself has available on the topic. Particularly he must avoid addressing any prolonged discussion by himself directly to the student whose question serves as the occasion for it. I have seen a student ask a question which the instructor was hoping for, and receive as a reward a 20-minute lecture which seemed addressed personally to him while he squirmed and others felt disregarded. To avoid this, one can readily make a limited response to a given individual and then deliberately address any further remarks to the whole group. It is likely to be particularly useful here to use the initial response by an individual student as a basis for brief discussion, then restate or review the question. This leads naturally to consideration again by the whole group rather than any one individual. ("Mr. A. suggests that the problem can be approached by . . . ; now, let's consider also . . .")

Perhaps the principal problem in using the leading-question technique is what kind of relationship to strive for, between the instructor and the class, and among the members of the class. The simplest relationship is one in which the instructor remains always the dominant figure in the discussion, with most questions and comments directed to him, or relayed through him, or redirected by him to other members of the class. At the other extreme, the instructor can strive to have the group take only general guidance from him and his questions, and to take over from him the responsibility for adequate treatment of those questions or substitution of better ones, with direct and maximum interaction among the members of the group. This puts the instructor on the side-line, so to speak, and may even put him in the position of not offering maximally useful resources to his students. One can only guess, in the absence of evaluation data, that the desirability of these varying degrees of group control will depend to a fairly large extent upon the situation, for some groups will be ready for or profit from relatively great freedom, at least on some topics, while other classes may need a relatively firm guiding hand. Whatever the situation, the instructor must take an active role in deciding how the situation should be structured.

Student questions. Implied at various points in the discussion of leading questions was the fact that good questions produce more questions. So do good discussions or good lectures. In conjunction with any other method of teaching, then, there may be a deliberate effort to utilize the questions from students to guide discussion by the instructor, or to secure response from still other students. Our emphasis now will briefly be upon getting and utilizing those student questions, not because they exemplify some special method of teaching, as the planned use of leading questions does, but because student questions may be helpful at any point with any method.

Perhaps the first thing to say is that students ask questions only when they have some degree of readiness or preparation. The instructor cannot expect to be able at any moment, especially early in his course or without warning, to say, "Now are there any questions?" and immediately receive useful questions upon which he may work. This simply does not allow for either the difficulties in formulating questions or the barriers to expressing them. Such an approach is likely to be even less useful in a large group, for if there are 100 or 500 people around him, only the most aggressive student, more interested in self-assertion than in subject matter perhaps, will give quick responses. The problem of the instructor, therefore, is to generate questions by his teaching and to reduce the occurrence of questions which are merely asked and answered in a ritualistic way.

To encourage student questions there are some rather well-tried procedures. Which ones are appropriate, or will work for a given instructor, cannot well be predicted, but they are suggested as possibilities. First, the instructor may adopt the use of a planned and predictable question period, such as the first part or the last part of a class hour, or a certain hour each week. The students are then reminded that they may utilize that period for their questions, and they may be given suitable praise for being prepared with questions. Two shortcomings of the procedure are likely to be evident, one being a certain lack of spontaneity or timeliness in the questions, and another being that in this more or less formalized setting the questions often do not materialize. I have tried calling for written questions at the beginning of each class period, or once per week, and have found, for example, that the questions appear not to have been written at home as they developed during study or review but rather were hastily phrased as a last-minute thought just before class. For those who like a classroom process to be somewhat orderly, this suggests another shortcoming of the procedure under discussion; typically there is a problem of relating questions thus presented to the main business of the particular class meeting. This kind of orderliness may be unnecessary in the opinion of some teachers, so that if consistent use of the planned question period makes it rewarding, it may be retained even if treated as a subperiod separate from the main line of the class.

More commonly the instructor will seek to elicit student questions in the context, and in the process of, an ongoing lecture or discussion. Several suggestions can be made respecting the stimulation of questions in this setting. The obvious method is to pause at suitable places in a presentation and ask as teachers have presumably asked since teaching began, "Is this clear?" or "Are there any questions?" It should not be necessary to make this suggestion at all, except for the fact that the question is so often put by the instructor in a way which suggests that it is rhetorical, or in such a fashion that the student suspects he had better not hold up progress (as seen from the instructor's point of view). The professor who believes he has given adequate time for questions by remarking "So . . . ?" in brusque fashion and looking around the room in a sweeping manner has simply not allowed the time necessary for question formulation and by his action trains his students not to respond anyway. And if he is not consistent about stopping to see if there are questions, he also trains students to refrain from bothering to formulate them at all. Another suggestion is that the best source of questions is typically a concrete example, a specific instance of some more general problem or idea. Concepts, as we have had occasion to remark before, get formed out of specific occurrences. If the instructor sees to it that his discussions include case materials, experimental demonstrations, or simply descriptions of specific behavioral events, his students are able to make a beginning with him, take hold of the ideas implied or presented, and formulate questions which carry them a step further toward understanding.

A third suggestion, applicable to some extent to a whole class, but to a greater extent where something is known about individual students in the class, is to utilize in a lecture or a discussion materials known in advance to appeal to particular interests or backgrounds of members of the class. Thus, when the instructor knows that his class contains a few commuters, or some young married couples, or persons from a foreign country, or students personally involved in politics, or whatever else may be identified as interest involving, he may slant his examples so as to arouse their interests and secure their questions. This of course is quite the same thing as utilizing materials of contemporary or news value, on the assumption that this will provide a good bridge to matters of more enduring importance or interest. As a final suggestion about securing student response, it may be of use to mention a device which must be used with care, that of setting a deliberate logical trap of some kind for students, perhaps warning them that it is coming and perhaps not, depending upon the instructor's degree of self-confidence in what he is about to perpetrate. (One instructor of whom I heard would describe an experiment. Then, in interpreting it, he would make a completely unjustified statement with a straight face, going right ahead without pause until or unless he was challenged.) The dangers are, of course, that the trap will never be perceived as such by students, even though the instructor is convinced it is one, or that some students will react negatively to the traumatic experience of going along with the presentation, comfortably nodding the head, then suddenly discovering that they have been led up the intellectual garden path. The device is perhaps more provocative in general than it is of responses directly related to the subject matter of the moment. In some cases this may be desirable, but the safer version of the procedure is that in which the instructor with proper introductory remarks formulates a problem or a puzzling relationship for students and involves them in the task of analyzing it, which in essence means that he is following our earlier suggestion that presenting specifics will secure student responses.

The implications of what has been said about question-and-answer teaching here can be summarized and evaluated rather briefly, and this will provide a good transition to the next topic. First, the effectiveness of questions and answers to them by the instructor or by class peers depends upon many factors: factors found in the nature of the material, in the instructor's interests or skills or knowledge, and in the nature of the individual students and their group relationship. Correspondingly, the perceived worth of the method will depend upon whether it appears to achieve whatever are the teaching objectives stated for the course or accepted by students or instructor. It may even be enjoyed by students at the same time that they state that it is relatively worthless, simply because they see it as time wasting, or as not yielding the experience of progress with respect to the stated goals of a course. Third, since the objectives of question-and-answer teaching, while they may occasionally include the imparting of information, usually do not, such teaching is most likely to be effective if reading materials, lectures, and other sources of factual or systematic material are both adequate and supportive of attempts to master the subject matter in an organized and insightful way. Fourth, the effectiveness of question-and-answer teaching depends directly upon the instructor's ability to discriminate when it is appropriate, his flexibility and adaptability in swinging to or from the technique, and his capacity for accepting a suitable amount of direction from the students with respect to what will meet their felt needs. Finally, it appears likely that while the amount of control exerted over a classroom group may for many reasons need to vary, the whole atmosphere of give and take between instructor and students tends to make for a good group feeling, for security feelings, and consequently for freer mobilization of interests and attitudes in support of learning than where student-instructor interchange is minimized or held to a rigidly formal or stress-producing pattern.

THE DISCUSSION GROUP

In the foregoing sections frequent mention has been made of discussion, but always in the context of specific or leading questions and such class responses as may revolve around them. This kind of discussion is typically fragmentary, in the sense of dealing with particular, and not necessarily related, aspects of subject matter, and it is typically discussion between the instructor and a given student, with only accessory remarks by other students, or with the interaction between students mediated by the instructor. With the freest atmosphere for question-and-answer teaching, however, and in attempts to deal with certain kinds of questions, we encounter what here will be called true discussion. (Ruja [232] has pointed out how varied are the forms of social interaction included under the label of discussion.)

By true discussion is meant first, an emphasis upon genuine group interactions, with the instructor present and effective, but with the usefulness of discussion depending in large measure upon what the members of the group have to contribute to one another. A second defining characteristic of the true group discussion is that it deals, not with segmental questions, but with problems which themselves are unitary and to which each member of the group is (or should be) prepared in advance to contribute. (For treatments which effectively stress this defining characteristic see [14, 16, 134]. The first of these references, by Axelrod, gives very practical illustrations of the difficulties encountered and techniques for getting discussion under way. The others are especially valuable for the wide range of problems they cover and viewpoints they reflect.)

In the discussion setting, evaluation, in the sense of judgment of individual performances for grading by the instructor, is no longer an obvious or easy consideration. Correctness of answers is sometimes an almost irrelevant consideration. The enhancement of understanding and the improvement of the quality of thought processes are primary aims, with each member of the group being responsible not only for his own understanding but also for that reached by the group. The probabilities are that when a true group atmosphere is established there will be greater freedom of expression than in any situation which is instructor dominated, and it is likely, as Maier [173] suggests in his excellent treatment of discussion techniques, that social pressures exerted by the peer group will have greater attitudinal influence than will occur in the instructor dominated situation.

We shall treat discussion techniques relatively briefly here, because many of the operating difficulties the instructor encounters are the same as those discussed earlier in this chapter. It must be recognized, however, that in shifting from an emphasis upon instructor-student relationships as such to a concern for these plus group structure and interpersonal reaction, the problems of the instructor are made more complex and his skill requirements raised. It is not merely a truism that lecturing is the easiest method of teaching.

Free discussion. By free discussion is meant the kind of situation where, typically, the instructor raises or sketches some problem for consideration by the group (although it may arise while some other teaching technique is being used). When encouraging free discussion, the instructor explicitly attempts to avoid structuring or directing the line of comment, but he sounds out members of the group who need to have a chance to get in on the discussion, he occasionally asks probing questions to break a fixed line of thought, and so on. His relationship to the members of the group is one in which he seeks to get them to express their opinions about the problems; he is therefore permissive, accepting, and encouraging.

We have all sat through and participated in such free-for-alls. We know that they usually contain large numbers of verbal responses, typically expressed in a nonorderly mixture of analysis, ventilation of feelings, interpersonal clashes on feeling or fact, incomplete and interrupted formulations, or expressions of dissatisfaction that nothing is being clarified or that no progress is being made. We are aware that without some minimum degree of control, usually by the instructor, aggressive or overly talkative persons take up too much time or antagonize other members of the group. We may question, therefore, the value of ever using free discussion as a teaching technique.

Its best use is apparently as a starting point for the more controlled type of discussion which will be described below. As such a starting point, free discussion does indeed help make clear the range of knowledge and attitudes in the group and varying conceptions of the problem at hand. It does permit airing of emotional reactions in a way which many times make the individual in question feel better, and thus be more nearly ready for a rational consideration of the problem. The free discussion may well lead spontaneously to agreements of opinion or fact, and very commonly it leads to recognition of disagreements. It always risks the danger of causing people to stand stubbornly behind their initially expressed opinions, as well as the danger of leaving behind it suppressed or overridden emotional reactions.

Controlled discussion. In this form of discussion, the problem typically is set by the instructor, although it may grow out of earlier experiences of the group, such as a free discussion. It is likely to be discussed against a planned background of readings, lecture materials, or directed observation. It is likely to exhibit, particularly as the technique is being learned by any group, more or less formal aspects of control so that the discussion is developmental (this is Maier's term [173]). That is, it will be intended to proceed in a planned fashion toward the analysis or solution (development) of the problem at hand. Controlled discussion may be likened to the application of generally accepted methods of logical or scientific analysis to a group-analysis process, and to the extent that the group has had prior logical or scientific training, is more likely to be easy to introduce. Initially, control and training tend to be exerted by the instructor, but as the necessary mode of thought is interiorized in the students, they begin to apply their own controls to the discussion process.

The principal element of the controlled discussion procedure is adoption of a reasonably planned mode of attack on the problem or issue. Just how this is formulated depends greatly on the individual instructor or group, but it is done knowingly. It is likely to include such familiar and announced emphases as formulation or delimitation of the problem; examination of the kinds of analysis or evidence which would be pertinent to the solution of the problem; a deliberate search for evidence, whether by commentary in the group or by use of outside resources or those of the instructor; formulation of defensible conclusions, and a search for implications of conclusions, for unanswered questions, for limitations upon the conclusions, and for action consequences. There is likely also to be a deliberate attempt to avoid prejudgments, semantic traps, the confusion of issues, and admixtures of opinion, feeling, and fact. The more of these guards against faulty thinking the group can come to adopt, and the more it can concentrate upon the devices which permit creative thought (such as learning not to get stuck in a rut, learning to fractionate problems or questions or deliberately put them in a larger framework, or learning to go back and re-examine the question if answers to it do not seem to be forthcoming), the more likely is the group to experience the satisfaction of making progress toward solving its own problem. This is a powerfully rewarding experience for the learner, and if it occurs occasionally will do much to motivate him in other necessary methods of learning, such as rote mastery of basic language or factual material.

The agility (and memory) required of a controlled-discussion leader, particularly in the training phases of such discussion, are rather great. He must keep the outline of the orderly thought process before the group, help prevent stymies in the discussion by delaying or shifting momentary subdiscussions, move the group forward by such devices as summarizing and reviewing and then setting the stage for a next step, and in general lead the group to do its own thinking rather than merely take it over passively from him. It is again necessary to remark that the instructor must be capable of self-restraint, so that members of the group have sufficient opportunity to work out what they think before he leaps in to straighten them out. He further must be discriminating enough not to utilize discussion techniques where there is really nothing that makes either free or controlled discussion useful to the students.

SEMINARS

The word seminar may at one time have pointed to a distinguishable method of instruction, but can no longer be said to do so. For example, the word may once have implied interaction among students, as well as between students and instructor. It typically did imply that a small group was involved. Also, it once commonly implied a relatively advanced group of students, dealing with some specialized version of subject matter (which might be narrow and circumscribed or, at the opposite extreme, very broadly defined). But various kinds of influences, not the least of which has been the overpopulation of colleges and the resultant compensatory reaction of seeking a return to smaller classes, have made the seminar into many kinds of things. Our purpose here will therefore be only to call attention to some forms which the seminar has taken in recent years, in order to suggest to the beginning instructor some possible starting points for planning his own. Three reference-point seminars will be mentioned.

First, and used very successfully by certain psychologists at both the graduate and undergraduate levels, is the kind of seminar which the instructor dominates, not merely because he is the master of the subject matter but because of the way he handles the class. By the use of leading questions in class, by the use of thought questions issued to be used in preparations outside of class, and so on, the instructor guides the class with a relatively tight rein through the appointed subject matter, he uses the class period primarily to clarify the readings, and he takes primary responsibility upon himself for seeing to it that the right readings are utilized, as well as for making certain, by rigorous examinations over those materials, that mastery and understanding have been achieved. Social interaction in such a class inevitably is limited to that between instructor and student, and the role of the instructor is that of tutor and judge. It is implied by the whole situation that the instructor knows what should be mastered, so that the method is particularly likely to be suitable where some exterior standard, such as the necessity for meeting professional proficiency requirements or preparing for a comprehensive examination, is relevant to the assessment of student progress.

Another reference form of seminar puts more emphasis upon student contributions, yet retains a goodly degree of control in the instructor's hands. In this procedure the weekly two-hour class meetings, just to take a particular example, might be divided always into two parts. One part is a lecture or lecturette by the instructor, to introduce a topic of discussion, or give an overview or summary of general ideas on the topic, relate it to other topics, and so on. The other part calls for reports by certain students on particular assigned readings, these sometimes being portions of books but more often a selected journal article which provides a specific illustration of what the instructor is concerned with. It is characteristic of this seminar form that give-and-take, particularly as it relates to the analysis and understanding of the concrete research reports, is designed to involve the whole group, not merely an instructor-student line of communication. The use of specific materials (which may, of course, come first temporally) generates many questions which are not only involving to the students reporting and listening, but also give outward practice in the rigorous processes of thought and exposition which we presume to be significant to both liberal education and to science. If this seminar method is further loosened up so that the student assigned a particular reading expects to do collateral reading and bring it to bear upon his direct assignment, and so that other students do overlapping reading and thus are prepared to be more critical, considerable teaching begins to be done by the students themselves, with the instructor playing progressively more the role of a true discussion group leader, rather than tutor. Nevertheless, since he retains control over the assignments and is likely to utilize examinations, term papers and so on, he is quite clearly the central figure of the seminar.

A third seminar form, perhaps close to the extreme where the instructor does not really control what happens (as in the true nondirective situation, to be discussed in the next chapter), is that in which, after one or a few introductory meetings of the group, the students themselves take over, and more or less formally are teachers in their turn in the various topical areas. In this procedure it is common for the instructor to set the stage initially for the entire program of the seminar, suggesting desired topics for successive meetings, with perhaps some alternatives allowed, and indicating in detail the responsibilities to be assumed by students. The students then elect the topics they will present, some bargaining always being necessary for the first few elected and the last few unassigned topics. Thereafter each student schedules private meetings with the instructor to discuss his own reading. After he does a wide range of reading, instructor and student jointly select those references which are suitable as requirements for the remainder of the class in preparation for the specific seminar. The student then brings in a seminar plan he proposes to follow, and after the class meeting there may be private discussion of strengths and weaknesses in the seminar presentation itself. During the presentation by a seminarist, the instructor of the course serves as one member of the group and thus does not dominate the actual class meeting. He has already let the seminarist learn largely through his own efforts what it means to make a literature search and to plan a presentation, and then finally he lets the student present it and cope with class reactions. Such a seminar plan of course runs the risk of poor presentations by student seminarists and an occasional resultant demand that the course instructor take over, but careful preparation, plus the use of carefully selected readings and restrained participation by the course instructor, can minimize this risk. On the other side of the ledger, it is certain that the experience of bearing almost entire responsibility for a seminar presentation is challenging to the average undergraduate, so that he may work harder than ever before in his academic history. As a matter of fact, this points to a very common problem with this form of seminar: each individual, outside class, is so engrossed in his own preparations that he fails to read for each seminar by others and therefore is not in a good position to contribute to their presentations. A judicious use of quizzes preliminary to each discussion and bearing upon term grades may help here, as may some sort of rating scheme for evaluating (usually, via the instructor's memory) the quality of contribution by each student to a class meeting which is not his own primary responsibility.

BUZZ

Following the lead of Phillips [209], in recent years a novel device now known as the buzz session has come to be used to secure certain advantages of small group activity, even where the actual group confronted by the instructor is moderately or even very large, as in the instance described by McKeachie and Kimble [192]. The name presumably comes from the fact that for brief periods and for particular purposes, subgroups of four to eight students are formed where they sit in the classroom and discuss a particular question to learn their subgroup reaction to it; and as the signal is given to start these subdiscussions simultaneously throughout the classroom, the audible effects are indeed like those of a giant buzz. To go behind the name, the purpose of the buzz session is to create within a larger and ordinarily more passive group an opportunity for small group participation in discussion of the matter at hand. Like other forms of discussion, the technique is less useful for teaching factual information than a lecture or other procedures, but it is known to be effective in arousing students and in giving them a feeling of being able to express opinion or analyze a problem even though the total group is large.

To utilize the buzz session, the instructor first divides the total group into subgroups, usually by designating seat and row divisions arbitrarily. He then instructs each subgroup to select its own recorder (reporter, secretary, the name being of no exact significance) and possibly a chairman, if the subgroup consists of more than four or five people. He then indicates the nature of what is expected, making it clear that each subgroup is to arrive, if it can, at an acceptable statement of group opinion or analysis, which the recorder or chairman will be able to express for the subgroup to the total group. The topic or question is then indicated and a period of varying length, sometimes as short as five minutes and usually not longer than ten, is allowed for the subgroups to discuss the problem. At the end of that time the instructor calls for reports from the recorders, and in this way he can achieve something of the motivational effect of having had total group discussion, while student interaction in the small group will have eliminated many of the less-well-founded ideas and made the residue of useful ideas or opinions greater than could be achieved in the larger group in the same length of time.

The technique can even be used with groups so large that all the reporters could not possibly be called on directly. In this case it is possible to sample the subgroups, and by asking for a show of hands from other subgroups, give them at least some feeling of involvement in the discussion. I have tried this at the first meeting of an introductory psychology class of 150 students, dividing them into groups of six each to arrive at a statement of what they thought might be the most important objective of the course. Relatively quickly the reports enabled me to list on the board the statements of objectives (including, interestingly enough, a heavy emphasis upon intellectual matters and upon science, not merely upon personal and practical things), and to learn by a show of hands that the subgroups whose opinions were not directly sampled agreed with those whose opinions were recorded. In such a situation, the effect is to make it clear that there is common ground in the reasons for taking the course, and in this instance, to make it clear that what the instructor hoped to achieve was quite the same as what the students wanted. This could not have been so convincingly made clear by a unilateral presentation by the instructor, nor achieved so easily or with such widespread participation if the group had been treated as one large discussion unit. (It would of course be slightly senseless to use the technique as here described if one had no intention of being influenced by what the students had to say.)

The range of problems to which the buzz session is applicable is quite wide. It is helpful to get discussions started; to provide take-off points for lectures; to clarify at the student level what has been discussed by a lecturer, or to feed back information on what is not clear; to reach decisions as to the best next step for the course to take, or the direction to turn; and to guide the instructor in his planning. It is also helpful just as a device to relieve the monotony of lecturing, if this is a problem, for involvement in subgroup discussion serves to alert students much as does fresh air introduced into a room full of drowsy people.

Certain problems must be kept in mind in using the buzz procedure. First is the point that students cannot sensibly discuss a question unless it is one concerning which they possess some information or an attitude growing out of prior experience. The buzz is therefore likely to be useless on questions of fact (except as opinion-polling facts are involved) and is not pertinent to the first presentation of materials not covered in reading or lecture, except as a buzz may guide the presentation. Second, a major reason for using the whole procedure is to arouse and involve students. To follow through in this spirit, whatever is reported has to be taken as rendered in good faith, preferably with signs of acceptance by the instructor. Certainly, critical or punishing comment about what the reporters have to say must be avoided or the reports will dry up or become merely safe from the student point of view. Third, since the technique is obviously intended to find out what students think, the instructor is committed to dealing with whatever is produced by the sessions. He may use the results to guide his own discussion, he may use them to set further discussions in motion or to elicit discussion between subgroups who appear to have differences of opinion, or he may set for the whole group the task of finding the common ideas in the expressions of subgroups. But deal with the responses he must. Fourth, in introducing the technique, as with any new or strange classroom procedure, the students must be given an understanding of what is to happen and of what the technique can be expected to achieve. At best, a few of the students are likely initially to regard the whole thing as a little silly, if only because it is so unconventional. The instructor must therefore be as sure as he can that there are no slips in his introduction of the buzz or in his choice of the initial topics for discussion. He will then find that all but a very few of the scoffers, if such there be, will be drawn into their assigned subgroups and, having committed themselves to some extent by this fact, will become participants like all the others. It may be remarked, finally, that depending upon the topics chosen for buzz discussion, the technique may be combined with a variety of methods of teaching, ranging from those which are essentially instructor controlled to those in which the students have a goodly share of control over what is done.

9

GROUP-CENTERED TEACHING AND CASE ANALYSIS

In the last two decades certain instructional methods have developed, or at least come to prominence in psychology, which may have an inherent suitability for certain kinds of teaching problems that psychologists or instructors in the other behavorial sciences encounter. Especially are these methods of interest when the avowed objectives of instruction go beyond the transmission of information to include influencing the values, attitudes, or other personal qualities of students in either instructor-valued or self-determined ways.

GROUP-CENTERED TEACHING

Origins of the concept. As Axelrod [15] has shown in some detail (and Lorge [167] and Wispe [283] have observed), several currents of thought about teaching and about the goals of education have tended to merge in a sometimes confusing way in recent years. From one direction there came a reaction of those who earlier would have been called progressive educators. They were against the instructor-dominated class and teaching process, feeling that education, to be effective, had to be centered about the needs of the pupil or student, and that the key to educational development was the life experiences of the individual. At the college level this attitude was reflected in classroom efforts to get away from the lecture, to free students to express their wishes or needs, and to use discussion, project, and other teaching devices in which nonverbal as well as verbal experiences would produce both nonverbal (e.g., attitudinal) learnings and verbal ones.

From another direction came an influence originating in the study of group dynamics. Certain of the earlier experiments in this field, especially by Lewin and his associates, had lent themselves well to the conviction that democratic interpersonal processes were conducive to more desirable or effective conduct, in the long run, than were authoritarian ones. These investigators and many others became very active contributors to our understanding of the social psychology of the group, and especially of the small group. From this source, then, came ideas for additional methods of utilizing the social setting of the classroom to produce or enhance learning. For example, it became apparent that for the member of the group there was significance in such learnable processes as group setting of goals, group effort to solve a problem, sharing or varying leadership roles according to competence or the task at hand, and so on. From the group dynamics direction as from the progressive education direction came the idea that the goals of education should include emphasis upon affective and attitudinal changes, that student participation was the key to student involvement or motivation and therefore to student development, and that conventional examining and grading procedures, with their disciplinary and competitive aspects, should be de-emphasized.

From a third direction came the influence of those who had developed the nondirective psychotherapeutic techniques. Their view is most effectively presented by Rogers [225, Chap. 9], and we shall give somewhat detailed attention to what he says, not only to explain what nondirective teaching is but also to show what its theory has in common with the two influences on teaching just mentioned. It is Rogers' view that educational programs and methods should be intended to produce students who can take self-direction, are critical learners able to evaluate the work of others, have acquired knowledge relevant to the solution of various problems, can adapt flexibly and intelligently to new problem situations, are habituated to adaptive problem solving methods, can work creatively, value co-operation and are able to give it, and in general are socialized to act under internalized controls and standards. It is evident that Cantor [58, 59, 60], who has been affected more obviously by a psychoanalytic view, accepts these same general kinds of educational goals.

Rogers suggests certain hypotheses about teaching and learning which provide clues to the nature of nondirective teaching as such, and we can see that those hypotheses would be congenial to educators concerned with the variety and impact of life experiences, as well as those concerned with the relation of the individual to the dynamics of his social group. It is Rogers' feeling, first, that we do not really teach others; rather, we can only facilitate their learning for themselves. On this hypothesis, much of the coverage which occurs formally in academic courses is waste effort, for this is teaching defined from the instructor's point of view, without allowance for the determining influence of the student's needs. A second hypothesis is that we learn to an important degree only things related to the maintenance and enhancement of our personal self-concepts. Correspondingly, unless what is to be learned is seen by the prospective learner as making a difference to his personal condition or status, it will be no more than superficially acquired, if at all. Third, it is characteristic of people that there is resistance to material which appears to threaten self-perception or the organization of the self, so that instead of changing (learning) flexibly under pressure, we typically become more rigid or even negativistic. These three hypotheses relate to a fourth: To be effective an educational situation must both keep threats to the integrity of the individual at a minimum and facilitate his perceiving his experiences so that what is important and relevant will be seen as such and no barriers to change will be engendered by threat or confusion. It is important to add here, to these statements taken somewhat out of context, condensed, and paraphrased, the underlying general hypothesis that the individual has within him the capacity for self-change and growth which is essential to both psychotherapy and academic learning.

With ideas coming together from such diverse sources it is only to be expected that a sizable confusion has sometimes existed about just how the various ideas and methods of instruction relate to one another. To arrive at our own choice of a label for the kind of teaching resulting from these idea mergers we shall need to be aware of some of the specific meanings (and labels) that are being incorporated. The principal point of reference, as we shall note in detail in the next section of this chapter, is the kind of teaching situation which is information oriented, relatively formal, and controlled largely by the instructor. In contrast to it, the kinds of ideas we have presented above have sometimes been called student centered. Another pair of labels for the contrast has been directive-nondirective. The newer methods have also been called democratic, to distinguish them from what was called autocratic. Woven in from time to time has been the idea that a psychotherapeutic teaching process was being distinguished from an intellectual or content-oriented teaching process. It is my feeling that in practice no one has made a sharp enough distinction between the various kinds of teaching processes set in opposition to the supposedly instructor-dominated process to justify adopting one of the labels we have mentioned. As I have suggested elsewhere [56], the most useful term for the methods collectively seems to be group-centered teaching, and a generalized analysis below will both give this term meaning and show why it is appropriate. It should perhaps be understood that this choice of term will not altogether please the originators of other terms or those who have called attention to the more specific contrasts.

Group-centered technique. What does the instructor who teaches in a group-centered way actually do in his classroom? (For example see [2, 3, 43, 58, 104, 116, 122, 150, 282]. For summaries see [34, 188]). At the very first class meeting he will set the stage for this kind of course and teaching by defining its nature and its place in the curriculum, the method by which the class is to be conducted, and his own role. But this is done in a limited way and in a particular spirit, for the sense of group-centered teaching is that almost immediately it is made clear to the members of the class that the responsibility for learning, and therefore for definition of goals, for progress in the course, and for conduct of the class meetings, belongs not to the instructor but rather to the whole group including the instructor. Although, particularly in the beginning but inevitably to some extent throughout the course, the instructor serves as a focus of classroom discussion, because some member of the group must serve in this role or only general bull sessions occur (see Whyte [278]), the instructor does not use this position or his age-title status as a means of deciding unilaterally just what the group will do, what detailed goals it will try to achieve, or how progress toward those goals (specifically, academic standing) will be evaluated. Rather, he works toward group clarification of goals and methods by drawing out and accepting all shades of opinion and by accepting any consensus that makes itself apparent as the discussion proceeds. He makes himself into a member of the group, not a superior officer. Yet as it gradually becomes apparent to the group that various resources must be drawn upon as a basis for learning in any subject matter, these typically including textbooks or supplementary readings, field trips and many other kinds of experiences, the role of the instructor tends to become clarified in a special way, for he is an additional and particularly well-equipped resource for the work of the group, although now students are free to take him as they will.

Perhaps the best way of characterizing the group-centered teacher is to contrast him with the most traditional (and possibly extreme) classroom teachers. The group-centered teacher, in this contrast, attempts to avoid enforcing his will upon students. He tries to get them to understand, not by argument but by his refusal to take responsibility for it, that they must finally take the initiative in their own educations. He is concerned to have his students utilize him, not as authority, guide, or judge, but rather as friend, participant, even confidant, and as resource person. He is likely to avoid lecturing and other techniques which imply doing the student's work or thinking for him, except as there are specific instances in which the class requests this of him as a resource on a particular topic. Central to the contrast is the group-centered teacher's concern for the emotional aspects of learning. So strong is this concern that dominant emphasis is placed upon accepting individual differences among students and their opinions, upon not punishing for but being permissive toward inadequate or inappropriate responses, and upon reducing ego threats to the point where the full capacity of the student for thought and self-discipline may be exerted. When the instructor is effective and adaptive in this kind of role, the correlate may be a student group thoroughly united and participating equally in trying to achieve the agreed-upon goals. From the free and relatively mature interactions among group members flow many motivational and stimulative influences. The classroom atmosphere is intended to be one in which the student is at the same time emotionally secure, independent, and co-operative.

At a "how to" level, Cantor [59, p. 66] suggests how the leader should behave in a discussion group which is conducted in the spirit of group-centered philosophy: 1. Do not argue. 2. Do not give advice. 3. Do not direct the discussion. 4. Do not force answers. 5. Do not take sides. 6. Listen rather than talk. 7. Try to grasp why group members do not participate. 8. Try to grasp what lies behind what the speaker is saying. 9. Do not make moral judgments. 10. Above all, try to communicate to the speaker your appreciation of what he says and how he feels.

Cantor's illustrative group discussions, and those cited by Rogers, indicate perhaps better than any less literal presentation the striking difference between the most traditional classroom procedures and those advocated by the group-centered theorists. I cannot help but feel, however, that to some extent the contrast is with a straw-man traditional procedure. By this I mean that able and sensitive teachers, allowed to teach reasonably small groups of students, have for a long time lived by much of the philosophy which now has been newly discovered. They have been responsive to student need, have yielded much responsibility for learning and for course direction to the students, and so on. The contrast therefore is one of degree, except for those teachers or those teaching situations, and I do not claim there are not a good many of them, where authoritarian methods and attitudes continue even now to be dominant, or where large classes or small budgets have forced the use of straight lecture procedures.

Deciding whether to use the technique. We shall discuss in the next section the relatively few research efforts to evaluate the effects of group-centered teaching. Here we shall discuss some of the factors which seem to be involved in the decision whether or not to use the method. One of the most central points is of course the instructor's own personality and aspirations as a teacher. Without the capacity to accept student definitions of goals, methods, or evaluation standards, the instructor can hardly succeed with a group-centered procedure (Albracht and Gross [3] have emphasized this). Furthermore, because of the novelty of various forms of the method and the probable contrast with what students are accustomed to or are simultaneously experiencing elsewhere in their academic programs, it cannot be expected that the group-centered method can be introduced briefly, partially, or lightly. Rather it must, except for conceivable experimental uses, constitute the method for a whole course. It may be noted [3] that the need for training or permitting students to take a full measure of responsibility may be made doubly evident in group-centered situations where a few students get the idea that everyone's opinion is equally good without concern for how opinions should be formed and evaluated, or where some individuals find it difficult initially to tolerate the method.

Another determiner of whether the method should be used is the nature of the content assigned in curriculum planning to a particular course. If the course is concerned with human relations or group dynamics, or if it has any responsibility for skills acquisition or attitude formation, the illustrative or practice values of group-centered procedures plus their commonly supposed emotional impact might make them very desirable. But if the function of a course is primarily that of assuring mastery of factual materials or of arbitrary systems of thought or expression (as in mathematics, or statistics, or the foreign languages), group-centered methods could scarcely be expected to be the most effective. Because educational goals the students themselves choose will in many instances naturally require it, there may be the pressure for the mastery of quantities of factual information, and thus the applicability of the group-centered method may be wider than appears at first glance.

A knotty problem is whether the instructor can or will permit students to determine grades, or even share in the determination of grades, in the process of giving a group not make-believe, but genuine, control over its own destiny (see Deutsch's study centered about this problem [85]). Since the existing system demands evaluations of students in relation to all sorts of institutional and real-life standards, it is practically always necessary that grades be turned in. Rogers [225] discusses the problem fairly, the sense of his solution being that students can accept as real the instructor's conflict between his responsibilities to the institution and his desire to give his students maximum opportunity for self-determination and self-evaluation. If the students then decide that resolution of this dilemma is a group responsibility, a compromise arrangement usually becomes possible in which the student first assesses himself and then reviews this evaluation with the instructor. Grades jointly agreed to and submitted for record may thus have the usual meanings. It perhaps should be added that the situation still is not simple, for the grade may refer to subject matter mastery or may, in contradistinction to other grades entered on the student's record, imply assessment of personal growth, attitude change, skill formation, and so on.

A somewhat related problem created by the decision to use a group-centered method arises in the relation between prerequisite courses and those that follow, i.e., the appropriateness of the background of the student who has taken a prerequisite course in which the group, rather than faculty policy primarily, determined the goals. The problem is more acute where there are several independent student sections of a given prerequisite course. Instructors of succeeding courses drawing randomly from these independent sections will face the possibility of extreme heterogeneity among their students. As one who has taught intermediate and advanced courses for a good many years I must admit, however, that students could hardly seem more heterogeneous than they do now, regardless of what new or different methods of teaching they might be exposed to in prerequisite courses. Perhaps relevant again is Rogers' implication that students can understand that certain limitations upon their freedom of choice or action are necessary without losing thereby the spirit in which the remaining freedoms are utilized. Students can therefore accept the necessity for common examinations in all sections of a course, or for a criterion examination at the end of a course or program, yet take upon themselves all responsibility for satisfying these limiting conditions. In this way the faculty would still exert its supposedly more mature judgment as to what aspects of subject matter or what problems must be included to define a field, whether student needs or interests lead to them spontaneously or not, and as to the hierarchies of ideas which imply sequences of study within the discipline.

It is also necessary to note that the group-centered method seems to make sense only in smaller groups, where it is reasonable to expect full acquaintance and participation, and where the instructor is reasonably sure to notice those students who retreat from the kinds of realities they are exposed to in self-controlling groups and can attempt to draw them into the work of the group.

Finally, for many teachers of psychology an interest in the group-centered approach has been counteracted by a concern that student determination of course goals would lead always to the same general sphere of self-concern, personal adjustment, and amateur therapy. In the opinion of those who have used the method, however, these concerns do not seem well founded for two reasons. First, the scope of a course is more or less clearly defined by its place in the curriculum, and the instructor, as an accepted member of the group, can and inevitably does influence movement of the group toward the goals assigned in general to the course. In practice there is not a great distortion of the to-be-expected content of the course, although there may be wide variation in how the students go at it. And second, while self-improvement is always sought by the developing individual, he is likely not to regard academic courses as established merely for this purpose, nor is a group brought together in an educational context likely to choose goals of a purely therapeutic character.

The accepting and friendly atmosphere which is sought in group-centered teaching may lead to outside contacts with the instructor as a therapeutic resource person, but this need not dominate the group meetings or activities. Of course, the very existence of this possibility does seem to make it likely that in the hands of a person to whom all teaching is new, or for whom therapeutic activities are incompatible with his self-perception of his role, or who is quite unfamiliar with problems of therapy, the method may generate student frustrations and concerns which cannot be properly dealt with, and in this way the method becomes self-defeating.

Evaluations of group-centered teaching. Group-centered teaching has been evaluated by comparing its results with those of instructor-centered teaching. The contrasts and conflicts here have motivated some of the most interesting research on teaching that psychologists have done, but as might be anticipated the complexities of the area are such that definitive research is difficult. Birney and McKeachie [34] have given a detailed report of what has been done, so that our discussion here can be limited primarily to such results as are available, with secondary attention to the difficulties encountered.

For most instructors, the first question about group-centered methods is: What is their effect on the kinds of achievement usually sought in college classes? The general answer is clear. For this kind of achievement group-centered teaching is not significantly superior or inferior to more conventional instruction [43, 85, 86, 116, 150, 162, 189]. Not all the results have been entirely consistent with that conclusion, for Faw [104] found that there was a slight difference, which the students themselves did not perceive to exist, in favor of the group-centered class on regular course examinations. Asch [13], on the other hand, found the opposite result, but his finding is made ambiguous by the fact that his group-centered class, which did less well, was told that the examination was merely for comparison purposes and would not count in any important way for them. Kelley and Pepitone [156] seemed to find that group-centered instruction gave an advantage in intellectual matters, although as they point out the nature of their measures was such that this may not be a valid finding. Guetzkow, Kelly, and McKeachie [122], comparing a recitation-drill type of procedure with a group-discussion and a tutorial type of procedure, found certain differences to favor the (directive) recitation-drill procedure; these achievement advantages may have stemmed from the more relevant and more frequent rehearsal of examination-type content in the classes taught by this procedure. Finally, Wispe [282] found that for superior students there was no performance difference between those in classes taught directively and those taught in a group-centered way, whereas poorer students profited more from direction and structure in the class procedures. The best guess we can make from the weight of the evidence, then, is that students who have been taught by group-centered methods have not lagged behind in their achievement, as conventionally defined. This is regarded as an important finding by those who believe that group-centered methods are aimed also at securing other and additional objectives, for it could mean that nothing has been lost in this added effort. On the other hand, as we shall imply in discussing research problems in this area, the lack of a difference on conventional achievement measures may simply reflect inadequate manipulation or measurement of variables in the research designs to date.

The next question about group-centered teaching then is, what of these other kinds of achievement? First, in the realm of changes in social-emotional attitudes, it seems quite possible that positive advantages are achieved by group-centered teaching, although this result is by no means a firm one. On the positive side of the evidence are such findings as these. Asch [13], comparing a group-centered experimental class with control classes, found that although the classes were not different initially or finally in degree of tolerance as measured by the Bogardus Social Distance Scale, the number of students who improved in their personal-emotional adjustment was clearly greater in the group-centered class, as measured by the Minnesota Multiphasic Personality Inventory. Gibb and Gibb [116], to judge by their short abstract, found that in group-centered instruction there were significant gains in ability to assume different social roles, in self-insight, and in ability to assume leadership. In a comparison of students taught nondirectively and by conventional procedures, Gross [121] found an apparently greater increase in self-insight in the former group, and Ruja [233] later applied an appropriate statistical test to Gross' data and found the difference between groups to be significant. In the work of Bovard [43] and McKeachie [189], it was found that group-centered teaching evidently produced superior ability to analyze and understand case material as presented in the film "Feelings of Rejection." Finally on the positive side, we may list the finding of Kelley and Pepitone [156] that interpersonal attitudes improved significantly in their group-centered course on human relations, with the reservation again that the manner in which their measures were taken may vitiate the finding.

On the other side of the scale we find considerable negative evidence concerning the ability of group-centered teaching to produce social and emotional changes. In the careful study by Guetzkow, Kelly, and McKeachie [122], for example, there were no significant differences in the conceptions of parenthood which the students showed, or in number of misbeliefs about psychological matters, or in the degree to which measured scientific and analytical attitudes were exhibited. Nor did Johnson and Smith [150] find any superiority in the degree to which democratic attitudes were instilled in a group-centered class (although the description of the way in which these classes were taught suggests something of a laissez-faire treatment, the results of which would not be exactly predictable). We are left with the feeling that there are indeed possibilities that group-centered teaching might have greater impact upon personal and social traits than does conventional teaching. But we are forced to say also either that such changes are rather specific to as yet not well-analyzed conditions or that the measures by which they may be demonstrated are not yet consistent and dependable.

We may also ask how students like group-centered teaching. The results again are somewhat mixed. On the side of a favorable reaction are results [e.g., 43, 104, 282] suggesting that students exposed to group-centered teaching like each other and the method better than in conventional classes. On the other hand, students evidently miss familiar circumstances or controls, for the students of Eglash [99] responded by rather favoring the lecture method (except on the question of what method most stimulated independent thought), while Milner's students [198] and those of Wispe [282] preferred more directive instruction. The mixed character of these findings suggests the very great importance of the milieu from which students come, as well as the way they are introduced to any new method of instruction, in determining how well they accept the new method.

It may be well to indicate as we did with the lecture method (Chap. 7) some of the difficulties encountered in researches of the kind we have just been discussing and some of the variables on which interpretations of results often hinge. We must immediately note the problem of introducing the major independent variable—the method of instruction—into the experimental design. This problem has at least four aspects. There is the question of instructor competence and bias with respect to the methods to be compared. This has not been adequately controlled in some studies [13, 33, 99, 104]; it has been assessed in others by having several instructors use in different classes each of the teaching techniques to be compared [122, 162]; and it has been controlled in others by having the instructor use only that technique he could best use and letting this be part of the definition of the method [86, 282]. As a check on any of these methods, observations and other records of the instructor's actual classroom performance have been used by some investigators [122, 282], and this seems to be a very desirable procedure. Second, it is always necessary, as we have already mentioned, to evaluate the effects of the uniqueness, novelty, and frustration value of a new teaching technique. In the overriding competition for marks, students are always made uneasy by any instructional system which they do not fully understand, and presumably to the degree that this sort of thing happens, the evaluation of the instructional method as such is distorted. Third, there is always the question of whether the experimental manipulations performed for the purpose of introducing a given variable actually introduce it into the investigation. For example, students may compensate in unknown ways outside of class for what happens inside class—the instructor may de-emphasize examinations or formal study of the text, only to have his students decide to take no chances and work harder at these aspects of the course outside class than they otherwise would, thus keeping their achievement on a par with that of students encouraged to work directly at mastering information. And finally, an experimental method of instruction is not adequately evaluated without using it sufficiently to permit it to have noticeable effects, as may have been true in some researches to date [e.g., 282], or to have been discriminably different from methods of instruction used in control conditions (possibly in [198]).

Another general kind of problem, discussed thoroughly by Birney and McKeachie [34], is that methods are only now being developed to measure some of the changes investigators have thought their experimental methods of instruction might produce. Without special measures the achievement of special objectives of teaching can scarcely be evaluated.

Wispe [282] has called attention to still another problem. It is necessary to evaluate not only the effects of experimental conditions of instruction on the actual classroom situation and behavior of students (for this is the way the independent variable is made operative in the experiment), but also the subsequent effects of this classroom situation or atmosphere upon the measured outcomes of the teaching. Early investigators of group-centered instruction tended to emphasize the first of these without giving sufficient attention to the second, which after all is the goal of instructional research.

We must also note that there are many sheerly practical problems which make research of this sort difficult, for college schedules and college students tend to come in what the investigator views as self-determined ways, so that only crude manipulations of variables, or uncertain controls, are possible in the experimental design, and statistical types of control, at the point of data analysis, are the only ones available. Where the circumstances are favorable, however, as they have been at Michigan and Harvard, psychologists have been able to do interesting and methodologically sound research on teaching. This gives rise to the hope that if there are specific differences between group-centered and other kinds of teaching procedures, they will have some chance to be identified more adequately in the future.

ROLE PLAYING

Role playing has been used increasingly in recent years as a method of providing, in the classroom, genuine samples of behavior and opportunities for directed observation and immediate analysis of them. Having the live behavior available for discussion at a relevant moment in a course, having the technique involve students to a high degree of interest, and being able to predict with relative confidence, despite the fluidity of the situation, that the content of the behavior sample will be pertinent to the topic at hand, appear to be important advantages. Role playing itself can be defined as the presentation of a spontaneously acted playlet by a few members of a group functioning in assigned roles. The technique originated in the realm of psychotherapy, where it was intended to give the patient freedom to express and work out his relations with other persons. In something of this same tradition, under the label of psychodrama, the technique has spread to industry, community leadership training programs, and many other situations [21, 135, 165, 173, 294, 295] where the goal of the role playing is first of all an impact on the individual who does it.

In some contrast with this emphasis upon change in the individual directly involved is the kind of role playing with which we shall be concerned here. It has been called sociodrama, to indicate that the focus is not on the individual role player so much as on the culturally defined role which he assumes and reflects and with the interaction among roles. Perhaps this variety of role playing should be regarded as less dangerous to the self-regard of the player; certainly it lends itself to the more generalized interests of an educational group. Thus, although it perhaps differs from psychodrama only in degree, it will be our main interest.

As will become evident in the ensuing discussion, particular role playing episodes may be used to achieve widely varying specific course objectives, in addition to teaching the ability to observe behavior analytically. On one occasion or another, for example, as Maier [173] has implied, role playing may be used to make students aware of the existence of a particular psychological problem; to develop sensitivity to the feelings and attitudes of another person; to illustrate particular psychological principles; or to add variety, interest, and involvement to the course. In role playing verging on psychodrama in certain respects, the objective may be to develop student skills in being permissive, in taking leadership roles, or in securing co-operation or social action from others.

Steps in the process of role playing. Because role playing as a classroom technique is both complex and unfamiliar to many beginning teachers, it may be helpful to organize our discussion of the technique around an analysis of the component processes through which a teacher and class go in using the method. There are a number of good references to consult [153, 165, 173, 295]. In advance it must be recognized that to plan, stage, and analyze a playlet, the instructor will ordinarily act as director. But the important thing is that he is director with regard to procedures, and functions only as a person who knows the necessary steps and stages in the role playing process. He is definitely not a controller of the actual lines and actions. These are the unrehearsed production of the student players, and it is the very unrehearsed or spontaneous character of this behavior which creates the authenticity of the behavior sample. When role playing is utilized, the following steps are likely to be taken, although steps may be combined or may occur somewhat out of order, and there will be numerous reversals as thought about the playlet develops or the scene itself is prepared for action.

Role playing begins with the formulation of the problem which is to be played out. This by definition in sociodrama is some problem of interpersonal relationships, chosen to relate to a current topic in the course. At this stage of planning, the problem is typically at the level of "What produces strong rebellion against parents in some adolescents?" or "What factors work against attempts at desegregation in a (given) community setting?" The problem must be formulated in a way limited or simple enough so that when it is role played details will be understood and remembered and audience involvement and participation in the discussion will come easily. The problem itself may come from class discussion or, more commonly, from the instructor's experience with what is likely to be useful at a particular stage of his course; it nevertheless may be shaped considerably by preliminary discussion, possibly by the whole class but more likely by those who are going to take a part in playing it out.

After formulation of the problem, a situation must be established in which the action is going to occur. This situation must be appropriate to the problem, so that the assumption of roles in it is perceived as pertinent. As simple examples, in the illustrative problem concerning adolescent rebellion, a natural situation could be that of a conversation between a girl who has come in late and the parents who have waited up for her, or between the boy who wants a jitney of his own and the father who would have to help pay for it. In the desegregation example, an appropriate situation might be the conversation between the principal and the parent of a Negro child who brings her child to be enrolled in what was previously an all-white school in some particular kind of locality. The situation, again, may be set by the instructor, or it may be worked out very usefully by those who are going to participate in it, or it may even be influenced at the planning stage by those who are later to be the audience. For certain purposes the instructor may find it valuable to rely upon relatively stereotyped and familiar situations [21], but the danger in this seems to be that the stereotyped situation may not be wholly appropriate for any given group. Sometimes a situation is selected because it clearly comes in phases which require separate actions and analysis (introducing the new Negro pupil to a largely white school), and sometimes because it has a very clear termination point and is relatively brief (an employment interview). In all instances the playlet must be capable of being interrupted, if not terminated, after only a few minutes of action, so that memory and analysis are not confused by the sheer quantity of action. Finally, the situation may be chosen so that its goal is clearly one of arriving at some resolution of interpersonal conflict (as in joint problem solving) or, with equal definiteness, the avoidance of any implication that a problem is to be solved by the interaction (as in exploration of attitudes, particularly when these are to serve as a point of departure for wider discussion after the role playing is terminated).

Casting must be considered next. For the purposes of sociodrama, persons are chosen because they are thought to be able to carry a particular role well, and not to feel threatened or exposed by it. The most unfavorable roles, if there are such, may well be given to persons with the greatest security or prestige in the group, on the assumption that they will be least threatened. What is involved in these considerations is what Grambs [120] has called the feeling of psychic nakedness. That is, the person who plays a role, especially for the first time, tends to feel caught in an unfamiliar or emergency situation in which he may expose his inner self to the group. The result, quite apart from its consequences for the individual, may be constricted and unspontaneous performance, so that the whole group benefits less by it. By using volunteers primarily or altogether, by stressing the cultural, not personal, definition of roles, by not pressuring any individual to take part, and especially by stressing an attitude of objectivity by the individual toward his assigned role and by the audience toward the role as it is played (always de-emphasizing the individual in it), it is possible to overcome the unease relating to participation and yet arrange for a cast suited to the problem.

A fourth distinguishable process in role playing is that of preparing for the presentation. The degree and kind of preparation can scarcely be described as following a prescribed pattern, for they depend upon so many variables. For example, brief oral sketching of the situation and a sentence or two naming the roles for the players may be sufficient, but at times a written layout of the situation and description of roles may be desirable for the players or for the audience or both. In a good many instances the preparations are different for different persons. For example, if the point of a playlet is to analyze barriers to communication, as in the desegregation example mentioned earlier, the person having the role of the Negro parent may be kept in ignorance of attitudinal instructions to the principal, or vice versa. Or, if the point is to analyze how private feelings such as suppressed hostility affect public actions, the motives of a person in the role of employment seeker may be structured but kept from the person assigned to interview him by removing the latter from the room during preparation for role playing. Bavelas [21] suggests that it may be desirable to structure all roles but the one which is of primary interest at the moment. It must be repeated that the preparations we speak of, or the structuring of the situation or the role, provide only the framework within which the role playing will occur and never the actual content of what is to be done or said. The latter, in its spontaneous form, is the point of the whole procedure, and its effect is thoroughly weakened if it appears coached or predetermined. As a final aspect of preparation for role playing two points may be mentioned. Oftentimes props are desirable; in fact, using a table as an office desk, a pointer as a boundary-line fence, and so on, helps achieve something of the stage atmosphere which is essential to adoption of a role or acceptance of it. The props, and in addition various kinds of relatively unplanned and somewhat irrelevant conversation, may illustrate the second point here, namely that warmup is typically desirable. For example, the persons assigned to roles may be instructed to begin, not by launching into the problem discussion which is to be their main business, but by talking about the physical setting ("this is the front door") or about their own role origins ("I am 40 years old and have lived in Brooklyn all my life"), and so on. The players may relax and fit into their roles the better for this, while at the same time the atmosphere for the playlet is being built in the minds of the audience.

The next process in role playing, the action itself, should be started by some kind of signal from the director, or by an initiating remark from some person whose assigned role permits or requires him to get the action under way (a person playing any sort of leader role may perhaps be assigned this responsibility). The moment of beginning the major action should be clear to all, if only to avoid having some thoroughly irrelevant remark detract from the main part of the playlet. The principal concern about the action, for present purposes, is with how long it should run. Brevity is desirable, as we have indicated before. Sometimes role interactions bring themselves to an early close, as at the termination of an interview; sometimes the drift of a scene becomes apparent and it can be interrupted without playing it all the way out; sometimes the players exhibit a blockage of some kind and the play itself peters out; and sometimes, without waiting for a clear termination point or pause, it is desirable for the director simply to stop the play because the quantity of action is right for useful analysis.

The process of analysis is of course what makes role playing of general pedagogical use. It commonly starts by the instructor's asking the players for reactions to their own roles and the roles of others. Their expressions of feeling and their analysis of what was going on between persons or roles set the tone for audience participation in the analysis. Furthermore, the ability of the actors to analyze their actions in their own roles, or the action of others, helps to stress the objectivity and the avoidance of judgment of persons which are so essential to undistracted analysis of the problem. All evaluation of acting ability or convincingness in roles is to be avoided. More directly, the analysis of roles should always bear upon what this analysis contributes to solution of the problem at hand (e.g., an understanding of why the Negro parent or the white principal performed as he did in his role is relevant to understanding the relationship between them and therefore to the broader problems of desegregation). It is also essential that the analysis of action make clear the individual differences among people and their reactions, both within the playlet and between those playing the roles and those observing. Sensitivity to even small individual differences in feeling, attitude, or knowledge should be stressed. While the analysis typically proceeds as a class discussion with the instructor involved, it should be noted that for pedagogical purposes the whole role playing technique should be used in a context of information secured from additional sources such as reading materials and lectures. And as a variant on the classroom discussion, the instructor may require each student player or member of the audience to prepare a written reaction to the playlet.

The role playing process as we have described it may be given a wide variation in forms and uses. For example, very often it is useful to follow the analysis as just discussed with a replaying of the situation, by the same persons in the same roles, by the same persons in exchanged or reversed roles (to get the feeling of, for example, the opposite side of the segregation boundary or the interviewer's desk), or by another group of players. In this way the different backgrounds of experience, different structurings of the same basic situation, the availability of different amounts of relevant information, or even variations in player personalities, may affect the behavioral material which comes out in the action and the analysis. Other variations on role playing, particularly in adapting it for use in large groups, are described by Maier [173]; by ingenious procedural measures he is able to involve whole audiences in subgroup role plays, or, by a sort of remote control, in a single playlet.

Whether to use role play. Although role play has been found, at least by those mainly successful practitioners who write about it, to be a novel, interest arousing, and illuminating technique, like any other technique it must be used under appropriate circumstances. It is suggested, for example, that best results are obtained in a relatively small group, where the feeling of involvement of both cast and audience is great, where all can participate in the analysis of action, and, possibly, where responsibility for taking roles is rotated so that an atmosphere of being in it together, with the consequent depersonalization of role taking itself, is achieved [46, 135]. Others have attempted to use role playing, sometimes by especially practiced groups, before very large classes.

Those who use the technique agree that it is expensive of time and energy, not merely for the instructor but also for the class; role playing should therefore be used only when the returns promise to justify the costs. One teacher whom I know has used the technique effectively but nevertheless has dropped it because it required more time than he could afford for outside preparation of situation and cast.

Evidently also [21, 46], not everyone can successfully direct role plays or capitalize on the analysis. A relatively great amount of flexibility and adaptability is required, in order to cope with what may come out in the play, and both imaginativeness and realism are required in working out the situations and roles that will make for understanding of the chosen problem. Those of us who still are not very confident of our classroom skill may do well to avoid the technique, as will those who value an orderly and systematic presentation of information, here to be contrasted with the less predictable, less controlled, more spasmodic character of progress toward understanding which may evolve during and after role playing.

Certain other limitations on the use of the technique have been suggested. Zander [294], for example, found that there was some tendency for show-offs to interfere with successful use of role play by their readiness to volunteer. This can be avoided to a large extent by using in the cast only individuals about whom something is known, or by using role playing only in groups where such a problem can be expected to be minimal (e.g., where there are presumably no strong tendencies for aggressive sideplay against the role taking idea by persons who accept roles). It must also be anticipated that sometimes a cast will produce a play which is simply colorless or nonarousing, perhaps because of the line their action happened to take or perhaps because they themselves are constricted rather than spontaneous in their lines. Another problem arises in the fact that only simple and brief situations may be used for role playing; compensation for this may be found in the fact that even simple situations, as the psychologist encounters them, contain complex material and may be illustrative of key points in the most complex of problems. Finally, it has been suggested [46] that the conventional 50-minute class period is overly brief for effective use of role playing. Experience suggests that half or more of such a period is spent preparing and staging the play, a little more in the action itself, and then, just as discussion gets going, the period ends. With more experience, of course, both instructor and class can be more efficient in the use of time.

Perhaps the most important consideration of all with respect to role playing is that the more it can be related to understanding or mastering some problem which bears meaningfully on achievement of recognized course objectives the more useful it should be. Problems, action and analysis, must all be constantly seen in this light. When the experienced instructor can so utilize the technique, and at the right place in his course, the motivational effects appear to be very favorable, as are the increases in basic understanding of behavior.

Evaluations of role playing. There appear to have been very few attempts at objective evaluation of the relative worth of role playing. In one of these attempts Coleman [72] used a basically sound design in which two classes were equated on a number of relevant variables and were then to be taught by the same general procedures except that one was to experience role playing on selected topics from time to time during the term. Unfortunately, on certain critical variables (e.g., knowledge of subject matter) the classes turned out not to be equivalent initially. Another kind of evaluation was attempted by Grambs [120], who secured a number of measures on her students at the beginning of the class and later; unfortunately, her published account does not cite the data, although it does give what may be conclusions drawn from those data. As in several of our previous discussions of efforts to evaluate techniques, then, we are left with the feeling that role playing probably has certain specific instructional advantages which are capable of being shown objectively. But to date we must rely principally on the belief of many users of the technique that it has some very useful features. Of its motivational or interest value there seems to be little doubt.

CASE STUDY ANALYSIS

A very interesting development in psychological teaching has been the introduction of the case study procedure with its emphasis on the learning process of induction. Berrien [29, 30] has done much to introduce the method, having been led to it partly as a consequence of personal contact with methods used in the Harvard Business School. (Donham [89] gives a good treatment of the reasons for its use there and elsewhere.) Materials appropriate for use with the case method are now becoming available in book form [e.g., 31, 103, 277] as well as in the article form appearing fairly often in the *Journal of Abnormal and Social Psychology* [e.g., 127]. Also, experience with close analysis of case materials is becoming a much more common component of graduate training in psychology, so that we may reasonably expect a wider use of the case analysis method for college teaching in the future.

This method has many features of the group-centered method, supplemented by direct emphasis upon training in problem analysis. The defining feature of case study analysis is of course a particular means of providing content. In the method as used by Berrien and at Harvard [10] there is much emphasis upon student responsibility. The role of the instructor as group participant and as reflector of feelings or opinions rather than dominant figure is stressed, and the desirability of dealing with real problems without a pedantic concern for correct solutions is made obvious. Case study analysis in a lecture is of course possible, but its use to provide illustrative material there would be very different from the uses now being described.

Although objectives that may be achieved by case analysis methods presumably will vary from one instructor to another, just as objectives always do, we may note in the published descriptions to date a concern for practice in analyzing complex practical situations in the hope of securing positive transfer of training. The atmosphere is one of reality practice only one step removed from the real-life situation of having to follow through on decisions for action and bear any consequences thereof. At Harvard [10, pp. 23, 25] the users of the case method seem rather proud of the fact that their cases are not selected to be illustrative of particular principles or theories, and Berrien, in his initial descriptive note [30, p. 149] has implied that he accepts this view. It seems likely, however, that Berrien's book [31], and the case analysis method in the hands of others [see 146], will yield ideas or concepts of generalizable value, as well as skills. Indeed, this will be the main reason for using the method, in the opinion of most scientifically oriented teachers.

Nature of the technique. We may ask again what the instructor actually does. One answer seems agreed upon: there is no set pattern of instructor behavior, either for introducing the case study method and getting a class under way or for conducting the individual case discussions as the course proceeds. Nevertheless, the introduction to the course may fairly predictably include such elements as a description of the general ground to be covered by it or the general objectives assigned to it within the curriculum, a general characterization of the method, and remarks which indicate the instructor-student relationship to be desired and the effective roles each must play for the experience to be a useful one. The necessary home study of the first case may be preceded by other, more systematic kinds of preparation for case analysis, as would evidently happen if one used Berrien's book, or it may be accompanied by readings or other relevant experiences. After that, responsibility for discussion and analysis goes over to the group. As in the nondirective procedure proper, the instructor avoids expressing his own opinions or giving direction to the discussion. (Hunt [146] is probably an example of a person who is *not* nondirective in the use of case studies.) He may summarize, as a device for testing understanding or agreement, but will not formulate conclusions in the process. By his own participation as group member he tries to cause students to analyze the multiple facets of any situation before coming to possible decisions concerning it, although he will not force this. Discussion and analysis are therefore emphasized as producers of learning in the classroom. This learning includes both the substantive field of interpersonal relations and the requisite skills of analysis.

Glover and Hower [10] suggest some of the important considerations for the case analysis instructor, in addition to those which might be expected from our earlier discussion of the role of the instructor in group-centered teaching. They point, for example, to the necessity for developing the concept of factual analysis and for distinguishing between fact and opinion, as a necessary prelude to discussion. Categorizations of material, perhaps into those concerning activities, those bearing upon the relations between people involved in the activities, and those reflecting individual sentiments or beliefs, may be developed by a particular group to aid in developing analytical habits.

The instructor must work for a growing appreciation of the fact that complexity characterizes real situations, frustrating though this may be. Individual members of a group need to learn that no two discussants perceive the case or the facts in it in quite the same way, and that this is characteristic of interpersonal relations problems. Glover and Hower also point out that a case grows and changes during discussion. As its meanings develop, somewhat differently for each member of the class, what comes out of the case analysis may be quite different from what was expected. To deal adequately with this the instructor must be convinced that students largely possess the resources for self-instruction, and he must have the patience to wait for this to happen. In addition, both instructor and class may find that those students who are most facile verbally are not necessarily those who best understand what is fundamental in a case.

Perhaps the overriding consideration for the instructor is one of the strong emphases of group-centered teachers generally: an atmosphere must be created in which each student's own needs dictate to him a necessity to understand better the problem posed by the concrete case, without the application of external motivation except of kinds accepted by the student and having only limiting functions. Under such circumstances, Berrien [30] believes, it is possible to see certain changes in student performance in class discussion and written assignments, such as increased continuity of theme in the analysis; progressive refinement of ideas, so that immediate evaluative statements are replaced by analytical ones; a reduction of "parallel experience" comments as the uniqueness of each case comes to be expected; and a generally more orderly, thorough, and judicious process of arriving at action decisions.

Problems in using case study analysis. To date, the problems associated with use of the case study method in psychology have not been discussed in detail. From the experience in the Harvard Business School, the writing of Berrien and others, the excellent article by Hunt [146] and from armchair analysis, we may perhaps anticipate some of the considerations which will confront the instructor who is thinking of using the method. (Most of the previous discussion of problems in use of group-centered procedures is directly relevant here.)

Studies by Castore [63] and Castore and Berrien [64], and the reports by Bailey [10, pp. 35-40], and Fox [110], suggest that the novelty of the case analysis situation, particularly as it involves nondirective handling by the instructor, is disturbing and frustrating to many students who seek to have the truth given to them in the traditional manner. The consequence is that after even a reasonably good beginning of a course there is likely to come a lower point in student morale. Evidently this kind of crisis in the relation of instructor to students, if adequately handled, can lead to a sort of conversion phenomenon in which, finally, the student really begins to accept responsibility for case analysis and the course may pick up considerably in tone.

It is perhaps evident on the face of it that the method cannot be used unless appropriate case materials are available in one's particular course area. Reference has been made above to materials now in book form, but it seems clear that the usual journal or textbook description of a situation or incident is not adequate to use in a case analysis course. Hunt [146] has emphasized that cases are not instances with worked-out solutions to be evaluated by the student, as is often true in, for example, medical training, nor are they exercises. Rather they are intended to lead to problem solving through processes which in effect will be validated only through later practical decisions and actions. Preparation of one's own case is likely to be necessary, and some of the suggestions given by Lawrence [10, pp. 215-24] ought to be helpful. (Hunt suggests criteria for determining the order in which cases are to be used.)

A further consideration stems from the fact that, since mastery of information is not the major goal of a case analysis course, the usual methods of evaluation of students are not directly applicable. Berrien's remarks about the kinds of changes to be expected in a successful class, as summarized above, and the discussion by Fuller [10, pp. 122-37] of what makes for an unsatisfactory examination paper in a case analysis course, suggest very clearly that the instructor who begins to use the method will need to evolve his own ratings or other methods of evaluation; whether these can be worked out jointly with students, as suggested earlier for the usual kind of group-centered situation, has not as yet been settled. There are of course standardized case analysis tests which may be suitable for certain kinds of evaluation (e.g., [143, 144]; see discussion in [34]).

We might expect that one shortcoming of the case method would be the smallness of behavior sample the students can actually deal with. Only a few cases can be treated thoroughly within the usual academic term, so that the almost inexhaustible variety of interpersonal relations problems seems hardly to be touched. The counterremark is, presumably, that there are circumstances where it is better to analyze a few cases thoroughly and learn the process well than to analyze a more representative sample of materials in less detail. Further, although only a few cases may be analyzed thoroughly within a given course, their very complexity and richness of detail ensure that a good many different scientific concepts must be utilized and many relevant variables understood, so that much learning may be generated by a single case.

Castore and Berrien [64] have suggested some of the specific tactical problems to be expected in dealing with students via this method. For example, some students persist in prejudging cases. Heterogeneity of students is at times an aid, at times a hindrance in analysis of a particular case. Some students persist in being politically minded in the way they make their own contributions or respond to contributions by others. And while they may very much want to retain the feature of immediate, nontheoretical attack upon a real, complex, and personally meaningful kind of case, students are likely to feel, somewhat incompatibly, that the course should have clear objectives so as to orient their work and facilitate measurement of progress toward those objectives. Castore and Berrien feel that it is not wise to force a statement of objectives upon a class, but that it is important somehow to get those objectives developed and clearly understood within the work of a particular group.

Size of class is an important consideration in use of the method. Fox [110], in whose study the classes contained about 40 students, and Castore and Berrien, whose classes numbered about 25, found these numbers too great for the most effective instruction.

Finally, the case method lends itself first and foremost to the acquisition of analytical skill. It presumably is not the most efficient carrier of information and therefore may best be used either after suitable preparation of the student by other methods or in conjunction with other methods or materials calculated to provide a firm factual or technical basis for the thought processes which are to be encouraged in the case analysis.

Evaluation of the case study method. There are as yet no data which compare the achievements of students using this method with those using conventional class methods, if only because the objectives which might be set are so different, particularly in comparison with the standard reference class which is oriented toward information and controlled largely by the instructor. Such evaluations as have been made, as by Castore [63], Castore and Berrien [64], and Fox [110], have assessed student reaction primarily, with the implicit assumption that students could compare the method with other methods they had experienced. As we have already implied, this approach shows that the novelty, practicality, and reality character of the method and materials have a definite impact. As might be expected, for some students this is a good state of affairs, for others something to be adjusted to only with great difficulty. On the whole and in the hands of those who have used it most, subjective evidence seems to be that the method has achieved positive consequences in, let it be noted, a skills area where conventional methods of instruction do not often penetrate.

10

CONSTRUCTING COURSE EXAMINATIONS

Examinations are one of the most important aspects of any course, especially from the viewpoint of the student who must take them. It is sometimes disturbing to the beginning instructor to discover that the subject matter in which he is so vitally interested, and which the students presumably wish to master, seems somehow to take second place to tests and marks. It soon becomes apparent that aspects of measurement, of public relations with students, and of pedagogy all focus upon the examination procedures.

Some reasons for this are easy to discern, if one has been brought up through an American school system and thinks back upon his experiences there. For one thing, in the pragmatic tradition, it has been regarded as desirable by parents and teachers alike for the school pupil to work for good test scores and thus for high course marks, the better to ensure getting a good job. Many other kinds of rewards and prizes have been associated with getting high marks, until it may naturally appear to be the reason for education itself. A second factor making examinations so important is the prevalence of large or relatively large classes in high school and especially in colleges and the general impersonality of the teaching situation. In this context, examinations may in a sense be the only point at which a student is really personally involved in a course, the only occasion on which he does something sure to receive the attention of the instructor, if only by remote control. And a third point may be that much subsidiary motivation is tied to examinations. There is competitiveness, and there is anxiety—about one's own capabilities, about the unknown questions which lie ahead, about the motives of the instructor, about the adequacy of preparation, or about the consequences of failure. It is no wonder, then, that students become deeply involved in examinations and that the instructor must treat the matter with thoughtful concern. This is probably no less true in psychology than elsewhere, if only because the psychologist typically has the competence, and therefore the temptation, to become preoccupied with securing suitably objective measurements, possibly at the expense of concern about other considerations in the examination situation.

We can illustrate the complexity of the problem, and also a lack of perfect equivalence between instructor and student approaches to examinations, by raising the question of what constitutes an acceptable examination. It is clear that what is acceptable depends upon institutional and departmental tradition, and upon the kinds of students involved. To give only two contrasts from personal experience, students coming to college from a large midwestern high school may regard objective examinations as suitable, fair, and familiar, whereas students coming to college from certain small eastern preparatory schools may regard them as abominable; or, students stressing the humanities and arts in their own educational programs may react more favorably toward the essay examination than do students in the natural or social sciences.

From the point of view of the student, however, we can

with some confidence expect that certain more specific criteria will commonly determine whether an examination is acceptable. The most important criterion by far is likely to be whether it permits fair competition (rather than whether it permits a fair self-assessment of mastery of the material studied). An examination which permits fair competition, in the eyes of students, does not contain unclear, misleading or tricky questions, is of seemingly reasonable length and difficulty, and is administered so that details do not get in the way of performance on the substance of the examination. It will be recognized, of course, that this concern of the student is akin to a concern for what the professional test constructor calls reliability of measurement. Students evidently accept implicitly the notion that examination results ought to be dependable indicators of who knew how much, albeit for the competitive purposes already described. A second criterion which often appears explicitly in student evaluations of tests is the relevance of content and form of the test to material studied. Evidently the student wishes to feel that the work of preparation was worthwhile, that it has had a chance to pay off in fair competition. The general idea here seems akin to the instructor's notion of validity of the test, but the student's idea may be distressingly oriented toward competitive uses of this validity.

We can equally well ask what makes a faculty member regard an examination as satisfactory, and here we find criteria somewhat at variance with what most concerns students. It is quite possible that the faculty member will give first emphasis to discrimination power in his examinations, in order to facilitate the all-essential business of assigning the marks which the students and the system demand. There presumably is an implication here that examinations should be valid for the material covered, but the more probable implication is that reliability is required first of all and, especially in view of the difficulty of validating a classroom examination in any way, may in effect be sufficient. We may as well admit frankly that in practice the faculty member regards as good the examination that causes him a low degree of pain: that produces few complaints from the students, and is not overly demanding of labor in construction, is not complex to administer, or difficult to score. To date, unfortunately, no magic will produce a test meeting all these criteria at once. The test that tends in certain respects to be easiest to construct (the essay) is easy to administer but laborious to score; the test that is typically difficult to construct well and somewhat complicated to administer, the wholly objective test, is easy to score. Furthermore, the type of test that produces few complaints from certain kinds of students will almost surely make others in the same class unhappy.

Analyses of this kind suggest strongly that it is desirable here to be more concerned with just what examinations do and how they do it than with the technical details of how to build them, and to be more concerned with examinations as instances of teaching and learning than with scaling or measurement problems as such. The sheerly technical aspects are in the main suitably handled elsewhere, and illustrative treatments will be referred to below.

PEDAGOGICAL ASPECTS OF EXAMINATIONS

Guidance of learning. We have already indicated that the student will be strongly oriented toward achievement on examinations. Our first problem, then, is how to direct this orientation toward the fullest attainment of the educational objectives of our course or curriculum.

It is clear at once that for every stated educational objective of a course there must be a corresponding effort to measure that achievement (Dyer [96] has made this point very well), and the students must be aware that such a measurement effort will be made. In the elementary psychology course, for example, a stated objective may be the attainment of some degree of technical language proficiency. This is easy enough to measure, it can be anticipated readily by students in their study of the subject matter, and mastery can be facilitated by self-created word or concept lists. But it is also common for the instructor to set an objective of learning how to apply scientific principles to practical or personal affairs. And here, as the experience cited by McKeachie and Kimble illustrates [192, p. 24], it is more difficult to create an effective examination form. We may expect to find a certain degree of ambiguity in the student's views respecting the stress he should place, for example, upon learning the basic principles or the elaborations or uses of them, simply because the usefulness of study, as shown in success on examinations, may not be distributed to the two kinds of topics the way the instructor says it is supposed to be. And, of course, if we set an objective such as improving the student's ability to think critically, direct attention must be given to making examinations which demand this kind of thought about the subject matter or the student will simply not give his attention to it at all (his critical thought more likely being directed at an analysis of the instructor's examination-construction habits).

Another important way in which examinations influence learning stems from the form of the examination itself. The essay examination, which demands the process of recall, provides a criterion of remembering which is more difficult than the criterion of recognition. It may well be that, in any specific course setting, one of these criteria of mastery is more appropriate than the other, so that we should not fall into the rut of using only one kind of examination for all purposes. It is also true that the typical essay examination demands a more comprehensive or organized view of the subject, a greater ability to fit parts of knowledge together. Organization may be more or less important than facts as such in a particular course or at a particular level of scholarship, and the learning of the student will be responsive to the appropriate choice of examination forms. There is, of course, an oft-cited research [194] suggesting that no matter what type of examination is actually administered, preparation for an essay test produces better achievement. It must be said, however, that in the interests of good classroom morale one cannot motivate toward essay examinations with the intention of using any other kind. The instructor must therefore select his examination type or types in such a way that he can publicly indicate their nature and make clear the appropriate type of study. Terry [262] has shown that students can and do adapt their study techniques to the type of examination they face.

Although the element of evaluation or assessment ultimately enters into any examination system, it is worthy of notice that in some institutions, at least, this has been de-emphasized, or at least lessened markedly in the context of everyday study and progress. In the College of the University of Chicago, for example [213, p. 299], routine course examinations have been taken only by those students who desire to do so for information about their degree of mastery of the materials. Final assessment of the learning has waited until comprehensive examinations are given at a later date. In this kind of setting it is clear that the only purpose of the routine examinations is to guide and assist learning. Much of the subsidiary motivation which usually is associated with examinations is simply irrelevant and the pedagogical function has a clearer chance to show itself.

Student motivation. An understanding of the ways in which student motivation may differ from instructor motivation is so important to a sensitive utilization of tests that more discussion of it may be profitable. No matter how successful a student generally is at taking examinations they are almost inevitably a conflict situation for him. On the one hand he wishes to do well in his own eyes and in the eyes of others, and even to discover whether he has mastered the material; on the other hand he is frustrated by certain questions, or by the examination situation itself and made anxious by various elements in it. The negative aspects of the situation, while they in general support study and preparation (as a form of anxiety-avoidance behavior) just as do the positive aspects of it, tend when strong to introduce distraction or a wish to retreat from the study itself. From this point of view we may conclude that reduction of the negative aspects of tests is probably desirable. How may this be done?

Some useful procedures may be these. As announced policy, we can avoid spot or surprise examinations, and thus avoid generalization from concern aroused in previous experiences with such examinations. Further, the student can be informed not only as to when the examinations will occur, but also as to what forms of questions will be used, how they may best be responded to, and so on. These suggestions might be characterized as illustrating a general principle of taking the mystery and surprise out of examinations and examination policy, or reducing the degree to which these are unknown, and therefore to-be-feared, elements in examinations. As a second principle, we may take steps to assure the student and ourselves that a fair sample of test behavior is collected. It is sometimes surprising to an instructor to learn that students prefer more, rather than fewer, examinations. They have evidently learned that with the longer sample of behavior a more representative result is probable. Such a reason for more frequent tests is nicely supplemented by the clear finding of Fitch, Drucker, and Norton [108] that students quizzed weekly outperformed students having only monthly quizzes, with ability partialled out. It is also possible to reduce concerns about unrepresentative performance, as when a student gets caught short on preparation time or does not feel well during an examination, by creating systems within which the poorest mark during a term is not entered into the totals for determination of final grade, or in which term papers or other special assignments may compensate for examination inadequacies. (The first of these two devices creates technical problems of its own; see p. 280.) As a third suggestion, some of the threat of examinations may be reduced by the instructor's evident willingness to teach all he can in preparation for an examination and by demonstrations of reasonableness about corrections of scoring errors or discussions of debatable points. A very important related point has to do with the threat of public announcement, by posting marks, or the like, which might indicate poorer performance than a given student (superior or poor) might wish to have known. Except where it is flatly contradictory to established practice, it may be better to return examination results to students in a private way, so that the instructor is not in the position of appearing to be willing to punish. Thus the use of number codes for identifying students on posting lists, or placing marks on the inside of papers to be returned, may protect the student and thereby reduce his concerns about examinations in general.

To further reduce the conflict about examinations, the instructor must also discover how to strengthen the appropriate positive motives toward them and thus to affect favorably the learning which leads up to them. The most important suggestion, obviously, is to use only examinations which are good in design and which pertain to the objectives of the course; this is harder to do than to say. Without in any way questioning the importance of this overriding idea, we can also search for concrete suggestions of immediate applicability. For example, one can encourage a favorable response to examinations by returning papers promptly, discussing them as necessary, and letting students keep them for purposes of record or review. (A little questioning shows that faculty members are often almost rude in their refusals to get papers corrected and returned; a feeling seems to exist that just getting the papers in is all that's important.) One can also take care to adapt the form of examination, with due warning to students, to the particular material at hand. This varies in kind from time to time in any course, and variety in examinations is not only appropriate but as a form of sampling the different kinds of test-taking capacities or skills in the class is a method of achieving a fair opportunity for those who are handicapped by any particular form of test. It is possible also to make the examination itself, if it calls for other than rote performance, serve as a period of further learning, reorganization of knowledge, and re-examination of concepts, and to have the student come out of that period feeling that the exercise itself was of value no matter what the mark may be. This is a particularly important possibility in final or comprehensive examinations, in which rethinking the materials of a course to meet the challenge of a question may be a satisfying or even exhilarating experience. We cannot escape, however, the necessity of returning to the point that examinations will be seen to have positive value in more than a measurement sense only when they clearly relate to clearly stated (and preferably accepted) course objectives. No rules are available to guide us here; it can only be hoped that the learning process can, by stimulating teaching, be made of sufficient value in its own right that the learning achievement, rather than the social, or the competitive, or the escape-from-anxiety achievement, becomes central.

Control of classroom processes. As an extension of our analysis of the motivational aspects of examinations, and assuming now only that we have correctly claimed that strong student motivation is involved, we may ask how the instructor can effectively put that motivation to good use in the classroom. (We are distinguishing this control of motivation somewhat arbitrarily and incompletely from controlling motivation for learning in the course in general.)

It is presumably apparent that examination motivation can

be utilized to support pre-examination reviews, summaries, conferences, question answering in class and information giving. In all these activities students who feel that what is going on is pertinent to an approaching examination are likely to be direct and thorough in their responses to the teaching. Many instructors therefore precede each major examination in a course with a review period in which there is the widest possible latitude for questions and practice of responses. There are, of course, certain problems in this.

For one thing, if an examination is nicely printed and laid away in the drawer for tomorrow's use, it is perhaps distressing to have students ask for exact clarification on questions already committed to the printed test. On the other hand, one can take the attitude that a fair answer to such a question during review will not wholly remove the variance in the responses to the formal examination question, but if it does, the relative position of students in the class is not affected. In addition it may be reinforcing to them that what they regarded as important enough to review is also regarded as important enough to be sampled on the examination. The instructor who allows for a review period will find that, particularly early in the students' association with him, the negative aspects of testing will thrust themselves into the review period and will not extinguish very rapidly. For example, a common question is, "Do we have to know . . . ?" Other queries commonly have to do with the number of questions the student may expect, the kind of questions, or how they will be scored. Rather than regarding such queries as irrelevant and therefore totally undesirable, the instructor will do well to regard them as indicative of the underlying state of mind of the students. He will then try to deal with them as directly and educatively as possible, and reduce the implied interference with more desirable kinds of motivation toward the examination. One can only try in various ways, persistently, and in the long run to change this underlying attitude toward teaching and learning. Specific methods for dealing with symptoms of it cannot very well be catalogued in advance. To the student who keeps saying, "Do we have to know . . . ?" and to all his various brothers in anxiety, one can only show a steadfast intention to be reasonable, to explain, to give a rational basis for rules or assignments . . . as long as strength holds out.

Although, for some students, interest in examinations and what they represent appears to drop off sharply as soon as a mark is recorded for a particular performance, it is safe to say these are exceptional people. Typically, students are eager for post-examination review and analysis of results, and the instructor may therefore well consider how to capitalize upon this interest in order to enhance learning in his class. True, the students may wish for the review (and especially discussion of the scoring key) as a check upon the accuracy and therefore the fair-competition aspects of the examination, but nevertheless an opportunity presents itself to accomplish something pedagogically. For example, errors of fact or interpretation may be corrected, and inadequate learning generally may be strengthened. (Pressey [216] suggests using a mechanical device which automatically and instantaneously informs the student whether he has chosen a correct answer among the available alternatives. This seems pedagogically good and very relevant here.) Actual checking of scoring, while it can be a nuisance, is in its way reassuring to the student. The test review period may provide an opportunity for the instructor to demonstrate his interest in fair scoring and in turning the examination to good use in the educational process. Willingness to revise marking or throw out a bad question is quite convincing evidence of the instructor's good intentions, and equally can be presumed to reduce the student's concern about threats to his own status. Related to this is perhaps the most important reason for reviewing an examination, particularly in an introductory course in psychology where the student may for the first time come into contact with formal efforts to construct good examinations and utilize them in the most valid ways conceivable. This has to do with the need for releasing student reaction to the negative aspects of examinations, often generalized from previous unhappy experiences, for permitting the airing of grievances, for showing that these grievances can be dealt with reasonably or do not have a basis in fact, and thus in the long run modifying attitudes toward the examinations themselves. (This process will be discussed in the next chapter.)

There is another way in which many instructors, especially of less mature or less well-motivated students, utilize both the guidance and motivational values of examinations. This involves use of the daily quiz, which may be conceived as a form of recitation, but can be assigned quite different purposes. Users of the daily quiz (who, typically, do not have to deal with large classes) feel that it helps to ensure regular study habits, that it creates a different and broader base for evaluation than does a formal and lengthy examination, that it helps extinguish the concerns about examinations generally, and that, most important of all, it possesses diagnostic and reinforcement value because it leads almost immediately to information about what was and what was not adequately mastered. Use of the daily quiz must be integrated with other aspects of the course, for it may come to dominate the organization of each class meeting (and may deliberately be used for that purpose), or it may become a mere disciplinary device. For advanced classes or more mature students, such a device may be burdensome or an outright distraction. A decision on this can only be reached according to individual circumstances.

Examinations as demonstration material. Since psychologists are in the almost unique position, in the undergraduate sphere, of both utilizing measurement devices and teaching about measurement in the field of behavior, they very commonly make demonstration uses of their own examinations. For example, in discussing how a particular test was made, scored, and utilized, it is possible to teach principles of measurement, analysis, etc. The data secured from a specific examination often make interesting material for use in the teaching of individual differences and statistical concepts. Such use, however, is easily carried to extremes, and must be done in successive stages during a course. The ever present temptation for the instructor is to wax technical, while the students want little more than to find out where they stand. In a different context, an instructor who has, or can create, the necessary favorable conditions may be able to use the student's very real and personal response to examinations as an instance of aggression, anxiety, or what not. (The danger in this is, of course, that the student will respond to it as merely a sophisticated form of the childhood taunt, "It's all your own fault.")

Evaluation of teaching. It often happens that examination results, quite apart from what they reveal about students, reveal whether teaching on particular topics was adequate. Thus, examination questions which appear on their faces to be appropriate and fair may be inadequately answered by almost every student in a class. One can then devise methods of correcting for the inadequacy, plan to change his approach the following year, and so on. The difficult matter here, of course, is the discrimination between inadequate teaching and inadequate testing, but this may often be determined by supplementary questioning or classroom review.

FORMS AND VARIETIES OF CLASSROOM EXAMINATION

We have previously suggested that a variety of examination forms may be appropriate even within a single course. Now, because the average instructor may tend to utilize only familiar or trusted examination procedures, it seems desirable to explore the range of possibilities open to him. In all this it is well to bear in mind that, as Cole [71, p. 462] has said, particular examination forms are not in themselves good or bad, but they most certainly can be appropriate in varying degrees for particular uses. Further, the desirable examination form depends upon many factors external to the examination itself—as what the students are accustomed to or expect, the way the instructor thinks and teaches, or the circumstances in which the test is given. There is, therefore, no firm and invariant advice about what procedures should be followed. They must be chosen in whatever is the intelligent way for a particular complex of circumstances.

The instructor who wishes to go beyond the measurement of conventional content will find it worthwhile to study the summary of available or suggested measures by Birney and McKeachie [34]. They refer to attempts at measuring changes in students on such variables as the ability to think critically or scientifically, the ability to apply principles, personality change, and interest in psychology. It must be anticipated that the measurement instruments now available can hardly be adopted without careful matching against the materials and objectives of the course in which they are to be used.

Essay examinations. Although usually condemned by the psychologist or anyone else who is markedly concerned about reliability of results, the essay examination is nevertheless reasonably appropriate for many purposes and the only suitable kind of examination for certain purposes. Particularly as emphasis shifts from the measurement aspects of a test to its educational implications is it likely to be seen that some form of essay is advantageous despite its possible inadequacies (see Marcuse [174, 175]).

What are the essential features of essay examinations? We may answer first by saying that they vary tremendously. At one extreme they may call for reproduction (merely) of materials read or heard, while at the other extreme they may be thought to demand creativeness or originality, ability to organize and summarize, skill in analyzing and interpreting, or in judging and weighing alternatives, or in integrating related materials by showing their interdependencies. Evidently the possibility exists that the essay examination can be used to stimulate and evaluate active thinking as well as careful expression on the part of the student.

It is equally evident that the assessment of the very traits which the essay examination is believed to encourage is the discouraging aspect of the essay, for fair estimates by the instructor as to what is original, or what is sound judgment, or keenly analytical, are difficult indeed to make. As is well illustrated in classical studies [e.g., 98, 148, 256, 257] and in a study reported by McKeachie and Kimble [192, p. 26], the standards by which essay examinations are read are notoriously shifty or inexplicit. These standards tend to change as one reads further and further through a set of papers. They reflect all too well the level of fatigue or the soundness of digestion of the instructor. Perhaps most of all they reflect any prior opinion the instructor has formed about any student whose paper he is presently reading. In addition, since essay examinations involve the slow process of writing, they cannot ordinarily sample very widely (except superficially) the material to be covered, and they usually consist of a relatively small number of questions. A misinterpreted question, or a question on which the student fails to read a word carefully, or a question directed at a small portion of reading which the student has by chance not had time to cover thoroughly, can therefore loom large in determining the mark earned. We may say, further, that the mechanics of writing may be exhausting, or at least interfere with the student's chance to show as much as he can of what he knows, and that almost inevitably his skill in expression, punctuation, spelling, and longhand writing will affect, whether intended to or not, his chances for a good mark. In the perhaps typical case where these matters are not regarded by either student or instructor as pertinent to the objectives of the course, they may nevertheless be thoroughly distracting.

The improvement of essay examination practices. To compensate for these rather devastating criticisms of the essay examination and make this examination form more generally defensible so as to permit its use with clear conscience where it is deemed educationally appropriate, it is necessary to improve the common practices in constructing and using essay tests.

To begin with, one must use good questions. They cannot be made out on the spur of the moment. They must be chosen for fair coverage of the assigned material. In addition they must be studied and restudied most critically to search out the common flaws: ambiguity; lengthiness; overqualification; just plain difficulty of reading; the whole answer hinging upon interpretation of key words, or upon remembering certain routine or isolated facts or formulas; the use of idiosyncratic and therefore distracting or unclear forms of expression; failure of the question itself to indicate the framework of the answer; or the direction the answer is to take (as in questions beginning "Discuss . . . ," and pointing in no particular direction whatever).

The instructor will find it helpful, albeit uncomfortable or even painful, to adopt the practice of preparing essay questions day by day as he prepares materials for his course, and then setting them aside until they are cold and so appear to him as they might to a student who has never seen them before. When an examination is next to be prepared, questions can then be scrutinized more effectively for their possible faults. It is often desirable to ask a colleague to go over proposed examination questions and criticize them. McKeachie and Kimble [192, p. 31] recommend (in discussing objective tests) the practice of having student representatives criticize questions in a confidential session with the instructor before they are finally printed for use in a large class. Both this and the related practice of asking students to suggest questions have the effects of pre-testing the questions, of encouraging review, of teaching students some of the problems of examination constructors, and of increasing the confidence of the class that questions are being prepared in a way they regard as fair and responsive to their interests. Perhaps the most difficult and necessary check upon the adequacy of an essay question is that of attempting to write out an adequate (or, preferably, the wholly correct) answer in advance of any administration to students. This process will show up, more clearly than repeated readings of the question itself, whether it is inadequately worded or takes too long to answer, or whether the assigned reading is not in fact a suitable basis for the demanded answer.

Preparation of a proper answer to each question also constitutes the first step in improving the scoring of essay examinations, for that answer can serve as a stable reference point (for one's self or his examination reader) in determining standards for the evaluation of student papers. To secure consistency and fairness it is essential to spend considerable time reading sample papers before marking any, in order to estimate the ways in which, or the degrees to which, student discussions correspond to what is expected of them. As a consequence of this process, one can often create a scoring or credit key, so that partial credits may be recorded for various aspects of, or various parts of, an answer to a question. If this process is carried too far, of course, the scoring becomes essentially inflexible and is not likely to allow sufficiently for compensating features of an answer deficient in other respects. To avoid the halo effect, or at least to reduce it markedly, it is desirable to read papers without clues as to the identity of the writers. For this to be done successfully students must be trained to avoid forms of expression or examples which serve to identify them as individuals. If the group is small, handwriting variations must be removed somehow (as by requiring that papers be typewritten), at least after the first test, because even incorrect or unintentional identifications of handwriting or reactions to varying degree of legibility are, after all, an unwanted source of bias. The necessary effort to achieve unbiased reading is rewarded, however, by a feeling that at least one has done his best to mark each student's efforts for what they are, rather than for what they are expected to be.

While all these procedures may be useful in making essay reading more reliable, the most important step may still be that of taking sufficient time to read carefully, to make cross-comparisons of discussions, and to judge only after fully understanding what is written. This is what the harried instructor finds difficult to do consistently, however strong his motivation. Brigham's report [48] shows that under favorable conditions the reading of essays can be very reliable indeed.

To maximize pedagogical good from essay examinations there are certain further steps that one can take. For example, it is ordinarily very desirable to write comments and criticisms, directly on the papers, to show the student how his paper was evaluated, and to serve as a basis for consultation between student and instructor. The more carefully they are thought out and the more detailed they are, the more useful these comments are to the learning process. Even where group methods of examination review must be used in the interests of efficiency, opportunity should still be created to go over papers with individual students as necessary, for it is in this context that education is made to seem personal and learning a matter of individual progress. In this context also it becomes possible to train students in effective discussion. This may be positive and diagnostic instruction about content or organization and expression of ideas, or negative instruction intended to discourage the unplanned and undiscriminating shotgun type of answer, the disorganized survey, or the verbose response. Measurement and marks are always important, but at least they can be made to recede from the foreground and give the details of the learning process a chance to hold more of the spotlight.

Variants of the essay examination. As we have already indicated, the range of question types is great in the essay form of examination. In addition, there are variations in the ways in which this general kind of examination is used, which may be of use to the instructor.

By deliberately restricting the coverage of any individual question we can create the so-called short-answer essay. This particular variant of the essay examination may be so narrowly demanding that it calls essentially for completion of a sentence. It can well permit, however, demands for interpretation or analysis, or for other thought processes, so as closely to approximate the demands made by the longer or more complete essay. Experience with the short-answer test indicates that it is rather superior to the general essay test with respect to coverage of material, for as many as 15 or 20 questions may be answerable in the space of time required for only two or three general essay questions, and the number of topics or subdivisions of the subject which can be sampled is therefore greatly increased. In addition, the short-answer essay test can be scored with relative ease and quickness. This advantage must be regarded as only relative, however, for the inherent demands for brevity of answer and conciseness of expression also create the need for greater care by the reader, lest he miss any brief allusion or any incompletely expressed idea which is nevertheless present in essence. Furthermore, and this is perhaps the most common problem in making and using short-answer essays, the questions far too often are not so much concise questions, capable of a brief answer, as they are rather more general or sprawling questions for which a preferably lengthy answer must be excerpted and compacted into a brief time period. This simply makes the student scramble. Limiting the space in which he may write, or giving time signals to indicate when he should move on to the next question, may merely increase the general incoherency of his answers to the point where the good qualities of this examination form cannot show themselves. However, practice at constructing short-essay questions has commonly proved to be rewarding, and the degree of flexibility available with this form of examination, as well as its rather good coverage, make it potentially very useful.

Another variant in essay examinations is exhibited entirely in the way it is used. This may be called the questions-in-advance method, and I am somewhat grieved to learn after many years of experience with it, working out its details, that the essential notion was published about the time I started using it [62]. It is especially useful for major examinations, such as midterms or finals. The procedure is this. Using all the skills one can command, one creates a list of essay questions covering the block of material or the course to be examined; for a typical test the number of questions might range from 15 to 25. The questions must be directed at all important aspects of the material, be these methodological, factual, or theoretical, for the questions are distributed to students two or more weeks before the date of the formal examination, and they constitute the entire basis for review and thought about the subject matter. On the day of the examination a sample of answers, perhaps two to four, is required, these either to be handed in already prepared (in which case the examination has in effect required 15 to 25 short term papers), or, more commonly, to be written during a regular examination period from notes at hand or from memory as for an ordinary examination.

This general method of examining usually produces a favorable response on the part of students. They not only feel secure in knowing that all the possible examination questions are before them, and in knowing that in the instructor's judgment mastery of these questions signifies mastery of all or part of the course, but react favorably to having the questions to use as guides in study and review. And since questions used in such examinations can be as broad as necessary to demand organized thought, critical analysis, summaries, and so on, the study and review can be prevented from taking the form of hopeful rote memorization.

The questions-in-advance essay is not without its own peculiar problems. Poorly motivated students may try to guess which questions the instructor will finally choose, and thereby reduce their own labors of preparation. This may be combatted by literally arranging to choose the sample by chance, or by choosing questions from clusters (defined by comparable subject matter, form or any other criterion) such that only a balanced preparation of all the major clusters will really serve the student best. Another problem arises in the fact that during the preparation period students may work together in ways regarded as undesirable, especially if some students sponge on others. I have found it preferable to face this problem squarely, to encourage students to work together as much as they like (or even form committees or teams), since this is a method for enhancing the learning, and to make it perfectly apparent that in the final analysis the evaluation must concern what each student has learned and where he stands relative to his fellows who may have helped him.

The common experience of instructors who use the method is that no matter how closely students work together, and no matter how much preparation time has been given to a set of questions-in-advance by a class, there remain discernible variations in degree of mastery and understanding. This, then, is perhaps as close to a power test as one can come in the classroom context. One can include within the explicit requirements for answers such matters as quality of organization and presentation, accuracy of evidence, completeness of formulation, and so on, which cannot so readily be demanded in an essay written under the usual spot-examination time pressures. A final commentary about the questions-in-advance examination is that it almost without exception creates tremendous student motivation. Making the questions available has the effect of increasing greatly the drive to master the material, and certainly does not lessen the competitive aspect. The instructor must therefore literally consider whether this type of examination in his course would put his students under undue stress in their other academic responsibilities—an unusual consideration in the experience of most instructors! (Presumably part of the motivational effectiveness of this examination form in its use to date has arisen from its novelty, and if it were used throughout a department or a college some or much of the effect would disappear.)

An essay examination form which perhaps needs only brief mention is the so-called open-book test. In it, whether with questions distributed in advance or in the usual way, the student is permitted to use reference materials brought into the examination room. These materials may be limited or controlled in various ways by the instructor, but the most common uses are for the checking of routine or factual materials (such as statistical formulas or designations of experimental groups), so that a more exact and more properly qualified essay can be written. The incidental effect, of course, is that of reassuring the student that he will not get caught in a crisis because he has momentarily forgotten some key item of knowledge. The motivational consequences of the open-book examination may be, on the positive side, to make it apparent that rote memory and mere factual material are of less consequence than understanding and ability to deal intelligently with whatever questions are set concerning the material. On the negative side, the open-book procedure makes it possible for a careless student to hope that even though his preparation is not good he can look up enough material to write a passable essay under pressure. The instructor can control this in part by his choice of questions, for he can make it quite apparent that no one could possibly do the essential thinking and locating of materials and in the same examination period write a useful response to those questions.

Finally, mention should be made of the possibility of using

an oral examination where classes are small enough to permit it and course objectives are such that its limited character is appropriate. With the oral examination, of course, there is the superficial appearance of flexibility, avoidance of laborious details of question writing and paper reading, and an opportunity, almost unique among examination forms, to learn how well the student can express what he knows when under fire. The oral examination is likely, however, to offer a good many difficulties. It is time consuming in administration. Comparability of the evaluation, from student to student, is likely to be unsatisfactory unless the interview is quite standardized (thus yielding up the supposed virtue of flexibility). The tendency to waste time on irrelevancies is rather great, and there is no opportunity to reexamine what was said, or to return to it in exactly the same way at a later moment. And of course anyone who has taken a Ph.D. oral can testify to how communication infelicities under induced social stress can leave one feeling frustrated.

The objective examination. As we have already implied, essay questions vary widely in kind, and it is readily apparent that they can be written so as to bear close resemblance to what are called objective questions. The latter label, it is well to realize, refers only to scoring. A question is said to be of the objective variety if different persons would score answers to it in exactly the same way (except for simple errors of a mechanical sort). It is also well to reiterate that, just as some students prefer and some despise the essay, so some students regard the objective examination as impersonal, mechanical, and terrifying, while others feel at ease with it and regard it as entirely appropriate for use at the college level. One can always expect it to be necessary to work toward acceptance, or at least tolerance, by all his students of the examination forms and procedures which he regards as proper for his course.

The most common forms of objective examination include three which most psychologists now tend to avoid, at least for classroom testing purposes. One is the true-false question, which can hardly be constructed so that answers can be defended satisfactorily, if only for the simple reason that in science the answers to few questions can be stated at the necessary high confidence levels. Furthermore (see p. 259), it tends to be detrimental to study habits. Versions of the true-false test in which other categories of response are permitted, such as "can't be answered," have not yielded much more satisfactory results. Furthermore, the range of scores on a true-false test tends to be restricted and the reliability is relatively low.

Another form of objective test which psychologists do not often find a use for is the matching test, in which names of scientists, for example, are to be paired by the student with their major achievements, or statistical formulas are to be paired with brief statements of their use or meaning. Perhaps the most direct objection to this kind of test is that not much of the material studied, or the thought processes we want to encourage, lend themselves to this form of evaluation; the inherent inadequacies of the matching test as such are seemingly not so great.

The third not wholly acceptable objective test form is the fill-in or completion type. For this the student is required to write appropriate words (or numbers or other responses) in blank spaces left in paragraphs or sentences provided on the printed test form. When this kind of item amounts unambiguously to pure recall, it of course can function very well, but it then resembles the direct form of recall question. ("Between the mean and plus or minus one standard deviation in a normal distribution are found _____ per cent of the cases" amounts to "What proportion of the cases . . . ?") But anything less than this degree of preciseness in a fill-in question is likely to produce answers of debatable degrees of difference from what the test constructor intended, and considerable judgment and time is required in scoring. Furthermore, there is the temptation to secure freedom from ambiguity of the question by using exact quotes, as from textbooks. The result may be to encourage undesired rote learning and recognition rather than recall or a reasoning approach to the questions. And if a completion passage omits a very high ratio of words, or key words on which the meaning of the whole passage turns, both the ambiguity and the degree to which general reasoning ability is measured increase sharply.

The multiple-choice question is perhaps more widely used than any other in psychology courses. For that reason we shall give it more attention than the previously described test-item forms (although a number of things to be said now can be generalized to those forms). Under varying conditions of construction and use the multiple-choice question may be made to measure almost anything from sheer rote memory to ability at critical analysis and interpretation, although it cannot very readily be constructed to afford the student a chance to show his ability to organize or express ideas. It may be modified into the multiple-correct answer form ("Mark *all* correct answers among the alternatives given"). It can utilize graphical material, in the question or answer options. It can be built on numerical or formula material, or even cartoons [192]. It can be coupled with short-answer opportunities to explain or justify answers. In short, its flexibility makes mastery of its characteristics by the instructor very worthwhile indeed. As we have said in relation to other forms of examination, the multiple-choice form can vary tremendously in quality. However, the precautions and skills necessary for the construction of good tests are well understood and are discussed in detail in standard manuals [1, 68, 133, 264], so that we can here treat this matter relatively briefly.

First, we can express certain *general* principles about multiple-choice item construction. One of these, with which all the test technicians' suggestion lists begin, is far too often disregarded by the classroom instructor: the proper way to build an examination is to start with objectives. These may be statements for a unit of work or a course, initially, but they must be reduced to specific statements of just what the instructor wants to measure in a particular examination. From this he can properly move to selection or construction of questions appropriate to his measurement objectives, whereas if he adopts the all-too-common procedure of picking up the textbook and starting to look for likely items he cannot expect to build an adequate examination, one which has face validity (i.e., which appears reasonable) relative to what the course and the students are attempting to do. It has been said that the main trouble in examination building is that the teacher seldom has a very clear picture of what he is trying to do. A teacher who tries to cover the subject will need one test strategy, but the teacher who is trying to uncover it will need another. Not until the teacher understands or clarifies his own aims can he hope to test whether students have met his standards of achievement.

One must learn from experience with his own items to gauge their difficulty and thus the number to be used in a given examination. Although the questions written by one instructor may be answered at the rate of one per minute on the average, those written by another person may require two minutes each, or one instructor may find that the difficulty of his own items varies from time to time or topic to topic. It is helpful to keep a frequency tally of the length of time required by students to complete an examination and to relate this to the later analysis of item difficulty so that one learns to adjust test length to length of examination period and type of material.

One must attend closely to the criticisms and comments of the students who have been subjected to a given examination. Particularly if it has been made entirely clear to students that the instructor has no intention of enforcing arbitrary decisions in scoring, students are likely to be capable of expressing quite objective analyses of the questions as such. In this process, as elsewhere in teaching, the instructor can learn something about thinking like a sophomore, the better to adapt his methods to the achievement of desired ends. Related is the point that students entering a course are likely to vary in their sophistication with respect to techniques for taking objective examinations, and unless one wants to measure this sophistication he must take steps to ensure that it is largely equalized. This he can do by briefing sessions, especially before the first examination, in which examination taking is discussed. McKeachie and Kimble [192, p. 32] go so far as to suggest that there be instruction on the probable flaws in examination construction, in addition to the to-be-expected material concerning the wisdom of changing an initially chosen answer, omitting confusing or difficult items in a first trip through a test, working by elimination methods on certain questions, and so on.

One should take precautions to avoid making students choose between two or more authorities in order to answer a question, especially if the authorities are the instructor and the textbook. Questions about controversial matters may, of course, be asked in such a way that the student must indicate he knows relevant points on any side of a given question, without being forced to choose sides. Questions which introduce elements of novelty to the point where they are tricky, i.e., depend on special or esoteric kinds of information, or special sets or expectations during the reading, should be avoided. Students violently dislike them, and they are in addition unreliable because in different members of the class they measure quite different things. This consideration is an important one for the instructor who wishes to measure transfer or insight, for he must by definition provide a novel problem or situation to test for these and thus runs the danger of being merely tricky.

The items of any given examination should be independent of each other in the sense of not measuring the same thing twice (this merely gives double weight to measurement of the particular point in question) or having the wording of one indicate the answer to another. As a general rule, the language used in questions should be appropriate to the material they pertain to; this is part of the appearance of face validity and bears directly on how relevant the question is to the study the student has engaged in. Questions should be grouped together by content, so that the student does not have to be continually changing his set in order to think about the next item.

Second, a number of specific suggestions may be made concerning the *stem* of the multiple-choice item (the question or problem part). It should ask but a single question, or state but a single problem, accurately and clearly, and it should not contain irrelevant material. If this is accomplished the stem will avoid, as it should, complexities which require mere verbal facility. Sometimes, to ensure clarity and directness in the stem, it should be broken into two or more parts, the first parts being complete sentences which state the problem or situation, and the last part leading directly to the alternatives. This last remark should be singled out and labeled as a second important suggestion about item stems: they should point somewhere, i.e., suggest what answer the student who knows the material should expect to find somewhere in the available set of alternatives. Failing this, he has to put the stem together in succession with each of the alternatives and examine each one as a true-false combination. Except where the opposite tack is deliberately chosen as advisable, the stem should call for the positive form of an answer; stems calling for a negative answer ("Which of the following is *not* a correct interpretation of . . .") tend to emphasize retention of incorrect information, which is usually less important than the positive and correct statements that could be made.

About the writing of *alternatives,* and especially *distractors,* a great deal could be said. We shall here confine ourselves to three general statements, the third of which will be developed in some detail. First, distractors should represent genuine but erroneous modes of thought about a problem or question in order to be plausible to the person who does not actually know the correct answer. We have referred earlier to "thinking like a sophomore," and that ability is nowhere more helpful than in inventing distractors that will truly distract those who do not know their subject matter. Second, distractors, like stems, should be as brief as is consistent with demands for clarity and adequate qualification. Otherwise, irrelevant dimensions, such as ability to solve verbal puzzles, are being measured.

A third general principle about the construction of alternatives is that specific but irrelevant determiners of thought about the distractors should be eliminated, or at least point away from the correct answer, not toward it, for the student who does not know the correct answer. A number of illustrations of this principle may be worthwhile. Similar wordings may by chance occur in stem and in an alternative, or similar pronunciations, and if the student chooses an answer merely on the basis of this kind of similarity, he should not have been led to choose the correct answer thereby. All the alternatives should come from the same general domain of thought; otherwise, any representative of an unlike domain will almost automatically not distract, and in effect the number of functional alternatives for the question is reduced. (For example, if the stem says, "The psychologist whose name is associated with early formulations of the Law of Effect is . . ." and the alternative answers are Guthrie, Thorndike, Hemingway, Tolman and Lewin, one might just as well not print Hemingway's name.) Terms which indicate absolutes or which are all inclusive (never, always, all, etc.) tend to imply that alternatives containing them are incorrect because they are not properly qualified; the student who does not know the correct answer is nevertheless moved toward it if the distractors contain these negative indicators. Grammatical constructions of alternative answers should be appropriate to the structure of the stem; if a plural is required by the stem there should be no singular form in a distractor to appear conspicuously incorrect, or if the stem ends with "a," no distractor should begin with a vowel, and so on. Unusually short or unusually long distractors are usually avoided as being insufficiently qualified to be correct or deliberately made to contain misleading information. Irregularities in the order of answers which form a natural sequence of possibilities (like a series of numbers) suggest that the out-of-place answer is a correct answer—else why take the trouble to put it out of sequence? This latter point relates to the final suggestion, which is that the position of the correct answer in the series of alternatives should be varied from question to question in a random fashion, to prevent irrelevant expectations from influencing the choice of answer.

With the previous discussion of the technicalities of item writing as a background we may look briefly into those aspects of objective testing which are involved in the classroom teacher's decision whether to use this test form or not. It is immediately apparent that, compared with the variants of essay testing, objective tests have two important virtues. First, the large number of questions they can include permits a very adequate sampling of the assigned material, especially if page or idea counts are used as a check on fairness of coverage, and thereby makes available a wide range of topics to stimulate post-examination review and reteaching. With a large number of questions the student is not much threatened by failure on single questions, and conversely he receives credit for careful study of everything assigned. Second, scoring of papers, whether by machine or hand-stencil methods, is fast and can be almost entirely accurate.

As all our discussion suggests, however, the labor of preparing an objective examination is great. The saving in scoring time, except as it enables one to be virtuous in the matter of returning results to students promptly, does not really compensate for this initial labor except in the larger classes. There the objective methods become almost imperative. It is also found, in practice, that despite the repeatedly demonstrated possibility of utilizing multiple-choice and other types of objective questions to test for many desirable kinds of thought processes, including some of the less readily defined ones, the typical constructor finds himself making mostly factual and vocabulary questions. The effort to rethink assigned readings or lecture materials so that more abstract forms of idea or bona fide applications lend themselves to objective testing, although difficult, is both desirable and possible. Securing good coverage, which is also clearly desirable and possible, is again not always easy in practice. One finds, for example, that materials on quantitative method or sensory function lend themselves well to objective testing, whereas materials on the topic of personality may simply not readily yield a number of questions proportional to the importance of the topic. An important reservation one must have about multiple-choice items (or other objective test forms, for that matter) stems from the consideration that, after all, the objectivity is partly spurious or misleading, in that it is based upon a firm subjective judgment as to what a correct answer should be. Furthermore, to the extent that skimming, sentence selection, and other forms of study are useful as preparation for recognition-type examinations (as shown by Cole [71, p. 451], and others), the objective test form may partially defeat the aims of the instructor.

To conclude this discussion of the construction of objective examinations, attention should be called to the necessity, for either or both of two reasons, of testing the test items. That is, the instructor may wish to analyze the individual items of an examination for information about difficulty or ambiguity or inadequate teaching to guide his next contacts with the class, or he may wish to compile a list of questions which are likely to be useful in the future for each of the major topics of his course. Rather simple techniques can be very helpful for these purposes, and we shall describe only these, leaving highly technical procedures to the testing expert and to the instructor whose special circumstances demand them.

The most important thing to learn about questions is their validity: do they really measure what we intended? But the best evidence on this point is usually unavailable, for it would depend on correlations with measures of student learning or response outside the test itself, and such measures we rarely have. As a substitute for this, it is typically assumed that the test as a whole has face validity, i.e., it really does measure in the area it purports to sample. On that assumption, the student's total number of correct responses on all the questions of the test can be used as a criterion against which to assess the way individual questions measured his knowledge. In practice this amounts to selecting a group of papers with high total scores, another group with low total scores, and then for each individual question tallying the numbers of persons in each group giving each possible response. To be regarded as an item homogeneous with the total test, any given question should be passed by definitely more of the high scorers than the low scorers. In addition, scrutiny of the proportions of each group selecting the various distractors will indicate particular distractors which did or did not work well, and very often it is possible to see why. If the number of cases on which an item analysis is to be based is suitably large, much more precise statistical procedures are available (see, for example, Adkins [1, pp. 180-86]). The end result of either the less or the more exacting kind of analysis can be the same. The instructor will learn which of his items are discriminating between students who know the subject matter and those who do not and can guide his teaching, or construct a question file for the future, as his judgment indicates.

As a by-product of the above kind of analysis, data on the total proportion of students answering each item correctly become available. With these difficulty data the instructor is enabled to detect items passed or failed by everyone (they contribute nothing to placing students on a relative scale), or by an excessive number of students. He can also ensure having a wide range of difficulties of items in his next examination over this same material in order to be sure of being able to discriminate among students of all degrees of knowledge, high or low.

11

ADMINISTERING AND GRADING EXAMINATIONS

In the previous chapter we were concerned primarily with the motivational and pedagogical aspects of classroom examinations, although certain administrative or procedural matters inevitably were considered as part of this discussion. In the present chapter we shall discuss what the instructor may do in preparing materials, or in returning examinations, or in grading, to make the whole process as useful and as little disruptive of education as possible.

THE MECHANICS OF EXAMINATIONS

In any class, but especially in a large and inherently complicated one, examinations may be presumed to be more effective if distracting or extraneous influences are minimized. Several different procedures may help to accomplish this.

Preparation of the test forms. In the first place, to make it easy for the student to spend his time in thinking about and recording his answers to the questions, the obvious thing is to make sure the examination copy is legible—which it should not be necessary to say at all, except that inadequately cut stencils and awkward formats are far too often used in mimeographing. For ease of reading an objective type examination it may be well to use a double-column format. Type face and many other aspects of readability deserve attention. If the test occupies several pages, special checks must be made before the papers are distributed to ensure that there are no blank or missing pages, for under examination stress a student may not realize until too late that a whole set of questions must be missing from his question booklet or leaflet. To ensure that all students understand the procedures to be followed in the examination, it is often desirable to print explicit rules or instructions on the test form itself. This reminds certain students who need it of what they are to do, reassures others, and cuts down markedly on the number of questions the instructor has to answer in getting the examination started. Since the sheer handling of the test forms may lead to confusion and occupy considerable time at the beginning of an examination period, it is advisable to mechanize the distribution process in any way possible. For example, if students occupy assigned seats and these are placed in the usual row pattern, one can count out examination forms in his office and stack them so that when the appointed time arrives for beginning the examination he can distribute small packets of examination forms to end persons in the rows of students as rapidly as he can walk up the aisle.

Giving the examination. Although the way in which an examination is given will depend upon local tradition, as where an honor system is operative, and upon the physical circumstances, even to the shape of the room, there are some generally predictable problems. The first is that the students will have questions to ask during the examination. We have already remarked that the number of these may be reduced by providing explicit instructions, and we have implied that a good examination is sufficiently clear that questions about questions are largely unnecessary. The anxiety of students typically is such, however, that under the best of circumstances some of them will wish to make sure they understand the meaning of statements or the procedures expected of them. In this instance, it is quite clear, the instructor is obligated to answer and might as well have decided how he will act.

To avoid undue movement about the room by students, or questions whispered huskily across the heads of people taking the examination, the instructor will probably have to go to each student who has a question, or send an assistant who is an acceptable substitute so far as the student is concerned. In his responses the instructor will have to display a certain amount of intellectual agility, for on the spur of the moment he must decide whether what he might say would give away the nature of a proper answer to a question or by properly clarifying that question would put the student on the same measurement basis as others for whom the question as first rendered was adequate. Fortunately, students are likely to respect a refusal to answer, when told that the answer would give away the point or give an unfair advantage over other students. It should be added that these queries from students may, even in the best regulated of courses, turn up inadequacies in questions or instructions which require attention in the interest of the whole class. Once such a difficulty is definitely caught by the instructor he may, anticipating that a steady stream of other questions is likely to be directed at the same point, decide to interrupt the examination, make his correction and, if necessary, at that moment announce the addition of a few minutes to the length of the examination period to compensate for the interruption and the time lost shuffling through examination forms. The technique is sometimes used of writing corrections on the board, and training students to look there before asking a question (or turning in their papers).

To keep an examination period running smoothly one must also learn to deal with other kinds of distractions. One of these is the latecomer. It may be possible to standardize a plan whereby such persons do not enter the body of the class but sit near the entrance to the room. Particularly is this helpful in the large class, where a dozen or more persons may come late to any examination and stumble their way to their regular seats unless other arrangements are required of them. Another distraction is caused by students who finish before the end of the examination period and then wish to talk about the examination either to the instructor or to each other. Here the only solution appears to be for the instructor to have emphasized in advance the right of those remaining in the room to concentrate. He can, then, if he chooses, make a point of not discussing the examination until the period is over, and of requiring those persons who have finished the examination and want to talk it over with their peers, or those who are just conversing while waiting for a friend to finish, to leave the room—and the doorway. The instructor will also do well to pay particular attention, on examination days, to the physical circumstances: to the ventilation, heat, adequacy of lighting, and so on. In the contemporary classroom there may be a problem created by smoking; quite commonly there are institutional rules about smoking in the classroom, and just about as commonly those rules are disregarded. Often rules that are followed strictly during term are put aside during final examinations. Our only concerns here have to do with the adequacy of ventilation and the probable undesirability, for the beginning instructor especially, of taking upon himself the enforcement of rules which the rest of the faculty may ignore, or which the students resent.

Cheating. Except in the rare institution where an honor system is so thoroughly imbedded in the culture that it works, at least to the comfort and satisfaction of the faculty, the instructor has to be realistic about dishonesty, whether he makes public display concerning it or not. It seems to be believed that cheating on examinations is the most common form of dishonesty. (In the present context, we shall not attempt to deal with cheating on reports and papers.)

Of the cheating that occurs on examinations, the greatest proportion is probably done by the marginal or the impulse cheater, rather than by the systematic planner. This leads us to the view that it is important to reduce the opportunity for cheating during examinations, more as a protection for the honest than as a penalty for the dishonest. Without being obnoxious about it, we can create arrangements for examinations which are well understood by the students as providing security controls; these controls are usually appreciated rather than resented.

In other than a very small class it is usually wise to have one or more proctors, if only because the instructor is likely to be occupied with answering questions, especially in the hectic opening and closing moments of the examination, and these tend to be the moments in which the unsure or the harried student tries to secure aid. As a matter of fact, there should be enough proctor aid that the instructor does not need to think of himself as functioning in this way. The problem with proctoring, of course, is to make it effective without having the students feel it a sporting proposition to see whether they can cheat in spite of the proctoring, and without having the physical presence of the proctor be a nuisance. Certain suggestions can be made, among them that as the class taking the examination increases in size, more proctors should be added so that they are able to keep reasonably close surveillance over the situation while remaining in a restricted location and so avoiding movement of a patrolling (or squeaky-shoe) variety. Also, the proctors should be coached in advance about what to look for and about other responsibilities, so that one does not find, for example, that proctors who are ignorant of the subject matter are attempting to answer student questions, or that proctors are clustering together in the corner for a smoke.

Because much of the impulsive cheating that occurs is in the form of glances at neighboring papers, particularly in objective examinations, there are certain precautions which one can and should take. If possible, of course, students should be seated in a spaced pattern. Barring this possibility, alternative examination forms should be utilized. These may be printed on differently colored paper, so that at a glance the proctor knows which examination form is being used by a particular student. The alternative question forms, it should be noted, are rather readily made by scrambling question orders, or by varying the order of available answers to objective questions, but it is likely that in changing the original version of the test in order to make a second form there will be subtle changes in the required thought processes and therefore in the difficulty of the test. In the next test one can, if impressed by this possibility, reverse the assignment of original and modified test forms, if his examination practices are such that he always knows who gets which form.

With all these precautions, however, it is likely that attempts at cheating will occur, or more commonly, be merely suspected. As will be emphasized in a later chapter concerned with disciplinary problems, it is not likely to be effective or desirable to make a public show of the person suspected of or detected at cheating, no matter how sure the instructor is about it, for this may rally not only the student's own aggressive feelings but those of other students who at the moment identify with him. The instructor may therefore decide merely quietly to caution a student to keep his eyes on his own paper, or suggest that he move to another (more isolated) seat. It may actually be possible to do this in a relatively painless way, with a mixture of the jovial and the firm.

It is impossible to catalogue all the forms of cheating on examinations, for students tend to be inventive, sometimes just one step ahead of the detecting activities of the faculty. Some of the more ingenious or interesting devices may be worth mentioning just for fun. I have known crib notes to be prepared as a scroll inside an empty pocket-watch case, or on a white shirt cuff, on the palm of the hand, in an extra bluebook carried into the examination room by the student, or on what appeared to be a dirty and trampled piece of scrap paper carelessly tossed nearby on the floor. One was even fastened to a slip under a sheer dress, so that the young lady in question could spread her knees slightly and thus raise that slip close to the sheer dress material so that the notes could be read, or bring her knees together thus dropping the notes away from the sheer material and making them less visible to the proctor. The cheating glance can be concealed in interesting ways too, by means of the hand to forehead, the well-massaged neck, the long green eyeshade, the cramped and turned position of the body in the classroom chair, or even the long hair allowed to drape artistically over the tipped face.

Special problems of the multisection course. In most departments there is likely to be at least one course that is large enough to necessitate its being offered in more than one division or section. The instructor of one of these sections is therefore likely to be in the position of teaching the same reading materials on the same general time schedules as are used in other sections, of planning lectures or discussions which cover the ground other instructors have agreed they want also to cover, and of utilizing at least some examinations which the group has set jointly. The difficulty with all this is not merely that the whole process of examining is made much more complex, but that no examination set by a group can with complete fairness assess the learning of a particular instructor's students. He thus is placed in a dilemma for which there is really no good solution:

If the common or multisection examination is all that is used, his own contributions to the learning process are devalued, or, as the examinations are made increasingly peculiar to the instructor, the contributions by textbooks and the other instructors are made to appear less important. The same dilemma is posed, it should be noted, by the type of course in which there is a lecturer for a large class and numerous discussion sections led mostly by other (and usually junior) faculty members or graduate students. In this case, the question is whether to treat examinations as emanating from the section leader and his way of teaching the material, thus demoting the lecturer, or as emanating from the lecturer as the chief instructor of the course, thus demoting the section man. The virtuous solution is presumably the middle ground, where examinations are constructed and weighted to reflect the different sources of teaching. This virtuous solution is difficult of attainment, however, and typically involves a great amount of consultation time, joint reviewing of examination plans, and attempts at very clear communication to the students as to just what the balance of emphasis is to be.

Some of the other vexing problems of tests in the multisection course are these. First, if several faculty members must prepare the examinations, and do so conscientiously, there is the chance that only innocuous questions will survive this joint screening. The innocuous questions tend far too often to be dull ones of vocabulary or limited fact, these being less often debatable. Examinations may thus not rise to the challenge of testing for reasoning processes or for originality in any sense, for the scoring would be a matter of argument. Second, the scheduling of all the necessary conferences and other routines tends to be difficult. It may become almost imperative to establish special administrative machinery for even a single course, and a calendar by which the staff will work in preparing examinations so as to reduce the problems encountered in the scramble method of meeting a deadline. This is likely to be especially important near the end of a term. Third, information about a given test will pass from the first class taking it to later classes, and to the extent that it does not pass equally to all members of those later classes, it must be regarded as invalidating their examinations. This is a point at which organized or deliberate efforts may be made to frustrate the examination system. I once knew a fraternity, for example, to require certain of its freshmen to enroll in an eight o'clock section of a large course, to memorize designated pages of the examinations while taking them, report these after class, and so as a team make available a complete copy of the examination for keying and study by students having the test later in the day. Short of administering the examination to all sections simultaneously, which can be arranged in some institutions for an evening or other special time, the individual instructor probably must content himself with the organized efforts of the staff to control the passage of information by making sure all papers are returned to him in the early sections. He can also make sure that the tests always contain material which is characteristic of his own teaching and not usefully prepared for by methods other than study of the materials he himself has covered.

To make attempts to pass information from one section to another seem less important, it may be desirable to establish the tradition in which all papers are finally returned to students and a considerable file of earlier questions or typical questions is kept in the library or in other locations where every student in the course can familiarize himself with what is likely to happen on any given examination. If this concern of his is reduced, he is less likely to seek to get information about specific questions from some other student. And if he spends an undue amount of time studying questions used in previous years, it can be argued that he is simply using a substitute (probably inferior) textbook for the course. This general practice means that no question can be re-used until a considerable file has accumulated. Further, its statistical properties, if known, are not utilized. Some instructors therefore turn from this to the opposite extreme of strictest security controls, with no tests left in the hands of students (if it can be prevented!). To me this unhappily makes measurement more important than instruction.

REVIEWING EXAMINATIONS

It has previously been suggested that examinations should receive classroom review after they have been taken, preferably after they have been scored, in order to enhance learning and also to release feelings which students have developed in relation to the examining process. The rush of aggressive responses which can occur, however, if one innocently undertakes to review an examination which otherwise would simply be put away, may be traumatic to the beginning instructor, and never becomes a comfortable thing for even the most experienced instructor. It is desirable, therefore, to learn rapidly what to expect in this situation and how to deal with it.

For review purposes, the first tactical problem is to discover what needs discussion, in order not to waste time on irrelevant problems. One can rarely cover all the ground suggested, so there is continually the problem of deciding what is most important. This can never be decided wholly by the instructor, or wholly in advance, and must always depend in part upon student reaction in the classroom. One can, however, read at least a goodly sample of essay examinations himself, and thus have advance warning as to what the difficulties are likely to be, or he can do some kind of quick item analysis of objective test items, to discern which ones are likely to be regarded as ambiguous or overly difficult.

After one comes into the classroom there are also usable procedures for locating the sources of trouble. In using essay examinations, a very effective device is to discuss the general scoring key, if one is used, so that students may see the standards by which their writing was judged; an ideal or adequate answer, prepared at the time the question was written, can be read aloud to make standards evident. In using objective tests it is very necessary to realize that one cannot start with the first question, discuss it and all the reactions to it, then move to the second question, and ever get in this fashion to the end of the examination within that one period—the students will not let him work in such an orderly way or with such dispatch. Two alternatives may be suggested. One is to read rapidly the key to correct responses all the way through, firmly permitting no discussion but asking for a show of hands as to which questions should later be discussed, and returning to those questions for which discussion is most demanded. The weakness of the procedure is, however, that it is difficult to use in a discriminating way, for students may vote to discuss a question because they themselves missed it, or because they believe an important misunderstanding, or an error in item construction or in keying, is involved. No matter what the difficulty, however, the instructor knows where it is and thus can do some direct inquiring and, maybe, some good teaching. The alternative diagnostic method suggested by McKeachie and Kimble [192] is to divide the students arbitrarily into small groups, these groups to spend the first part of the period settling disagreements and discussing answers among themselves, leaving to the later portion of the period a review of remaining or disputed points by the instructor for the benefit of the whole class.

The second problem is, of course, coping with the difficulties located by whatever technique one has used. Four suggestions can be made about this. The first, obvious, and supposedly unnecessary suggestion is that one should never be surprised at student interpretations of his questions or scoring, and should never show temper about it. The whole situation is one in which aggression is a likely student response, and can turn into one in which the students attempt to stampede the instructor. The second suggestion is in its way equally obvious. The best method of dealing with student questions about or objections to an examination question is to take the offensive and to explain as precisely and completely as time allows exactly what reasoning or datum was involved. This is a method both of clarifying the situation for the student and reducing his tendency to feel aggressive, and of reteaching the subject matter. The third suggestion is to try, whenever possible, not to defend a particular question or method of scoring but to let some student who understands it provide the defense in the form of an explanation as to why he did what he did. (This contains the possible danger that some students, especially good ones, may appear to be favorites or toadies.) The fourth suggestion is related to the first, and it is this: Be reasonable, so that if students have a valid case against your question or examination, their work can be rescored or reread, or credit given where it is due. The aggressive behavior implies in part a distrust of the instructor's motives. Sooner or later it must be dealt with at that level, and convincing evidence must be given of the instructor's good intentions.

On the score of willingness to be responsive to student criticism or suggestions, however, certain additional points of precaution are worth mentioning. One, as implied above, is that the instructor, the younger one especially, may be pressured or stampeded by students into agreeing that their criticisms or suggestions are better founded than they really are. It is therefore desirable that, unless the case for changing one's judgment about some aspect of an examination is very clear indeed, one adopt the practice of agreeing in class only to reconsider and to report at a later class meeting just what his decision finally is. Of course, failure to follow through on such an agreement is doubly unfortunate. It is also desirable to make it very clear that when scoring standards or keys are modified, someone is always the loser, so that it is not merely whimsy on the part of the instructor to decide that a minor scoring inequity must remain in order not to do greater injustice by a change in the key. One of the interesting but painful commentaries on student attitude is that the student who gets credit for what later turns out to have been an incorrectly credited answer is likely to be one of the most aggressive about the injustice which he feels when his answer is correctly evaluated. Finally, in subjectively scored tests, and especially in the essay judged partly for such relative intangibles as quality of organization or clarity of thoughts, it may not be possible at all to reconsider the scoring of individual papers. That is, the original subjective judgments were made relative to the frame of reference established by reading *all* the papers that had been read up to any given moment, whereas to reread a single paper is to do so against a different and uncertain frame of reference. How much of a purist to be on this technically correct point each instructor will have to decide for himself.

GRADING PRACTICES

Concerns and misconceptions about course grades. Most of what has been said previously about the student's concern for examinations applies very directly to the grades he receives on them. It is inevitable, therefore, that in addition to giving information about progress or adding to the genuine satisfactions of the learning process grades have disciplinary and possibly other somewhat unpleasant features. All too commonly, it must be admitted, grades are used by the instructor as a weapon in the perceived battle with students. By means of his grading system the instructor can keep his students in line and can reassure himself that he is a scholar of high and unimpeachable standards, or he can seem to make himself well liked by easy marking, or he can even disarm a particularly critical or demanding student by giving him the better mark, rather than dealing directly with him. The beginning instructor does well, therefore, to analyze his own grading motives and practices and the student's reaction to them, to the end that what he does will be both just and educationally meaningful.

The aspect of grading systems to which students most often object is grading on the curve. Instructors in disciplines where the frequency distribution curve is a familiar item to the professional person, as in the various behavioral sciences, may not understand what students mean when they use the expression, or why they may so intensely dislike the whole notion. The key to the student's concern here is the relatively common instructor practice of using performance by the group, rather than performance relative to the subject matter of the course, as the reference point in deciding who shall receive what marks. The instructor is motivated, of course, by his knowledge that in the absence of an absolute reference point for his scoring scale, he ordinarily must adopt a relative reference point, such as the average score, for use in interpreting scores on his tests or in his course.

What he overlooks is the logical point that, while he can use such a relative reference point and relative measures of dispersion about it for scaling the results of a given test or series of tests, this is not necessarily a grading system and usually is not. Rather, scores, however scaled, have to be transmuted into grades or given grade equivalents. And then this part of the grading system, whether of the letter variety or numerical in character, reflects the instructor's personal judgment as to what proportion of students ought to receive what sign of proficiency in the subject matter. If the instructor overlooks this point, as have so many in the past, he may merely decide that a certain proportion of the students must automatically fail each examination, or each course. (If he decides a certain proportion must receive the highest category of grade this is equally restricting, but rather less galling and therefore not complained about so much.) It is this seemingly mechanical and heartless method of assigning grades to which students refer when they complain about marking on the curve.

The students have a point. Samples or classes of students vary widely, performances on one sample or examination with a given group of students may vary widely, and all the factors influencing the quality of examination or the marking of it may vary widely. Therefore *any* device which automatically turns the recorded performance into grades without some attempt at the most intelligent and comprehensive judgment as to what is desirable or what is required in the distribution of those grades is simply not good teaching practice, regardless of the amount of sophistication in measurement or statistics upon which it may appear to rest. To state the problem in a slightly different way, while human performances very often are found to yield a relatively symmetrical and even bell-shaped distribution of raw scores, *this* distribution is *not* the grade distribution. Much of the concern and misinterpretation center about the way the grade distribution is related to the score distribution. The practice in some institutions [e.g., 207] of suggesting proportions of marks to be assigned at various proficiency levels is merely a reflection of the confusion between measuring and grading. It must be hoped that the new instructor, realizing the complexity of the grading process and the largely subjective and necessarily judgmental character of the marks assigned, will not gloss this over or deceive himself and his students by appearing to use statistically automatic means to grind out the grist for the registrar's office.

Grading standards. If it is now clear that distributing grades is a different process from the compiling of raw scores indexing relative standing in a class, we are in a position to say that one of the first things an instructor must learn is how he will set *grading* standards. Both the average grade and the relative number of grades at different levels are after all adjustable, within limits, so that they reflect not only what the students have done but also what the instructor feels they deserve. The meaning of the standards the instructor sets is determined largely by the practice of others, so that he must learn as quickly as he can what are the general practices in his institution, in his department, and in the kind of course he is teaching. He may learn, for example, that senior classes are in effect graded on a different scale than freshmen, or that the work of a major student is graded differently than the work of a non-major. The circumstances may indicate that some average degree of stiffness in grading standards is the most appropriate one, or that another practice is indicated. It may well be that the beginning instructor should attempt to be typical in the grades he assigns, thus to be inconspicuous until or unless he decides on what he is certain is the correct practice for his particular situation. Particularly to be decried is the attitude sometimes found in the newest instructor that because students are so miserably far below the standard of achievement he has been accustomed to expect of himself and his associates in graduate school they should be given marks which "show them where they stand" (and himself how superior he is). The other extreme, that of lowering absolute standards to fit the population, is probably also undesirable, for it is hardly a scholarly thing to pass students who do not deserve it. This matter, however, is far from easily handled, for it relates to one's over-all views on the objectives of higher education (see Chap. 2).

Even though the instructor has made himself reasonably clear as to the general standards he will employ in grading, he will still have to cope with particular distributions of scores and will find that the standards problem is still with him. Let us assume he has an approximate notion as to how many students should fall in different categories, and that he is willing to adjust this notion for any good reason, such as the belief that he has before him an unusually able class, or results indicating a very poorly prepared assignment. He may nevertheless, as an example, meet the question of where in a distribution to draw the dividing lines between 70 and 75, or between A and B. He must then decide whether to give a disproportionate number of grades of one kind, so as to take advantage of any natural clustering of scores and a gap before the next cluster, or argue with students who do not like his dividing a cluster of scores exactly as his preconceived notion demands they should be in order to be distributed properly into the higher and the lower of two grade categories. The compensating factor is here usually assumed to be the probability that over the span of a course liberties taken with standards on individual examinations or papers will average out so that one can finally assign grades which meet the demands of his conscience, without being unduly troubled by it on each individual test.

A second aspect of grading practices centers about the student's understanding of those practices. As part of the general policy of taking the mystery out of examinations and marks, it is desirable that the instructor communicate everything he can to the student with regard to marking procedures, details of the procedures or judgments by which scores are turned into grades, and so on. Although it has been discussed previously, it is desirable to say again that the essential independence and conventionality of grades as such has to be recognized by both student and instructor. In setting his grades the instructor is both free to exert his own best judgment and required to do so.

A third aspect of grading practices, related to the original statement of course objectives as well as to the construction of examinations, is that they should reflect with proper weight all the scorable aspects of course performance. If, for example, the instructor encourages and evaluates attempts at self-expression or critical thought, grades should reflect this, and in a way which is open to inspection by the student, not concealed behind or within a mark ostensibly given on some other dimension of evaluation.

Every effort must be made to be explicit and open about what is expected of the student and about the grades which are assigned to him for what he does. Two remarks must be added here, on points which may possibly prove to be troublesome if one approaches grading in this spirit. The first is that if improvement by the student (with reference to his own initial status) is sought and graded, there may be complications in the use of such a standard—once the word gets around, some students are likely to make sure their initial performances are low enough that spectacular improvement is evident. The second is that if the instructor strives for attitudinal changes in his course such that his students become more tolerant, or more objective, or more favorably disposed toward his discipline, he may find himself in a moral dilemma if he attempts to allot credit for such changes (assuming he can measure them, which is not often true). He may well decide that while he hopes for those attitudinal changes, he cannot require them, or signs of them, without depriving the student of an essential freedom to feel as he pleases about ideas presented to him. He may then retire to the position of demanding that the student know and be able to express ideas, without asking for commitment to them. This is neither an easy thing to do nor an unequivocally clear resolution of the dilemma (see p. 28 and p. 83).

Tactical aspects of the assignment of grades. In his day-to-day dealings with students the instructor will find that he can make his own work easier or his system more understandable if he does certain things not yet mentioned here. One of these is to develop some kind of cumulative grading system for his course, so that the student is able to learn easily where he stands, not merely in a particular test but in the course to date. Such a cumulative system in practice tends to carry with it a small dividend in the form of eased clerical burdens at the end of the term, merely because totaling or other tasks have been carried on throughout the term; in a large class this dividend can be quite appreciable.

The instructor must decide just how he will cumulate or average the work of the term in deciding how to assign final grades. There is a technical problem here which is sometimes not appreciated and which may involve adverse student reaction if it is not understood. To summarize the problem, if the instructor decides to assign tentative grades on each test or assignment—each time basing his marks on the usual distribution of scores—but then to assign final grades for the course on the basis of a total summation of all the raw scores earned during the term, he will find that the student does not allow (nor does he himself, oftentimes) for certain predictable consequences of this procedure. Specifically, because of the unreliability and variability in scores earned by an individual, the typical expectation is that if a student is extremely high or extremely low on a given test he will regress toward the mean on other tests. Such a student causes no particular problem if his marks are averaged or totaled, for he receives a passing mark in any case. But a student who by chance does not follow this typical pattern, perhaps receiving a succession of D's, that is, not failing any given examination, will by virtue of that somewhat exceptional consistency be found among the lowest in the class in the final tabulation of scores. Like the runners in a relay team, each man nearly the slowest in the leg of the race he runs, and in their combined performance turning out to be in last place, such a student can fail the course after having failed no individual tests. He is sure to be disturbed by a system that permits such results. (It is equally possible to find that a student who receives only B's has the highest final total in the class and receives the highest available grade; he rarely protests.)

If the instructor elects to drop the lowest mark(s) each student earns during a term this too will have certain predictable consequences. A person who was steadily near the top of his class, but not at it, will find he has competition, in the final analysis, from students who otherwise might have been pulled down below him by a single poor mark. This is less likely to attract attention than having a consistently low performer again turn out finally to be last because most of the people near him moved up in the standings when their poorest mark was discarded.

Confronted with these problems, the instructor really has only two options. The first he chooses if he feels that it really is very important to base the final mark only upon the total sample of work by the student. This is to take every step to make it clear that marks during the term are tentative, that they do not with confidence predict the final mark because the latter will be based on a final *score* total, and that technical phenomena such as regression, and failure to exhibit regression, are involved. This tactic, while it is intellectually honest, is rarely very satisfactory to the student who is impatient with explanations of why he does not receive the grade he expects, especially if someone appears to be trying to make a virtue of this fact. (The fairly common device of using summated raw scores as the basis for a final mark, but allowing for regression effects by giving a disproportionately large number of extreme grades on the separate tests, has the unfortunate effect of keeping some students partly misinformed during the course.) The other option for the instructor is to assign a grade for each item of work as the term progresses and merely to average such *grades* to indicate the cumulated standing at any point or to determine the semester total. This to some extent conceals the phenomena we have been discussing but has the value of letting the student know exactly, from the grades earned to date, where he stands and what his final mark would be if assigned at that moment. Since the practices of nonpsychologists, to which the student is accustomed, are likely to be of this second kind, it may be that this is a place where it is not worth fighting a battle; in other words, better to mark by the method the student expects and turn one's greater efforts to more important aspects of the teaching process.

Such a suggestion might imply that the different components that determine the final grade all receive equal weight, by simply being averaged. This of course need not necessarily be the case, for a weighted average could be derived for any set of components by arbitrarily weighting, say, a certain examination mark by a factor of two, or a term paper by a factor of three. Multiplying the students' scores, or their divergence from the average, by a constant will emphasize superiorities or weaknesses on the components in question, that is, a student who is far above average or below it on a certain examination can have this count twice (or any other number of times) in evaluating his total performance over the term, and any student who was not as superior or inferior as he on that test will benefit or suffer relatively less by the same weighting process. Furthermore, this procedure can be communicated to students in advance, so that there is nothing deceptive about it. On the other hand, if one has chosen the option of combining *score* components before assigning final grades, one must remember that different examination distributions weight themselves when they are combined, since the possibilities of score dispersion, and therefore for built-in weighting, tend to vary with test length. Typically, it appears that not much is gained by more elaborate weighting schemes, and it is laborious to prevent this natural weighting from occurring. Just averaging the marks as the course moves along, with heavier weights for midterm examination marks or other special components, is probably satisfactory for the great majority of teaching situations.

It has been suggested, in relation to final marks particularly, that the student may be asked to estimate his mark in advance. Then any wide discrepancies between student estimate and instructor estimate can be noted and steps taken to resolve the disagreement or see that it is understood and, preferably, accepted by the student.

One tactical problem for which there is no good solution is what to do about make-up examinations. They are almost always required, since almost always one or more students will miss any given examination. In rare circumstances one can use exactly the same examination as for the original group, hoping that there has been no passing of information or other influence upon the performance. Then the make-up can be treated as though it were an original. Under all other circumstances, however, there are complications. The make-up examination typically differs from the original in content and even in form. It cannot be given marks falling on a scale comparing closely with the scale used for the original test, since there is no common point of reference for the measurements. Furthermore the make-up test, being given to a small and often atypical segment of a class, does not produce enough data that one can confidently decide upon a new set of norms. About all that can be done is to admit the worst about the examination (at least, to one's self), read and score it as though endowed with supreme and absolute wisdom, and hope for more defensible measurement and grading of the remainder of the student's work.

On changing grades. Under the American system, where the grade obtained is so important to the student and where one wishes to be fair and reasonable in assigning grades, it is difficult to know what to do about requests that grades be reconsidered or changed. The beginning instructor needs to be forewarned about what can happen, and amusing warnings can be taken from Selle [245] and from McKeachie and Kimble [192].

In particular, the teacher needs to realize that some relatively unscrupulous students, or some students perceiving themselves in dire straits (such as being ineligible for athletic teams, or, horror of horrors, election to a sorority), may be quite skillful at eliciting agreements to change or to reconsider. One may have the experience, for example, of finding his every sympathy appealed to by a student who is "in need of" a better mark. To learn to feel calm in the face of this, he has only to have one or two students go through this act and then, upon being turned down, turn entirely cheerful, shrug their shoulders, and remark as they leave, "Well, you can't blame me for the big try." More commonly, the purely personal reasons which motivate the pressure on the instructor are concealed and requests for reconsideration involve attacks on the fairness of the questions, the adequacy of the reading of the examination, and so on. It is necessary therefore to discriminate sharply between justifiable points which the student can make on his own behalf and marginal arguments which he utilizes to put his performance in better light. In moments of utter exasperation one can take rude pleasure, if not a good example, from the story about the professor who agreed to reread every examination which students asked him to reconsider. He then uniformly found fault to the point where the total mark on the examination, after allowing the student credit for all his criticisms or complaints, was nevertheless lower than it had been before it was reread.

To avoid pressures to change grades there are certain things one can virtuously do. The best and most difficult, of course, is to create a classroom atmosphere in which it is accepted that the instructor intends to deal as exactly and fairly with each student as it is in his power to do, and students will expect grades to be assigned thoughtfully and judiciously. In such an atmosphere it is possible to discuss discrepancies between expected and actual grades in an unaggressive and reasonable way, without the student's feeling that he has to find pressures and arguments, and without the instructor's constantly feeling that he must be iron-firm and on the defensive. Many of the procedures discussed in this and the preceding chapter, particularly those aimed at keeping grading systems unambiguous, examinations up to a high standard, and communication between student and instructor effective, will reduce the student's feeling that he has been unfairly treated and negate the all-too-common tendency to find out whether the instructor can be moved. Many of the considerations in the following chapter are equally relevant.

It should not be forgotten that, as has been suggested several times before, a grading system in addition to its evaluative aspects has information aspects. The developing individual of college age needs such information for his own guidance and control of his own learning. Grading systems therefore should not become an object of derogation merely because they offer many problems, but should be taken seriously and improved as much as possible so that they serve their intended functions well.

12

MAINTAINING CLASSROOM MORALE

Treatments of certain topics in previous chapters, among them the problems of examination review, may have indicated the general tone to be expected now in my discussion of morale and discipline in an academic course. Our present concern is for the way a student feels about a course, and the way he behaves and works in it. The basic position adopted here is that in the teaching process humaneness, sensitivity, and maturity rather than harshness, unreasonableness, or whimsicality should be dominant themes. The reason for this basic position is the obvious assumption that humaneness, sensitivity, and maturity will provide a climate to facilitate the learning process, whereas the opposite kinds of instructor behavior will, in perhaps subtle or devious ways, retard the learning the instructor intends or cause undesirable learning such as a dislike of the subject.

We have stressed reducing negative aspects of examinations as a first step toward allowing their positive aspects to become pre-eminent. Now, in discussing morale, the search for factors producing the positive or favorable result must be foremost.

THE DETERMINERS OF MORALE

The word *morale* is used here as an inclusive term for all aspects of motivation and feeling which bear upon the degree of zest for learning the subject matter of a course. It is perhaps not amiss to define *zest* also, for by it is implied both strong motivation appropriate to the learning situation and the absence of detracting or competing motivations or feelings. The individual who is said to take part zestfully in a particular course is one who enjoys it, works hard at it, takes pleasures in its rewards, and all in all finds the learning process to contain a degree of excitement for him. Morale as a term can apply to an individual's reaction to a course, or it can apply to the reactions of a class as a whole. We shall use it here rather more, but not exclusively, in the latter meaning, and make an effort to identify some of the determiners of class morale, together with some of the manners of variation of those determiners.

Subject matter interest. First we may look for the positive motivation which draws a student into a course and carries him along in it. We can hope that this is a direct intellectual concern for the subject matter. We are likely to find, however, all manner of subsidiary (sometimes competing) motivations: the course may be thought to have practical, job-getting uses, it may satisfy a specific degree requirement, it may fall at a convenient hour, the instructor may have a reputation for being amusing, or one's good friend may be going to take it. The important thing about these motivations is that they do help to bring the student into the course and will hold him there so long as the course holds promise for satisfying these particular motives or new ones instilled by the course itself or by other circumstances.

Psychology is in the fortunate position of dealing with a subject matter which is inherently interesting to people of college age. An interest in people, in self-analysis, in psychological forces in the world about us, in the psychological aspects of a career or of personal decisions or adjustments to military service, marriage, and community life—these are concerns which characterize the typical college student and in a sense are legitimized for him in a psychology course. In one way or another his psychological instruction will relate to these concerns. He will respond positively except as the instructor or the text or other aspects of the course frustrate him by turning interesting topics into boring ones or by doing other things which create negative motivation.

Something of a problem is created here for the instructor, of course, by the fact that much modern literature, and much motion-picture and newspaper material, whets the student's interests by spectacular (and typically nonscientific) treatments of various topics, especially the bizarre or seemingly mysterious. If the teacher does not then directly and promptly engage in discussions of perversion, hypnosis, insanity, telepathy, and so on, it may be difficult to make his students see why he starts where he does and approaches problems of behavior in the spirit that he does. Be that as it may, there are basic interests the instructor can capitalize on, so that he needs primarily to develop skills in showing students how their basic interests will be satisfied by his approach to the subject matter.

Presumably morale will be heightened or maintained in proportion to his success in doing this, and it is the mark of a good teacher that he is aware of what he can do to keep interest high—and does it. He will, for one thing, make liberal use of concrete examples or demonstrations in his classroom presentations as the best way for making clear the connection between general principles and the ever present student concern with the individual instance (often, his own). He will take time for deliberate analysis of the relevance of certain topics or discussions to student needs or interests. He will see to it that students feel involved in the course, whether by way of their classroom participation or by their aid in setting, or at least modifying, class objectives or procedures. As we have said before, he will take special pains to develop sensitivity to how a sophomore thinks, i.e., for the particular forms which late-adolescent interests take in the groups he must deal with, realizing that these are not the same in co-educational as in monosexual institutions, or in municipally supported adult-education classes as in private liberal arts colleges of the expensive variety, or in students drawn from different basic curriculums of his own institution. He will be concerned for the maintenance of variety in classroom style or presentation or procedures. He is likely to ensure as best he can that essential but less interesting topics are not clustered together in some particular portion of the course (especially at the beginning) where they may extinguish the interest of those in whom it is weakening anyway. And if he has the capacity to do it, he will style his own behavior in such a way that it makes attendance at class the more attractive for his students.

Knowing what can be achieved. Our discussion of subject matter interests has referred to factors which psychologists would classify as both drives and incentives. Nevertheless it could be written to show that it is centered primarily about the first of these, particularly as the (mainly social) drives relate to underlying drives which in turn are closely related to the individual's biological development. We shall speak now of the role in morale of the student's understanding of what he can hope to achieve in a course. This is a more direct reference to the incentives which he may attain in the satisfaction of whatever drives bring him into a course and carry him along. The point here seems to be that motivation is more effective when activity is stimulated and directed, not merely by the goading drive, but also in an effective way by the goals or incentives offered. As these are made more specific and clear-cut, more readily perceived or discriminated, their consequences for individual action tend to be more predictable. In the context of teaching, then, we may expect student motivation and morale to be higher where the goals of a course are clear and acceptable to the student, where the subgoals such as assignments and examinations are clear and specific, and where the day-to-day activities of the course are made to pertain to the attainment of the accepted goals. Confidence that the job to be done in a course is a reasonable one, i.e., that a person who is willing to work can attain the objectives, is a necessary consideration in evaluating the effectiveness of goals, for a clear-cut but definitely impossible goal is likely to be self-defeating. This is perhaps a way of saying that the knowledge a student has about what he is to do, or what is expected of him, should not include items of information which arouse negative motivation unduly. (In the collegiate world as elsewhere work has both negative and positive aspects. It is likely to be found that a student does not mind working extremely hard if he can feel that something good is being accomplished or will finally result, and contrariwise, the negative aspects of work become prominent only when the consequences of the work are not satisfying.)

Personal status protection. The student, being in the position where he does not know and is expected to learn, is by definition capable of being exposed to criticism, ridicule, or other punishments for inadequacy. By the time he has arrived at college status he has learned to want to protect himself against such consequences of relations with other people, and his positive motivation for a course will be weakened if he must spend energy and concern on self-protection just to remain in that course.

One of the ways of making a student feel that his self-esteem is protected has been suggested earlier: giving information about marks and similar measures of status in a private way, if it is at all possible to do this. If a student wishes to announce his own marks, he can of course do so, but the instructor at least is not then in the position of having done it for the person who wished privacy.

One of the most important protections to the student is to make it clear that he has the right to be ignorant, provided that he does not insist on being ignorant about the same things for the duration of the course, or on imposing on the rights of others by the way he chooses the time and place to expose his ignorance. Criticism directed at the personality of the student who in good faith asks a question, or advances a counter-idea of his own which is not well founded, or about which he is supposed to have read, is not nearly so likely to make him wish to learn better as it is to make him resent the implication that he is not working in good faith, or that he is stupid. Voeks [271] has shown in student questionnaire data that of all the measurable differences between teachers rated good and those rated poor, one of the most obvious is the greater degree to which the latter use ridicule and sarcasm in the classroom. The right to be ignorant should also include the right to approach the instructor. This is discouraged not merely by aggressive or coldly indifferent responses to student remarks or questions in class, but also by such behavior as coming at the last minute to the classroom, fleeing immediately at the end of the period, and otherwise not being available to students for consultations or discussions.

In the American code competition is everywhere a dominant theme, and the developing individual is taught very sensitive reactions to the way the competition is carried out. Since the classroom with its grading system is a competitive situation, no matter how much one may wish to avoid that, an important element in status protection is protection of opportunity for fair competition. To turn this around for the moment, the instructor cannot afford to threaten the main group in a class by special favors to any subgroup or any individual in the class, at least as respects the main object of competition—grades. The instructor may not realize that attendance at social functions of the local chapter of his own college fraternity makes students dubious as to whether he will give equal breaks to all students when he hands out grades. He may unwittingly be too generous or too severe in dealing with a Negro student, a crippled student, a beautiful girl, or other minority group members (who, after all, may deserve either the lowest or the highest marks he can give), and it is very easy to depart from what appears to be equal treatment for all when dealing with the college athletes, or the departmental majors one has in the front row. Usually a distinction can successfully be made between, on the one hand, giving extra attention to students who need it or less attention to students who do not really need it and, on the other hand, the process of making judgments upon students, that is, grading them. Furthermore, it is possible to demonstrate this distinction to students, by making it clear to the whole group that one will give all the attention necessary to any student who wants to master the subject matter, that all are equally free to demand this attention, but that this variable has nothing to do with the final assessment and grading. If such an atmosphere is created, the athlete may thereafter avail himself of special conferences, or the bright and pretty girl may ask a disproportionate number of questions in class, without the notion that either is currying or receiving special favor threatening the competitive aspirations of the remaining students. Perhaps another way of viewing this is to say that one should make clear *all* the ground rules under which the fundamental goals of the course are to be achieved, and then be entirely certain to stick to those rules.

In relation to protection of the personal status of the student we must mention one further problem which is almost peculiar to American psychology. This is the problem of exploitation of the student for the purposes of research (see the related and more general considerations by Berg [26] and Sinick [246]). It is widespread practice to use students in this way, and in many instances the experience is educationally beneficial. All too often, however, the experience is partly or wholly a mere exploitation of the student for the presumed good of the science or, more bluntly, the good of the investigator. In larger departments, where communication is not close between researchers who may want subjects and instructors who supply them, it may even be that the investigators (including Ph.D. candidates) view it as one of their rights that they shall have the time and responses of undergraduates for use in their work. Even if the instructor takes the initiative and warns his colleagues about the problem, he may find that periodically (corresponding approximately to the length of a student generation at the Ph.D. level) his colleagues return to exploitive practices. Especially if he is a junior member of the faculty he may find that a senior member may attempt to pull rank on him in a rush effort to gather data in a study not foreseen when the instructor was planning how to use his course hours. Some of the specific sins of psychologists in this setting (see the booklet on ethical standards [7, pp. 95-96]) have been: seeking student co-operation by promising information in return, then failing to follow through; lying to students or using painful or unexpected stimulation; insisting on retests the student had not contracted for; pressing for very personal data in a routine way; and so on.

To protect against exploitation and upsetting schedules the instructor will have to lay a heavy hand on the choice of projects in which his students will be invited to participate. He will have to be careful to permit only projects for which there is educational justification, i.e., they illustrate or teach, or the investigator can and will teach, or the instructor can teach, something related to the course objectives. He will have to make it clear that service as a subject, or that quality of service from the investigator's viewpoint, has no bearing on the grade which he assigns—unless he is willing to ask his college faculty to approve graded service in experiments as a component of education suitable for being counted toward the bachelor's degree. He will have to make sure that investigators keep appointments; inform students as to the meaning of the procedures they go through (sooner or later, depending upon what the timing might do to the data); do not do unpleasant or surprising things to students without their advance consent to this kind of procedure, and even then do not breach ordinary codes for decency or humaneness in interpersonal relations; do not ask for excessive amounts of time; and above all, take steps to ensure a positive reaction on the part of the student, whether this be a feeling that he has learned something about how psychologists work, or that he has contributed to science even though he does not comprehend fully how he did it. In part these steps may be taken via a printed code for investigators, as McKeachie and Kimble [192, pp. 50-52] suggest. I have done this for a good many years, and think it necessary and worthwhile, but in need of supplementation by personal vigilance and communication.

Confidence in the instructor. In any situation structured so that there are both leaders and followers or group members, it is reasonable to suppose that favorable expectations both about the leader's ability to lead on to goal attainment and about the methods he uses are conducive to conviction that the goal can be reached. Translated, this seems to mean that students ought to have confidence in the person who heads their class work. It then becomes worthwhile to ask what traits he may exhibit to enhance this confidence.

There is a very large literature on student reactions to and evaluations of instruction (from which the following are selected as representative: [24, 25, 38, 69, 81, 93, 115, 126]). The methods of sampling and analyzing student reaction, and the samples of students studied, are so varied that it is difficult to summarize the results in a way that would be acceptable to more than a few of the authors cited. I shall nevertheless try here to choose what seem to be important nonmethodological findings (problems of methodology are discussed in Chap. 14).

In the earlier discussion of status protection certain instructor traits were mentioned, prominent among them being fairness in dealings with students. Fairness is an eminently desirable trait, to judge from student questionnaire results, and the instructor needs to take pains, not merely to be fair, but to be perceived as fair—through, for example, making perfectly plain how he arrives at the grades over which he expends so much conscientious worry. In addition to this, it appears important that the teacher be perceived as professionally competent and well prepared for organized presentation. The appearance of self-confidence is involved here; students become concerned if the instructor seems overly unsure of himself. Conversely, a willingness to admit an occasional error and correct it is regarded as human and desirable evidence that a fundamental self-confidence exists. Bluffing or covering up, if ever detected, is fatal to the student's attitude toward the instructor; inevitably he recognizes these as signs of incompetence. A third trait conducive to confidence in leadership is the degree of enthusiasm and conviction which the instructor evinces in his subject matter and in his classroom procedures. The parallel is an absence of cynicism, of boredom, and of touchiness. The instructor may at times become tired of hearing that he ought to be enthusiastic, especially in repeat sessions of a single course, or during his fourth class hour of the day, but he must nevertheless admit that signs of strong motivation in himself are likely, through the social learning his students have undergone, to arouse a supplementary motivation capable of becoming central, as enthusiasms can, in his students.

A fourth instructor trait very worthy of mention is that of empathy with or responsiveness to students. We can include here, not only the approachability and responsiveness to questions or criticisms mentioned previously, but also signs of an up-to-date understanding of typical student problems and attitudes. This latter characteristic is something which develops with experience, it appears, for the way in which an experienced instructor understands and responds to student problems, or student modes of thought, is likely to be quite different from the way in which the newly fledged Ph.D. perceives and responds to student problems. Assuming this interpretation is correct, the instructor's responses to the student must show that the student's world is adequately perceived by the instructor, else how can he deal with exactly those matters which the student needs to have clarified? As a fifth distinguishable trait bearing upon student confidence in the instructor we need to mention the essential ability to maintain intellectual leadership. This after all defines the reason for having an instructor. So it is that he must in the main be superior in knowledge, in analytical power and other intellectual and personal resources, without being so superior that he scares off those who might be led by him, and without attempting, in an egalitarian society, to presume he has other kinds of superiority. He must maintain ordinary social discipline, as will be discussed below, but this in the interests of intellectual discipline. All in all, he must be sufficiently sensitive socially to maintain a degree of social distance that helps structure the situation for students, i.e., helps them to know where they stand and where he stands in relation to them and the attainment of their goals, without creating barriers to effective communication. Perhaps one could put all of the traits discussed above into the one general category of traits which in the classroom as elsewhere in social intercourse make for the appearance of maturity and attractiveness, and thus for social effectiveness. This way of viewing instructor qualities helps to put in proper perspective the effect on teacher evaluation of such matters as dress, voice quality, rate of speech, and mannerisms. These, short of extremes producing annoyance, are evidently not fundamental.

Atmosphere. By the social atmosphere of a class is meant the kind and quality of interpersonal relations in it between instructor and students and among students. It would have been possible to reorganize much of the foregoing discussion into an analysis of classroom atmosphere and its effect upon the learning process, but at the present time it is not clear whether that would have been a better way to present those ideas that have been presented. The concept of atmosphere, possessing the degree of generality that it does, however, leads us to mention here two additional factors relevant to class morale.

The first factor is found in the characteristics of individual students who make up a class, particularly the smaller one where individuality as such can make its mark. The atmosphere of a classroom is definitely and immediately affected if the group happens to contain a chronic griper, an overly talkative or sociable individual, or a few students who are patently uninterested. It is here that the skills of the best teachers show themselves most quickly and subtly. They find ways, disciplinary or other, of responding to the basic characteristics of the students (not necessarily the surface signs) so as to involve the deviationists in the work of the course and to remove or reduce individuality hampering the work of the group (or of the individual himself) while leaving untouched such individuality as is irrelevant to these objectives.

The second determiner of atmosphere not included under the heading of instructor behavior or individual student characteristics is that of the extra-class or pre-course setting in which the course is given. By this is meant such things as local expectations as to how instructors in general operate, or as to how classes should be organized and conducted, or expectations (reputation) concerning the particular instructor. Such expectations contribute to the success or failure of any method of instruction, whether conventional or experimental, and also to the success of the instructor whose reputation is known to all or part of his students. There is always a fast-travelling student lore according to which certain courses, departments, or instructors are expected to be easy or stiff, queer or good fun, and so on. Unfortunately, it sometimes appears, this lore is reinforced by the faculty and administration at registration time by the advice they give students in consultations about courses to take. However these expectations develop, the instructor must be as fully cognizant of them as he can and allow for their effects among the multiple determiners of the morale he can expect in any particular group. If he knows his last group of students valued his course, he can be more jaunty in his expectations of the next group. If for any reason he, or his predecessor, had trouble in the course, he had best redouble his efforts to overcome the effects of rumor and casual comment and make clear from the beginning just what the course is now like, preferably without references to previous versions, which put him on the defensive unnecessarily.

DISCIPLINE

By the word *discipline* here is meant the maintenance of a degree of order, attention, and responsiveness in the classroom and in the relation between instructor and student that is conducive to carrying on the main business of an academic course. Unfortunately, the word for most of us has mainly negative connotations, relating to the punishments meted out to children. The position taken here will stress the opposite view, namely that discipline is best achieved by positive influences which attract the individual to his task, rather than by negative ones which merely repel him from the distracting interest or the undesirable kind of behavior. The instructor is here regarded as working in the service of, not in command of, students. A mature kind of interaction between him and his students, implying mutual trust and respect, is assumed to be the desirable state of affairs. Even where specific discipline in the regulative sense is required, the emphasis should be on learning the underlying causes of undesirable behavior, if it is at all reasonable and possible to do so, and dealing with these rather than with the symptoms as such. This effort is basic to making discipline bear upon changing the behavior of the student or the class, rather than merely making the instructor feel better. In a sense, all the advice which can be given to the beginning instructor, in this context, is contained in a nutshell: Do everything possible to build good morale in your classes. Then disciplinary problems as such rarely occur, and if they do, in occasional atypical individuals, the problems are easily dealt with because the remainder of the class is not even covertly aiding and abetting the individuals who are causing themselves or others trouble.

Discipline in general. It is nevertheless necessary not to be surprised if marginal or outright disciplinary problems occur in any course, particularly in any institution which does not have a dominating intellectual tradition or firm control over admissions policies. The instructor must deal with such problems when they occur if he is to maintain in the eyes of his students the position of leadership which they are initially willing to accord him. The way each problem is to be handled obviously depends upon the circumstances, but certain very general principles may be stated.

The first is that disciplinary action against a group or an individual is justified only when educational objectives are being defeated. Matters of social custom, to be specific, do not become objects of control or discipline by the instructor as an individual unless they in some way are distracting and prevent attention to the main objects of a course or a classroom procedure. For example, questions of dress, in which college students tend to be thoroughly faddish and at times extreme, are hardly the business of the individual instructor unless something in the adoption of a particular manner of dress (to take an interesting fantasy, well-formed young ladies wearing bathing suits to class) interferes with teaching and learning. This is not to imply that the institution as a whole, concerned as it must be with its public relations and with the all-round development of its students to the point where they are ready to assume their places in ordinary society when they leave college, should have no regard for the personal behavior of students. It may happen, in fact, that the institution may find rules necessary to govern dress or conduct (e.g., smoking in classroom, as mentioned previously), and then it may indeed become the business of the individual instructor to work for compliance with those rules, if only because deviations from them again become a distracting object of attention in his own classroom. Even though he does not feel that it is his place to enforce any rules of this kind, or when there happen to be none bearing upon what he regards as nonadult conduct, he may, in a natural way if his position as leader in the group is clear, express his opinions about such conduct; he may at the same time find it necessary to reiterate that such opinions do not bear upon marks in his course.

A second general principle is that disciplinary action is not justified unless there was prior knowledge of the rule or custom which has been breached. It may safely be assumed that most college students know most of the time when they are breaking ordinary rules or customs concerning social intercourse—talking out of place, cheating, disruptive horseplay in class, and so on, are the sorts of behavior which have been regarded as undesirable since childhood. On the other hand, most academic situations contain a good many less generally known social rules, and each instructor, or each course, may have particular rules governing conduct. It is in relation to the latter two classes of rules that the instructor must be careful to have given the clearest possible initial statement, lest he do an injustice with respect to what, after all, may be a breach of no more than an operating convenience. (The rule "No make-up examinations given without a *medical* excuse," which is ordinarily used to prevent wholesale absences from class, should not be interpreted as regulating absences justified on some other ground, such as need to help in a family crisis.)

The third general rule can be phrased: "Don't start anything unless you know exactly why, and where it can or will lead." In other words, discipline based on impulse rather than diagnosis and executed with lack of foresight as to its implications, or discipline which does not take full account of local tradition or administrative backing, is very likely to be self-defeating. In addition, it is well to remember that the kind of disciplinary action required in dealing with young adults is quite different from that which the new instructor may have used in dealing with the only persons over whom he may have disciplinary responsibility previously, namely children, and he may not so confidently expect that he can predict the outcome of his attempts at discipline. They can often backfire and embarrass him in dealing with individuals who, after all, are very nearly his age peers. I recall here the instance of a young colleague of mine who became exasperated, in an evening class, with a young man who at each weekly meeting dropped off, not merely to sleep but also to snore. In irritation one evening he tossed a blackboard eraser at the young man. His aim was bad but the clatter awoke the man, the class was amused and enlivened, and the whole disciplinary action could be called a success, at least in a way. A few weeks after this, however, a young lady fell asleep in class. Almost unthinkingly the instructor reached for a piece of chalk, to be tossed not at her but in her general direction. Unhappily, the chalk unerringly disappeared inside the top of the young lady's dress, just under her nodding chin. This particular type of disciplinary action thereafter disappeared from the instructor's repertoire in favor of more predictable methods.

A fourth suggestion to the beginning instructor is that he should be as consistent as he reasonably can with himself and with the rules he has accepted or adopted for his course. This point can be analyzed further. Suppose that on one occasion a class is getting somewhat restive because a single student dominates the question asking, but is quieted and rewarded for its patience by redirection of the questions to the class so that others have a chance to participate, while on another occasion the question asking by the dominant student is broken off only after the restiveness becomes so great that he cannot readily be heard, and then the instructor simply goes on to the next lecture topic. Here the members of the class are rewarded once for being quiet, once for being restive and noisy, the stimulus occasion being approximately the same. Consistent behavior thereafter by students can hardly be expected, since the instructor is himself inconsistent in his handling of problem situations as they arise. (Note that the kind of consistency here recommended—consistency in matters defining the *type* of relation between instructor and students—is not intended to stifle variety or even unpredictability in the types of behaviors acceptable within that relation.)

One more suggestion can be made to the beginning instructor: "Be firm about it." If an instructor can be bluffed out of a disciplinary intention, the student is likely to perceive this as indicative of a lack of self-confidence. Uncertainty of disciplinary action may of course indicate nothing whatever about the teacher's competence in his subject matter, but there is a good chance that some students will nevertheless generalize to that aspect of teacher behavior in a way which is unfortunate for conduct of the class. It should perhaps be unnecessary to add that firmness, as recommended here, is hardly synonymous with willful or whimsical stubbornness, but rather with the quiet and unwavering follow-through of whatever disciplinary action is thoroughly required by a situation.

Discipline in particular. Ruefully recalled experiences of classroom teachers in a wide variety of colleges suggest that there are certain predictable problems in discipline, and certain situations conducive to the development of disciplinary problems. To the extent that we can anticipate the problems, or what can happen in the situations, we enhance our confidence that this aspect of teaching can be coped with as necessary.

There is often a question, for example, about what to do concerning attendance at class. In rare instances attendance is completely optional, by institutional practice; in other rare instances, attendance is completely required, and the institution rather than the instructor provides the enforcement mechanism. Between these extremes is the far more common situation in which the instructor, partly governed by unenforced or partially enforced institutional rules and partly activated by his own concerns for mastery of his subject matter, frets over attendance. Several suggestions can be made to him. One is that when attendance is made necessary by rules, it can be expected that the rules will be resented and by-passed (the self-evident virtue of good teaching is nowhere more evident than in its ability to cause regular attendance at class). One therefore cannot institute a set of rules without going the whole way to allow for all contingencies, nor can he get away with enforcing the rules halfheartedly. Provision must be made for someone to take attendance regularly and without exception; for deciding whether a student shall be marked tardy or absent when he comes in, e.g., 15 minutes late for a 50-minute class; for recording justified absences, saying what the justifications are, and indicating how many of them may be taken without threat to credit for the course; for recording make-up work; or for any other variation in conduct from the perfect attendance record. It becomes evident that enforcing attendance regulations in the necessary legalistic way easily becomes a nuisance and an interference with more pleasant or important functions. Many instructors therefore, unless they are somehow forced into it, prefer to concentrate on the positive aspects of teaching and let this take care of attendance. After all, they can say with a reasonably clear conscience, students forced to come to class are likely to learn very little while there.

Even though one may not require attendance at class, he is likely to have students who are tardy much more often than is conducive to good performance on their part, or who are tardy in greater numbers than is conducive to a good beginning of a class hour for the whole class. In large classes a formal rule may be instituted according to which any student entering the room after the class has begun must sit in a special section provided near the door, so that he does not push his way to a regular seat in the main body of the class. If, when the rule is established and clear, a student nevertheless happens to interrupt the work of the group, the instructor can use the technique of making the interruption so conspicuous that the individual in question is made to realize that he bothers his peers, whether he cares about bothering the instructor or not. For this purpose, and this applies to any size of class, the most polite and perhaps the most useful device is for the instructor to stop talking, preferably somewhat dramatically in the middle of a sentence, or to make a gesture holding up any discussion which is in progress, and merely wait and watch while the offending individual finds his place. Sarcastic remarks or other signs of aggression are hardly useful because while they might suitably embarrass the offender, they run the risk of arousing the sympathies of other students and thus alienating the class from the instructor. Repeated tardiness, like repeated infraction of any necessary rule or common custom, is best dealt with by private summons to the individual in question for discussion outside of class. It fairly often turns out that such cases stem from what will be regarded by the instructor as reasonable causes (such as a previous class in a far building, an unfavorable commuter train schedule, a job of a kind not to be left by a clock schedule in order to attend class). Frequently, also, the behavior is merely symptomatic of some other kind of problem, which the instructor may be able to help solve. In any event, the private talk is likely to make the regulative influence upon the student's conduct more pointed and less arousing of defenses. It is therefore likely to be more effective than a publicly administered rebuke.

Every now and then, even in classes where morale is good, there is likely to be some action which competes unduly with the main business of the group. This may take the form of knitting, lengthy whispered interchanges, private mumbled conversations with an outburst of muffled laughter, obvious reading of a newspaper as a sign of boredom, or whatever else may strike the fancy of a restless young man or woman. This kind of classroom disturbance usually occurs when a few students are not at the moment strongly interested in what the majority is interested in. (If it is the majority which is uninterested, the instructor had better look to his teaching, not to his disciplinary skills.) Such behavior should not at all be confused with the noise, argumentation, and subconversations which can arise in a class where all this furor merely reflects the involvement of the students in the subject matter rather than any essential lack of control or order.

Perhaps the most useful suggestion that can be made, where lack of interest is the nub of the problem, is to make the asocial action perceptible or conspicuous by becoming quiet, or momentarily quieting the main discussion, watching the individuals who are causing trouble, and thus drawing the attention of the whole group to their conduct. This sort of technique obviously is better used where the offending student is actively doing something than where his offense lies mostly in a retreat of some kind, such as hiding behind a newspaper. In the latter instance remarks (again, not sarcastic but rather pleasantly joking if possible) may be necessary, merely to draw attention. And there is always the classic example of the student who repeatedly goes to sleep in class. In all likelihood, such a student should be summoned for discussion outside class. Both the guilty reaction of a student awakened in class and the reaction of others who sympathize with him are sufficiently unpredictable that the instructor will do well not to expect a useful result from classroom pouncing. Generally speaking, the instructor needs to develop tolerance for misconduct in just the right amount to permit overlooking the occasional or the random event, yet not to cause carelessness in dealing with distracting deviations.

A frustrating problem for the instructor becomes evident fairly often in the student who, according to everything that can be learned about him and his situation, simply does not work hard enough, who means well but is distracted by countermotivations, or who hasn't yet learned that successful college work is neither child's play nor a four-year pleasure jaunt. Assuming that all the positive things that can be done in general already have been done to make the course and the material in it effective, what can the instructor do for, to, or with such a student? All suggestions obviously have to be taken with a grain of salt, but here are some. First, taking a direct interest in the student, without stressing the fact that he has not been working hard enough, and doing this by calling him in for conferences, personal quizzing and review, and so on, all on a time schedule which will require him to work or look foolish, may dislodge him from his neutrality. Second, finding a special assignment, task, or commitment for the student so that he realizes that he as an individual really counts, both in the class and in the teacher's perception, may enliven him. And third, acting on the assumption that in the American credo laziness is akin to sin, the instructor may simply tell the student he has been lazy and that better things are expected in the future. (A good many immature students, who in college are for the first time in their lives free of schedules and timely injunctions to get their work done, and in whom self-discipline has not yet developed, may actually feel relieved to have the instructor become something of a stern father-figure who says: "Now you get busy, and I want to see this job done by such-and-such a time," and will respond by getting to work. This is not necessarily bad for the student's development toward maturity, particularly if this very aspect of his behavior can be dealt with subtly, and in due time, in his relationship with the instructor.)

Perhaps the most important disciplinary problem of all in our relations with students, because it may involve the student of high morale as well as the student of low morale, is more nearly on the intellectual than on the social level. By this I refer to the common occurrence of disorderly or nonsequential thought, the introduction of irrelevant ideas into discussions, striving for the spectacular rather than the sound conclusion, leaping to a conclusion or a practical judgment before it is warranted, trying to bluff or overpower another person rather than paying attention to his ideas, and similar devices. One of the greatest contributions an instructor can make to the development of his students is the encouragement in them of orderly and thorough habits of thought. These we all regard as necessary attributes of scholarly practice, but we may forget that in addition to aiding the student to memorize the substance of ideas, it is necessary constantly to exemplify and help him achieve the scholarly approach to thought itself. For this reason, although it is a different order of problem than that involved in missing lectures or disruptive laughter in class, the instructor needs to introduce discipline by pointing out whenever necessary the immature or inadequate modes of thought or expression, and in this way to conduct a course which is both substantial and intellectually clean-cut. And, as might be expected, this ability to deal with both the ideas that arise and the manner in which they are arrived at develops with teaching experience. In the beginning the instructor is likely to be very busy sorting out the ideas as such, accepting and rejecting according to his own standards, and thus not becoming familiar with or learning how to deal with the sometimes weird and wonderful ways in which students can arrive at or formulate ideas.

MORALE, DISCIPLINE, AND LOCAL CULTURE

The discussion of this chapter may in a sense leave the new instructor in conflict: he is evidently supposed to be democratic and sensitive to the rights and feelings of his students, yet he may feel he is supposed to be a consistent and conscientious disciplinarian. The resolution of any such felt conflict comes about when he realizes that to a large extent his problem is that of finding a proper role for himself in his classroom and of handling that role in such a way that the work of others is facilitated. In this context, both responsiveness and firmness, or both reasonableness and unwavering resistance, or both friendliness and maintenance of the right to criticize and evaluate may in their time and place be adaptive and appropriate behaviors. With this as background one small heresy must be declared: It does not appear to me that uniformly and always an altogether democratic approach is sure to be best in the classroom, or that any other single approach is best. Rather, for certain kinds of instructor personalities, or certain groups of students, or certain aspects of subject matter, or at certain times in a course, a relatively authoritarian approach may be best, or even a laissez-faire attitude on the part of the instructor. (Wispe [283] anticipates part of this.) Thus, freshmen learning to think independently and to speak up for themselves are different from a group of senior majors reviewing the history of their discipline in preparation for comprehensive examinations. A young, outgoing instructor personality is different from an austere middle-aged one. Grammar is different from logic, Fordham is different from Bennington. It all depends upon what one wants to achieve and in what context. What one should want to achieve should depend, certainly, upon factors over and above the wishes of the instructor—not alone the wishes of the class, but judgment as to what the class needs and as to the role the course fulfills in the over-all educational development of the students or in the over-all program of the institution. What is the best relationship with students follows from such judgments.

13

ADVISING AND COUNSELING

This chapter is not written for the specialist in advising and counseling, but rather for the person who must carry on such activities as part of a job devoted primarily to other responsibilities.

Although it has been given a multitude of meanings in recent years, the word *counseling* is to be used here as a term for person-to-person relationships with students, in which either one may give or seek information, render opinions, or reach decisions, but the sense nevertheless is that the faculty member is more mature, or better informed, or capable of fuller understanding than the student, and thus can aid him. In the discussion which follows, no particular point of view is assumed about the nature of the psychological processes involved, nor is there any overriding assumption about what kind of role the counselor plays in his actual contacts with the student. The term *advising* is the common one in the academic world for the variety of counseling situation in which simple academic problems or routines are handled. In such situations only relatively simple matters are treated—although it might be more accurate to say that the problems and routines are treated *as though* rational solutions were available with only the addition of relevant information to that already possessed by the student. The average faculty member in the typical department tends more often to serve as adviser than he does as counselor, but the two expressions will be used somewhat interchangeably here.

It is apparent from what has just been said that counseling situations may at one extreme hardly require any counsel at all, in the sense of aid to decision making, because the relationship between student and instructor is brief and noninvolving, sometimes requiring nothing more than a signature. Ranging to the other extreme are situations which are deeply involving and require much time, or which are so complex or serious that they raise immediately the question of whether they should be handled by an ordinary faculty member. It is also apparent that the skills necessary for competence in academic counseling vary all the way from simple knowledge about the institutional catalogue and rules to those which are basically psychiatric and therapeutic in nature. The American college has not yet come to present a consistent picture in the way the faculty and staff are assigned to the range of problems they are competent to deal with. Thus the individual faculty member bears most of the responsibility for deciding how much student advising and counseling to take upon himself, and when to do so, and how much is the affair of institutional orientation, counseling, tutoring, reading improvement, financial, vocational guidance, and psychiatric services. Unfortunately, all too often this individual faculty member does not realize that these services exist, or does not discriminate the point in his relations with students at which such services ought to be utilized.

The position of the psychologist. The psychologist is in a somewhat unusual position in relation to counseling and student personnel problems. He is more likely than most faculty members to be sensitized to the existence of student-aid services, and in addition he perceives himself, and is perceived by many others on the faculty and in the student body, as having at least some degree of professional competence to deal with certain classes of student problems. (As Wrenn [290] has remarked, the kinds of problems college students have are diagnosed differently depending upon the officer of the institution who sees them; financial officers tend to think of the problems as financial because those are the ones they encounter most often; deans of students often believe that social adjustment is the common problem; mental health specialists see the widespread influence of personal adjustment problems; and so on.) The psychologist might feel somewhat flattered at the expectation others seem to have of him were it not for two factors. He, like other faculty members, is harried for time and does not like to inherit an undue proportion of the student problems others have not dealt with; and in these days of specialization and professionalization in psychology, he may realize he has not had the training of an expert, regardless of how laymen may regard him. Considering his background and everyday duties, his position as regards problems of counseling is perhaps more like that of a nonpsychologist than it is like that of psychological experts employed to work in that field. Yet he cannot disregard the fact that advising and counseling as faculty activities grow very naturally out of any genuine contact with students, and have an important bearing on morale and discipline in a course. He must therefore feel the same responsibility for going as far as he should and has time to go in this sphere of activity as he does in others—such as preparing the materials he is to teach. Another way of saying the same thing is that the good teacher uses every means at his command to facilitate the learning of his students, and very often it turns out that some degree of counseling, in some degree related to what has occurred in his course, is required to free or direct a student toward better learning.

A few years ago, within the first few lectures in the elementary course which I began to teach almost upon arrival at a new university job, I was asked the common question about the differences among clinical psychology, general psychology, psychiatry, and psychoanalysis. Somewhere during the process of discussing this question, and I do not even remember how, I happened to make a rather casual side remark complimenting my new university upon the fact that in it a concern for mental health and the use of psychiatric services seemed to be entirely socially acceptable and ordinary. I learned some weeks later that these remarks had been reported by some six members of this class of less than 150, when these six persons presented themselves to the mental health department, as reassuring them to the point where they finally sought the help they felt they needed. The incident illustrates a further and unique problem for the college teacher of psychology: He must be aware that his choice of subject matter, the attitude in which he deals with various topics, and the kinds of relationships he builds with his students all will have a bearing upon the expressed need of those students for further exploration of the self-applications which students continually make of the academic and pure psychology they supposedly study.

A half-hour spent on problems of social acceptance or upon parent-child relations stands a very good chance of arousing anxiety in some student, or reassuring him about the reception he might get, to the point where he wants to talk further with his instructor about the matter, and usually in relation to an identified individual. (Very commonly, he consciously displaces his identity, at least initially, upon his roommate or someone else to make it easier to discuss the problem.) This is a chance to do very effective person-to-person teaching; it is also a situation in which time demands, or demands for professional skill both in unraveling what lies behind the approach and in dealing with it, may go beyond what the instructor can meet. It is for this reason that unless he is appointed to do counseling and given time for it he must always in his teaching consider the extent to which he should avoid discussion or reading which arouses feelings about which the institution and the instructor are not prepared to do an ethically defensible job. It is necessary to realize that institutions vary widely in their attitudes or facilities in such matters. Some provide systematically for all the necessary services and specialized staff. Others labor inadequately with the problem because they do not have funds or are not free from antiquated custom. And still others are like an institution in which I once taught, where the president was reported to have said that money need not be wasted on psychiatrists and their ilk because the upstanding young men and women who came to that institution were not such weaklings as to have problems they could not handle by themselves.

KINDS OF PROBLEMS

On the assumption that we are here dealing with a relatively restricted conception of advising and counseling, one not including major personality modifications, we can discuss the most common problems which the new instructor can expect, some of the kinds of causal factors that may be involved, and what may commonly be done about them. Problems more complex than these, or problems unique to the institution, will require other learning by the instructor or the utilization of specialists.

Difficulties in a course. Just as the grade a student finally earns in a course tends to be a composite of all the evaluations of his work, both expressed and unexpressed, so the fact that he has difficulty in a course tends to be produced by a composite of both understood and not understood causes. The student, in the great majority of instances, opens his conversation thus: "I don't know why it is, but I study harder for this course than any other, and it's very well taught, and still I just don't get it." It is likely that the student, who by this statement gives no information that the instructor does not already have, has tried to diagnose his own difficulties. He may be quite accurate in this diagnosis and merely feel a need to have someone encourage or force him to follow out the cures he has readily available—such as studying more, or getting more sleep—or he may literally need help in reaching both an understanding of his difficulties and a planned solution to them. The experienced instructor expects in an actuarial way that certain factors may be involved, and either gets the student to analyze them or leads him into an analysis of them. Yet just what really brought the student in may remain bafflingly obscure. Only more talk, more explanation, more analysis, is likely to help. In such cases the student is not very likely to turn up at long last a neatly placarded explanation of his presence. Hence the emphasis, in what follows, on patience, on inference, and on continued good personal relations with the student so that optimum conditions are provided for eventual mutual understanding of the problem.

Very commonly the student, especially a freshman or sophomore, has not yet built study habits appropriate to the college level. He may attempt to study under unfavorable physical conditions—with the radio roaring or with people talking, he may have irregular hours or places of study, or he may not realize how his physiological condition bears upon his ability to concentrate, as when he expects to finish football practice at 6:30, eat the large meal of the day, then study effectively for the next two hours. He may have learned little about the needs or skills for note taking, in reading or in class. He may worship the outline in a rigid way or be ignorant of its virtues when discriminatingly used. And very commonly, the student does not realize that for college learning and college competition it will not suffice to study the few hours per week that did suffice when he was one of the ablest individuals in his school class. The Holtzman-Brown-Farquhar study-habits questionnaire [142] may provide an instrument to guide evaluation, although it evidently is not equally useful in all types of colleges.

Comparisons of students of high and low standing do not to date show any convincing differences in the ways they behave. Brown, Abeles, and Iscoe [49] found, for example, that high-standing students were readier to respond to invitations to take part in special testing sessions or to fill out questionnaires, or to study possible examination questions in advance of administration. The authors believe the poor student is likely to lack decisiveness of action, to procrastinate, to conform, outside the classroom as well as in, so that traits of some considerable generality are postulated. However, several other interpretations of the traits of poor students are equally plausible. For example, they may be generally defensive and conflicted, and hence do not volunteer as subjects but protect themselves against criticism by not responding, and so on. Or, students who know they are of lower ability are both likely to get low marks and be reluctant to try new and uncertain tasks. The study of Duncan, Bell, Bradt, and Newman [95] does not demonstrate clear differences between the study procedures or motivations of good and poor students. Probably we may expect to find that it is the *pattern* of abilities and habits that distinguishes one good student from another, and each from a poor student, rather than decisive differences on specific or isolated variables (assuming only that gross ability differences are not operative).

If there are not special orientation advisers to work with those whose study habits seem inadequate, the individual instructor is likely to find that helping his students to make general improvements in their study habits and thus specific improvements in his course is very rewarding. He has to learn, however, that such habit changes are sometimes slow in coming about, are often but symptomatic of something more complex, and in any event have to be set in motion early in his course if there is to be any chance at all of profit during the one term or the one year that it lasts. Fortunately, there is a considerable literature in this field, and the instructor may find that it suffices, either altogether or as a first step, to recommend selected readings to the student or to make them available on loan from the library or his office [e.g., 224].

Frequently involved in the problem of study habits, but deserving separate mention, is the problem of reading skill. In the social and behavioral sciences the student is commonly expected to be able to master upwards of 100 pages per week of text material in a given course, and to do all the necessary integrating with lecture materials and other offerings of the course. (The page demands may be very different in courses in the literatures or history, as may be the sheer number of intellectual operations required per page read in mathematics or the sciences.) The student who reads slowly is likely to be in trouble from the beginning, and it is relatively easy to detect the extremely slow readers in one's own kind of discipline and material. Often it turns out that the student has already made his own diagnosis—although it may be used to support alibis, rather than being put to constructive remedial ends. Since the rewards from work with speed of reading seem to be relatively great and, one might almost say, surprisingly easy to attain as habit changes go, the instructor may well advise the student to secure special help in the matter, or again, if he is not an expert in this field and no specialist is available, direct the student to representative self-help materials [e.g., 252, 265].

It is also advisable to expect that scholastic problems, including those of study habits as such, may reflect motivational difficulties. These may take innumerable forms, perhaps the most painful one for the instructor being the one where the student regards the subject matter or the teaching as just plain dull. More commonly, since even the dullest course has its moments of interest and since the general excitement of going to college carries students through even disliked required courses, poor motivation in a given course reflects the subtractive influences of conflicting motives. Thus the student does not study regularly because he wants to do too many other things, or he cannot read well because his thoughts are constantly drawn to other matters. In psychology, particularly, it must be realized that for certain students some of the subject matter may be disturbing or frightening, as it touches upon deeply rooted guilt or anxiety feelings, so that the instructor can hardly disregard the motivational conflicts his students may exhibit.

Realizing as he does that the student's surface motivation rests upon a complex base of motives common to young adults or late adolescents, such as the needs for social and economic security, for clarity as to career line, for self-esteem and social acceptance, and for reassurance as to sexual role, the instructor will not be overly optimistic about remaking his student in a fundamental way. (These kinds of motivation, plus an interest in the bizarre, the exotic, or the morbid, have been evidenced repeatedly in surveys of student reasons for studying psychology.) He will nevertheless try to capitalize on the favorable motivational elements he can detect, thus drawing the students more firmly to the work of the course and reducing the importance of competitive elements. The favorable motivational elements will consist of expressed and inferred interests. To encourage these interests the instructor may use special assignments or competitions, tasks executed for the instructor or on behalf of the class or as a member of a team, or just sympathetic and interested inquiry which will arouse the student and start him working. These suggestions are all predicated on merely having to deal with an ordinary human being of a certain age in our own culture. Anything the instructor can do to make this classification more specific ("socially ambitious," "sports- or music-minded," "practical") will suggest more specific approaches to motivational arousal.

With surprising frequency, scholastic difficulties center about the art of examination taking. We have discussed previously (Chap. 11) the need for making sure that measurements of performance are based upon equal opportunity to perform well, and we need refer here only to the student who is extreme in his fear of examinations or in his lack of understanding as to what it takes to write a good examination. Reassurance, discussion of the techniques for taking examinations of any particularly troublesome kind, analysis of the relation between preparation and the examinations, and other procedures are available to the instructor. Since he more than anyone else ought to know how students should respond to his various examinations, he is the person to give counsel regarding them. (He may find, interestingly enough, that his own analysis of what it takes to do well on his examinations is sometimes not so acute as the analysis by one of his A students.) The very concreteness of examinations makes them an interesting and useful starting point for many kinds of discussion between instructor and students.

The task of the general academic adviser. In addition to confronting problems of students who take his courses, the faculty member very commonly finds himself to be counselor in a quite different setting, that of assigned general adviser to students in the early portion of their college career, before they have chosen a major. Such advising may be done with freshmen or sophomores, or even with transfer students, but in helping students decide upon a curricular program the adviser quickly learns that many kinds of problems are involved. Especially conspicuous are questions of vocational or professional choice, since the college is the principal route to the professions and a determiner of initial status or ease of entry into many other occupations, such as business. Furthermore, students in their earlier college years are likely to display more prominently than later their needs for independence of family judgment or influence and the conflicts related to satisfaction of such needs.

It is clear, therefore, that the demands upon the faculty adviser are likely to be more complex than those made in relation to a single course. It is further clear that while the advising of freshmen or sophomores is frequently turned over to junior members of the faculty, it is exactly the kind of work which ought to be done by the most experienced persons available. Regardless of who is assigned to the task, however, he will have to equip himself in certain ways. For one thing, he will need the broadest and most detailed information about his institution, its rules, and its course offerings, the available majors and other programs, and about the relationship between courses or majors and later careers or advanced studies. Such information can be gleaned to a great extent from the college catalogue, but will have to be supplemented by discussions with the experienced members of the staff, by additional reading, and by observation of students and the consequences of their choices. It is important to remember that information about possible careers is not, or may not have been, equally available, either with regard to all careers or for all students, and that information of this kind is likely therefore to be especially useful. The average student, for example, is not likely to realize that the social or behavioral sciences exist in their present rather fully developed form, or that they offer career opportunities other than those in college teaching. But the student who expects to enter medicine, engineering, or business has known about these fields for many years and may have decided on one of them without considering its basic suitability for him or what the alternatives might be. He may be quite unclear as to the prior demands some choices—for example, entrance into medical school—make upon him. Even where information is adequate, the student's basic interest patterns may still be changing as he matures, with or without his realizing it.

The amount of motivational clarification which the freshman or sophomore is likely to need, and the amount of information he needs in order to make basic decisions, give rise to a high probability that many choices will be tentative and unstable. The instructor who counsels with lower-division students has to learn to expect this changeability, often for reasons which to him may not seem very important. For this and for many other reasons, he has to develop in objectivity, and he must orient himself toward securing all the pertinent facts about any problems presented to him. He must learn for one thing how to reply to queries about his own field without proselytizing for it. Furthermore, the behavior of his students will teach him, if nothing else does, that decisions may best flow from the student's own initiative, for decisions urged upon a student or handed to him as requirements tend very often to be rejected at once or discarded later. And we must say again that in evaluating and dealing with the problems presented by a student to whom one is general adviser, the possible complexities and the possible needs for securing the help of specialists must always be kept in mind.

Advising the majoring student. By the time we see students who have chosen to major in our discipline the preceding college years have eliminated many of the students who are our severest problems: those who are most completely confused, or who have the most inadequate study habits or motivation, or who are in the severest and most distracting of personal situations. For that general reason, and because the students are interested in more of the same things that we are, or because the problems or questions they present seem more familiar, advising the major is regarded as an easy, often as a desirable, assignment. An excessive devotion to majors may even be assumed as a way to avoid dealing with problems arising in courses as such, or to escape from general advisory assignments.

Of the problems commonly encountered in counseling with majors, perhaps only one deserves special emphasis. This is the problem of the transfer student, who shows up after one or two years in another institution. He deserves more attention than he commonly gets, for he has not only the standard problems of choosing courses and instructors but also those of adjusting to a situation which is quite new to him but familiar for those with whom he works or competes in the classroom. The evaluation of his background and fitness to enter certain advanced courses may require particular care, in order not to launch him into, for example, an advanced course in small group dynamics when his supposed prerequisite course taken in another institution under the name of social psychology in fact provides no clearly relevant background for the advanced work.

Briefer enumeration of some of the remaining most common problems in advising the majoring student will perhaps be sufficient to alert the beginning instructor. One of these is the question of how much variation in the standard program for the major is to be allowed. For purposes of entry into graduate school, or for simple identification of the field of concentration of the student, it is usually desirable that a relatively restricted program be followed, one in which each student is quite like the other, and all could be ready for the same comprehensive examination at termination of the program. The longer one teaches, however, the more likely he is to perceive that formal similarities of program do not make educational progress alike for different students, and that variations in program can achieve a good deal for the motivation of students. He is likely, therefore, to become rather skilled in helping students achieve departures from orthodox course lists, although he should not often be so helpful in this that the student escapes what are generally regarded as essential courses, or, within his department, merely the more difficult courses (e.g., statistics, in psychology).

A different kind of problem is presented by the student who wishes to overconcentrate. He may misperceive the value of specialization, desire to feel secure in having taken every course that could possibly be expected of him upon entry into graduate school, wish to take no chance in presenting himself for a comprehensive examination, or wish to avoid taking certain courses outside the department. Here the adviser who understands what is going on can help the student see the folly of this kind of overspecialization. The adviser can help the student see (sometimes in an authoritarian way) that at least some mastery of other disciplines in addition to his psychology will really give him a much stronger hand.

Probably the most difficult problem of advisement in the major is that of working toward the most meaningful relationship between the program, both outside and inside the major, and the plans of the student for a career. This is particularly true for the student who is not going to become a psychologist. Information is simply lacking, for most purposes, on what aspects of education achieve the most useful balance between adequately specific preparation and general broadening of the student. Nevertheless, it is the responsibility of the adviser to take the time to think about this with the student, and not merely sign the card which the student pokes at him after having made personal judgments about what he wants to study. One of the most specific kinds of occupational planning is needed, of course, for the student who is considering becoming a psychologist. We have already discussed professional recruitment (Chap. 4), including the role of the relationship between instructor and student in this, and now need only to call attention to the necessity for ensuring that the pre-professional student has all the information relevant to his plans. It is particularly important, as Gustav's survey shows [123], to make sure that the majoring student does not think he can make a living at professional psychological work with only a B.A. This information should certainly include reference to the need for getting an early start on German and French (or Russian), since most graduate schools require them, and for doing at least basic work in most of the fields closely related to and supportive of psychology (mathematics, sociology, biology, etc.).

THE NATURE OF THE COUNSELING RELATION

There are currently many schools of thought about the nature of the relationship between counselor and student, and many good specialized books on the subject [e.g., 47, 279, 290], but the following discussion is not intended to make any special assumptions about theoretical positions. What is assumed basically is that the counseling relationship comes about primarily in and by means of interviews between counselor and student, supplemented by briefer contacts of various kinds and by information which the counselor may secure through channels not known to the student or by means which the student helps provide, such as aptitude tests.

Perhaps the first way to describe the counseling relationship from the faculty standpoint is that it is supportive, objective, and friendly. This must be true even when the problem is of the kind usually called disciplinary, if there is to be maximum chance for getting useful responses from the student. (By useful response is not necessarily meant what is regarded as correct, but only a response that can be worked with; the mute or passive student gives us restricted opportunity to sense how he thinks or what he wishes to do.) Certain other terms can be added to describe the effective situation: in it the instructor must often be patient, a listener willing to wait while a student clarifies his thoughts or gets up his courage to speak them or, quite commonly, finishes the long diagnostic speech he has prepared and is strongly motivated to finish to the bitter end. He must be tolerant and unsurprised at the kinds of thoughts which get expressed. He does well not to be hurried, not to push for exactness or consistency. He does well not to identify initial statements, or for that matter any student statements, with the objective truth of the situation, but rather to regard as one of the major purposes of counseling the process of moving toward truth and its acceptance. And he does not leap forward prematurely with well-intentioned advice.

Information getting. If counseling is regarded as a process for arriving at truth in the sense of the best possible course of action for the student, it can equally be regarded as a process in which suitable information must be secured upon which to base an adequate amount and kind of thought before decisions are reached. We have then to consider what sources of information are available and commonly prove useful. In the first place, there is the talk volunteered by the student; he is likely to have given thought, however one-sided, to his problem, and is quite often aware of most of the relevant information. Thorough opportunity for him to present factual information and air his feelings is therefore the most useful beginning point. Second, questioning by the instructor very often brings out information which the student possessed but did not realize could be relevant. A beginning usually is made with innocuous questions about matters which the student is certain to regard as pertinent, e.g., marks in various courses. Students very often know exactly their records in other courses, or in previous curricular programs. In many cases they know their own aptitude test scores, although whether this is good or bad is not always clear. They are specifically aware of the extracurricular activities, especially the social ones and athletics, that they carry on, or the number of hours per week they hold down a job. They know better than anyone else whether home and family circumstances or finances are a source of friction or worry. They know pretty well how they go about their studies. Less dependably they can record their interests, their motivational status generally, and their degree of interest in a particular course. How much of this information is sought will of course depend upon the problem which appears to be presented. The faculty member must be conscious of the possibility that he can overdo in exploring a problem, perhaps because the problem does not warrant it, or because the student does not want a big production made of what he regards as a minor affair, or because the instructor with many other things to do cannot afford to go completely into every matter brought to his attention by students, or even because the appearance of prying into another's private business is all too readily given.

In the third place, so far as it is indicated, information can be sought from sources other than the student. Either with the student, or privately, rules and regulations may be explored to see how they pertain to the problem, or it can be determined what help is available from other offices or other agencies on the campus. The instructor may seek out details of entrance examination scores or information from the student's previous advisers or residence hall supervisors. The useful sources will have to be learned for each particular institution, and each instructor tends to build his own list of favored sources and resource persons as experience grows. A major item of general information will be the additional resources which the institution affords, in the way of psychiatric services, reading clinic, loan funds, or other services.

Plans for dealing with the problem. Presumably counseling begins because decisions are required for future conduct. Fairly often plans or decisions are arrived at merely by the acquisition of relevant information. It is quite clear that the student must arrive at a plan or a decision in such a way that he accepts it as his own, and preferably feels that he has arrived at it himself, with only expert help from the counselor. Telling a student how to handle a major problem, without his acceptance of the telling, is likely to achieve relatively little that is lasting or consistent with the broadest objectives a counselor holds to in his work with others. (Perhaps it is pertinent to speculate here, as in relation to the conduct of a classroom, that in our culture the authoritarian method works only when embedded in a larger context which is willingly accepted by the student.)

In the academic counseling situation, plans or decisions must usually be arrived at in some degree of workable detail. Conversely, the counseling process has not gone far enough if dropped when the student does not yet know how he is going to follow through on his general intentions. More specifically, for example, if he intends to improve his study habits, he should think far enough with the instructor that he knows what he is going to try first and what he is likely to try next. If he needs to review or clarify his understanding of certain portions of subject matter, he should know whether he will attempt to do so through regulated study, with the aid of a tutor, or by some other concrete plan of action. If he is going to secure a loan or find a job or change roommates or arrange to see a physician in the student health department, he should have learned how this can be done, or know how he can find out.

Involved in the question of planning for future actions or for specialized attention to the student's problems is very often a referral of the student to some particular agency or office on the campus where his needs may be taken care of. In the main, only two principles seem to be statable here. One is that the relation between instructor and student is better maintained, and the whole process of referral made more efficient, if the instructor takes a hand in making the arrangements. Often a telephone call while the student is in the office will suffice to get him into the hands of someone else; preferably this will be a specific individual by name, so that the student does not merely regard the referral as buck passing. Also, the method ensures that the person to whom referral is made will know that he has, if needed, a useful source of information in the instructor involved. A second principle is that the referral is useless if the student does not regard it as acceptable and sensible.

In relation to this second point, special comment perhaps should be made about one particular kind of referral, this to a mental health expert or agency of any kind. The resistance to this kind of referral is of course well known, and it often happens that the resistance is intensified in the individual who is aware, consciously or unconsciously, that he could well use this kind of assistance. Therefore a blunt statement, such as "This sounds serious to me; you'd better go see a psychiatrist," is more likely to raise defenses or increase anxiety than it is to secure the hoped-for reaction. If this kind of referral seems likely to be desirable, in the great majority of cases it is best arrived at gradually by mutual discussion of methods of securing help with the problem, and then handled by the instructor-contact-with-expert method. In this way the likelihood of favorable circumstances for diagnosis and treatment by the professional therapist is enhanced. In what may appear to be the more serious and complex problems, the instructor will do well to seek the guidance of the professional who might be involved before continuing in his relationship with the student. It must be repeated that quite apart from the probability that unskilled or superficial treatment will produce no positive results with the person who is mentally ill or tending that way, the psychologist must feel morally bound not to assume responsibilities which he is not competent to assume in his relations with students. And to lend still more force to that injunction, let it be said that failure to handle a case of student maladjustment in a reasonably professional manner may permit a seriously paranoid or suicidal student to do serious harm to others or self or institution. Such consequences of unprofessional conduct would be personally and professionally damaging to any psychologist involved.

Ordinarily it is desirable to plan for, or create opportunity for, a follow-up on any counseling done. This again assures the student of friendly interest, supports him in his good intentions, may provide opportunity for improvement or correction of the plans or decisions initially arrived at, and may also show the counselor whether his work succeeded, thus making him a wiser man. Perhaps the guiding principle of the planning and decision making that occurs in academic counseling and the follow-through should be that whatever is done is intended to increase the student's understanding of himself and his situation so that his energies are freed for his academic work. Instructors vary considerably in the kinds of problems they feel competent or obligated to help students with, but the ordinary faculty member must discriminate the kinds of problems which bear primarily upon academic work from those kinds which more generally involve personality change and adjustment or are more properly the sphere of interest or competence of other persons.

Cautions concerning the counseling relationship. For the protection of the instructor who becomes involved in counseling to any degree, it may be desirable to call attention to some of the precautions that must be observed in it. First, it is possible to go too far in being helpful to students, even to the point of gaining a reputation as a good string-puller or conniver and a person likely to square things for the student in difficulty. Implied here is a lack of objectivity about what is good for the student and about where the individual student's rights leave off and the rights of others begin. Implied in this is also the tendency of some students to put themselves in the position of seeking advice, sometimes on a genuine problem, as a device for gaining sympathy and thus improving their marks in a course. Again, objectivity is the best protection in the evaluation of student motives. One should avoid making one's self into a father-figure, in the counseling process, as an unwitting way of seeking maturity for one's self. The fatherly character may, as reputation, draw undue numbers of students or draw them for the wrong reasons. An enlargement of the preceding point is that counseling with students should not be a means by which the instructor works out his own problems; his own momentary or persisting needs to be aggressive, or his own needs for acceptance and friendship, should not bias his relationship to students or distort the relationship which develops any more than can be helped.

Further, if counseling is to be engaged in to any considerable degree, its cost in time and energy should be recognized and definite arrangements made to have other aspects of the instructor's responsibilities lightened. If this is not possible, the instructor must realize it is a calculated career risk to be unusually devoted to his responsibility for counseling students, for as the academic culture now stands, progress up the conventional success and prestige ladder is rarely aided by concentration on any such activity. There must be note of the possibility that, under time pressures and pressures of other kinds, counseling may be done halfheartedly and without sufficiently careful thought. The instructor may come to settle for type students and corresponding type solutions as a shortcut around the lengthier process of finding out what is unique to each case, or he may pull out of any problem that appears to be getting complicated with just a little good advice firmly given, or with an explanation that he cannot take on that kind of problem. There is a problem of ethical responsibility here; the instructor can be clearly not involved, or he can take responsibility, but he is not ethical if he dabbles merely to frustrate.

Counseling, dealing as it does with personal problems, occasionally deeply involving ones, is subject to frustration, distraction, abuse, or misinterpretation. The physical circumstances can enhance these possibilities if they do not permit of appropriate privacy. There is also the point that, just as a physician does not ordinarily examine a woman patient without a nurse present, so the counselor must take precautions against abuse of the conference situation. This means that the setting must be incapable of misinterpretation by anyone. Locked doors, recording equipment, appointments of male instructors with female students in the evening, visits to student living quarters, are some of the items especially capable of misinterpretation by the student or others. Attention must always be given to the maintenance of a professional type of relationship with the student. Particularly must it be made clear that security will be maintained concerning the conversations between student and instructor except as these bear directly on academic status and may therefore become the legitimate business of others having an instructional or administrative interest in the student's welfare or conduct. Use of student remarks in faculty gossip at the lunch table, enticing as the opportunity may sometimes be, is an abuse of student confidence—and may well be a report based on biased or misleading information. Introduction of commentary about other faculty members, or their courses, into the counseling relationship has to be done most discriminatingly. Where the matter may be regarded as factually correct and within the province of information it is the student's right to have, there is no problem, but when the student seeks evaluation of other instructors or their courses, or evaluation of other students or staff, or merely criticizes other instructors, the counselor may find it very difficult to know what he may and may not say. Fundamental honesty should govern the counselor's conduct, and this may at times require courage to give the student some unpleasant facts of life, or an unfavorable prognosis concerning his own situation, or a firm commentary on gossip. And finally we may mention, as an aspect of professional conduct of a counseling episode, that it may be desirable to have a clear-cut termination of it, for clarification of the relationship between student and instructor and for indicating the status of the instructor's interest in and responsibility for the problem. Even a follow-up may be made in such a way as to avoid the impression that loose ends of a problem, or of an interpersonal responsibility, are still dangling.

14

KNOWING THE STUDENTS WE TEACH

In this book the beginning instructor has from chapter to chapter been advised, if only by implication, to adapt his teaching to his particular students. It becomes important, then, to anticipate in as many ways as possible just what these students will be like, although of course the characteristics of any class will be known with some degree of confidence only after a considerable exposure to them. We have discussed in a rather subjective way the motives that bring students into our classroom (Chaps. 12 and 13) and we can now add to our picture of the student information from several kinds of research studies.

MISCONCEPTIONS OR FALSE BELIEFS

Almost from the beginning of his psychological studies, even as an undergraduate himself, the instructor is likely to have realized that students approaching the study of behavior have a great number of mistaken notions. The instructor's realization is of course not without its analogue in economics [261] or anthropology [263] and other social or behavioral science disciplines. Much of our behavioral folklore is simply not true, wholly or in part, in the light of modern data, although part of it *is* true, as a distillation of folk experience.

Areas of misbelief. Psychologists have found it amusing, instructive, motivating, and sometimes just plain frustrating to measure the kinds and numbers of misbeliefs present in their beginning students. Most of the studies in this area [114, 141, 183, 203, 219, 269, 274] have provided lists of true-false statements for students to check. The earlier studies were technically not very rigorous, as in wording all statements so that the correct answer was "false," although later studies [e.g., 80] used carefully constructed measuring devices or questions screened for their ability to measure what a total test purports to measure [141]. Many of the studies reflected debatable beliefs prevalent among psychologists themselves at the time and would now be challenged for the way certain questions were scored. (Consider the cycles of opinion among psychologists on the correctness of the statement, "The IQ is innately determined.") But in the main, students have enjoyed trying to outguess the psychologists on such tests, and have been startled, not to say nettled, at a good many of their mistakes. The pre-test of misconceptions is therefore a good pedagogical device to dislodge students from the feeling that they already know most of what there is to know about behavior and so make them readier to learn the new ideas of a course. For purposes of the present discussion, however, the chief point about using a test of misconceptions is that it reveals what students believe and therefore guides the instructor in what he does.

The total number of mistaken notions that might be searched out is so large that no one has yet been able to present a good summary picture of the typical domains of misbelief. Two studies have made preliminary suggestions. Holley and Buxton [141] administered a 100-question true-false test to introductory psychology students, then by means of a special form of factor-analysis (Q-technique) identified four factors of misbelief in their sample of students. The first factor was thought to be one of general psychological naïveté, a general confusion in knowledge about behavioral matters. As illustrations of this kind of ignorance, students frequently misevaluated statements like these: "The printing on this page is upside-down on your retina." "Rats, cats, and dogs have the power to reason." "There is little that psychology can do for the normal person." Another source of misunderstanding (i.e., another factor) centered about special or technical terminology. It was illustrated by the missing of questions like these: "Half the people in this country are below average in intelligence." "The unconscious mind is located just above the roof of the mouth, directly back of the nose." The third factor was labeled conventional morality by the authors, for it was illustrated by misses on questions like these: "The majority of adult criminals are feeble-minded or very nearly so." "A child is born with a sense of good and evil—this is his conscience." "Being spanked may be pleasurable to a child." "A person who won't look you in the eye is probably untrustworthy." A fourth factor seemed to be an overvaluation of the possibilities of learning, particularly in children. It was illustrated by misses on items like these: "Children memorize much more easily than adults." "The average infant would learn to walk two months earlier than he does, if he were given the proper training." "The sense organs of touch, in a person with normal vision, are just as sensitive as those in a blind person." Anyone reading these illustrative items is likely to ask why, for example, ignorance of memorization rates in children and adults is not closely correlated with the factor called general psychological naïveté. There are as yet simply not enough data to answer such questions, although the techniques for careful exploration of the patterns of misbelief are now available.

Other groupings of specific psychological misbeliefs were suggested by Valentine [269] on the basis of a tentative logical classification of the questions he used (not the empirical-statistical kind of classification of Holley and Buxton). An important area, possibly not reflected in the Holley-Buxton study because not enough questions represented it (which would mean for reasons inherent in the factor analysis technique that it could not readily be identified), was that of misbeliefs about the biological bases of behavior. Valentine found, for example, many mistaken notions about the degree to which physical traits—such as body shape or appearance or physiology—or heredity may determine certain aspects of behavior. ("Long fingers indicate artistic temperament." "A weak chin signifies a lack of will power.") This kind of belief may exist, of course, alongside an equally firm overvaluation of learning as a determiner of behavior, without perception of the contrast or even the inconsistency that may exist. Valentine also found many misbeliefs that could only be called superstitions about behavior. ("Dogs recognize death and give voice to their grief." "Positions of the planets at birth influence the character of the individual." "Lines in a person's hand foretell his future.") In addition, there were many strictly behavioral misbeliefs, analogous to those found by Holley and Buxton. In sum, the very sketchy idea we have to date is that misbeliefs can be viewed as existing in clusters, but it is clear that we cannot confidently delimit these clusters. And it is highly likely that the clusters differ from one kind of student sample to another. Even within a given sample, as the data of Valentine show, students who have been in college longer have fewer misconceptions, as do those who have had more psychology, and a number of studies suggest [e.g., 78, 203, 269] that men are more skeptical than women, not by much, but in certain areas of interest.

A dramatic and surprising instance of a specific type of misbelief has been described recently by Dennis [84] and explored further by Crannell [80]. Dennis asked various samples of students (graduate students in education, introductory psychology students, a class in child development) whether the following things were alive: a match, a lighted match, an electric clock, the sun, a 5-cent piece, a pearl, gasoline, the ocean (with some students, clouds were substituted for one of the other items). From 37 to 48 per cent of the various groups named said that one or more of the objects was alive. On further questioning it appeared that this was no simple confusion of life with movement. For example, a third of the subjects attributed consciousness to the sea. Crannell improved on the questioning technique, and confirmed Dennis' findings. In a large psychology class a third of the students elected a multiple-choice alternative indicating some degree of animistic belief in Dennis' objects, and in a second year zoology class, interestingly enough, just fewer than a third of the students exhibited one or more animistic notions.

Correction of mistaken beliefs. It has been strongly argued [94, 241] that a major objective of introductory teaching in psychology should be the correction of misbeliefs and misconceptions. To a greater or lesser degree, certainly, every beginning instructor must deal with such mistaken notions as arise in his classes. How successful are our attempts to correct misbeliefs? Five studies give us some idea.

Valentine [269] supervised an introductory psychology course in which an explicit objective, among others, was the correction of misbeliefs by teaching the scientific method thoroughly. In general he found a considerable drop in the number of students accepting any given mistaken notion at the end of the term, and this did not seem attributable to artifacts such as selective dropping out of students. (There were no comparisons with changes in nonpsychology students.) Dysinger and Gregory [97] found that in three categories of misconceptions—popular, semipopular, and technical—the scores of their students improved during the beginning course. Their interpretation was that positive transfer occurred from the materials taught. Sanford and Hemphill [236] gave an 8-hour course to naval cadets, incorporating such topics as problem solving, motivation, individual differences, selective learning, group dynamics, and social psychology. As part of their evaluation of the impact of this course (plus some uncontrolled hours of discussion of leadership problems by the military, due to scheduling difficulties) they gave before-and-after tests of "common sense," using a 30-item true-false test, similar to the ones previously mentioned. Changes in a control group of cadets who did not have the lectures or the accompanying special reading were significantly less favorable than in the cadets having these materials. It was the belief of the investigators that this result reflected, not specific teaching about wrong common-sense beliefs, but rather the development of a more critical and generally analytical set toward statements about behavior.

Both of the latter two researches give reason to think that transfer occurs from teaching to specific items of misbelief about which there was not direct teaching. Valentine [269] found, however, that there was little such transfer. McGarvey [183] found that it occurred in statistically reliable amounts, but the total amount of change, in either beliefs subjected to discussion or beliefs not so treated, was nevertheless small from a practical point of view. So transfer is evidently not simple to obtain here any more than it is elsewhere in psychological instruction.

This inference is reinforced by a finding of Magaret and Sherriffs [172]. In a carefully designed study these investigators used a pre-test of common-sense beliefs related to eight potential areas of conflict in an introductory psychology student, and also an interview planned to identify in advance the presence of bias or anxieties related to the content of the course. At the end of the course an application or transfer test was used. It consisted of an essay response to a practical problem in each of the eight areas of potential conflict that the authors had believed to exist. For example: "Give your best guess as to what you would do in each situation and tell why. . . . You are the parent of an only child. The child is seven and has seemed peculiar in his reactions. On being asked for a diagnosis, a psychologist informs you that the child is a low-grade moron with an IQ of 53." Responses to these transfer problems were rated for the degree they corresponded to the teachings of the course. Although students identified in the pre-test and the interview as likely to experience conflict with the teachings of the course were not reliably inferior at the end of the course in their total achievement score, nor in college grade point average, they were reliably poorer in ability to make the transfers required in the practical-situations test. That is, when answering questions about the teachings of the course in their familiar form on an achievement examination, the conflicted student knew the right answer; when dealing with a relatively unstructured and new problem of application he showed that he functioned according to a belief or an attitude he held when he originally came into the course.

That the evidence about changeability of beliefs in the academic setting is not totally hopeful may be due partly to the fixity of the beliefs in question. One of the besetting difficulties of the behavioral scientist is the seeming conviction in most of his students that when they come to him they already know a good deal about human behavior. "After all," each has behaved, and each has lived with people. The student, therefore, as he would not in nuclear physics or medicine, only reluctantly gives up old ideas or accepts new ones, merely because in a certain personal sense he himself knows better. Furthermore, much of what he "knows better" he knows with considerable, even extreme, fervor (as is so often true of the emotional learning about race differences or other illustrations of prejudice). Furthermore, a good many of the ideas he accepts he first heard from someone else and then had fixed in himself by one or two instances of what Dudycha [94] called "inconsequential coincidences"—chance happenings, or by observations biased by expectations as to what would be seen. Finally, we may suggest, parents and other prestigeful figures, literature, the movies, and television, all tend to fix behavioral beliefs firmly in the individual. Unhappily, many of these beliefs are incorrect.

This general kind of problem may be attacked in many ways, presumably, but no one would presently do more than suggest possible solutions. Perhaps the most potent attack, pedagogically, is to begin by teaching methods for testing statements or hypotheses about behavior generally, to the point where such methods are well understood and accepted, then gradually using this methodology to attack questions which are more confusing or emotionally loaded for the student. He will then be led to examine his own beliefs by scientific methods which he himself understands and is able to apply. In the process he may develop a genuinely critical and objective attitude about any statements purporting to describe or explain behavior. This suggestion, it should be noted, is in line with the not altogether successful efforts of Valentine's group at Ohio State University; from the published reports we do not know, however, just how effectively and persistently Valentine's staff taught in this way, so we cannot be sure the idea has had a good trial.

A second suggestion stems from the fact that the instructor who wishes to correct misbeliefs will note that these ideas are not exhibited uniformly and constantly, to be recognized or diagnosed. Rather, they are latent within the student until evoked by something that goes on in relation to the instructor or the class. Many misbeliefs are in such a form that even when they are evoked the student does not readily perceive them to be related to his psychology course, this being especially true of misconceptions about behavior acquired in the setting and the language of religious upbringing, or through literature. A student may believe that conscience is an inborn trait. The concept of personality traits will probably be discussed in his psychology course, and it will become apparent that nurture as well as nature has much to contribute to trait development. But the specific misbelief about conscience is not likely to be voiced or self-recognized unless the opportunities for personal expression by the student are unusually good. We must conclude, then, that opportunities for discussion are essential to instruction intended to get at latent ideas, whether these are called misconceptions or something else.

Perhaps the most frustrating aspect of attempting to correct misbeliefs is the sheer stubbornness of the human animal in resisting changes he does not want to accept. It is the ability to compartmentalize and to rationalize that enables students to participate in a discussion of "the will" in a psychology course, readily accept the psychologist's view of will power as motivational balance and nothing more, yet retain the theologically rooted conception of free will and later show that this biases his attempts to view behavior in a psychological (not theological) way. Skinner [247, 248] has demonstrated most convincingly how widespread is this particular inconsistency in our culture, and we have earlier referred to Dennis' [84] finding of animistic beliefs among students as an example of belief relatively untouched by college-level education. We can hope that it is possible to teach in a way which generalizes to the correction of such ideas, but evidently we have much to learn. Some courage may perhaps be taken from the evidence of Newman and his associates [201] that students performing best on the achievement examinations of an introductory course, and students in that course who were ablest on an intelligence test, were also those who tended to exhibit fewest misconceptions. Valentine [269] also found that ability correlated favorably with skepticism about folk beliefs.

VARIATIONS IN ABILITY

In any course, and particularly in one in an institution where the instructor or the institution has little control over who is admitted, a wide range of abilities is to be expected. The abilities pertinent to a given course will naturally depend upon the nature of the course to some extent, but we shall confine ourselves here to discussion only of "general" ability as measured by standard entrance-examination types of intelligence tests.

It has been shown repeatedly that standard tests such as the Ohio State University Psychological Examination, the Otis Self-Administering Test of Mental Ability, or the tests of the American Council on Education provide a reasonably good prediction concerning performance in the beginning psychology course, and may thus be said to detect students likely to have trouble or to identify exceptionally promising students. The efficiency of prediction is probably as good as that with which college work in general is predicted. Correlations between intelligence test scores and total or final scores on examinations of the objective variety have been reported as high as .68 [212] in introductory psychology, although they are more typically in the .30's [201] or .40's [61].

It is sometimes said that the degree of correlation between grades and ability indicates the efficacy of instruction. This assumes that good instruction gets every student to perform to the maximum of his ability; that is, it implies that the knowledge of every member of a group should increase during a course in such an amount that each person assumes the place in the rank order of knowledge that he has in the rank order of ability. In practice, of course, many variables make this assumption all but untenable. Data from the study of Carlson, Fischer, and Young [61] are illustrative of findings on this point. They found, first, that scores on a pre-test of psychological knowledge (the same test to be used later as a final examination) correlated .556 with an adaptation of the Otis test of mental ability, but that the amount students would gain in psychological knowledge could not be predicted by either the ability (*r*, −.039) or the pre-test score itself (*r*, −.01). As these values imply, scores on the post-test correlate less closely with the ability measure than at the beginning (.429, compared with .556). And, as the leeway in all these statistics makes possible, scores on the post-test correlate quite closely with gains during the course (.712). The investigators considered various possible artifacts as interpretations of the results but consider them less likely than the ". . . interpretation . . . that improvement following tuition is largely dependent upon non-intellectual factors. Among the more important of these we would expect to find interest and motivation, opportunity to study, study habits, personality traits, and emotional conflicts at the time of study and at the time of taking the examination. These factors call attention to the importance of non-intellectual processes in accounting for differential improvement in achievement." One could go even further than these authors and say that since so many variables other than ability are relevant to what a student can or should learn, a very high correlation between performance and ability might indicate merely that the teaching has not been adaptive to the non-intellectual variables, so that only inherent ability enables some students to survive it better than others.

It may be useful to ask how the ability of students relates to their reactions to various forms of instruction. The data here are meager, but their trend seems fairly clear. Remmers [221], for example, in two of three studies, found that superior students and students of lesser ability profited about equally from lecture and lecture-recitation methods of instruction. Longstaff

[166] found that the correlation between performance and ability was unaffected by the use of lecture-quiz as against all-lecture methods of instruction. In a later study he also found that superior students (in this instance not compared with others of lower ability) did not profit from a discussion period as compared with straight lecturing. This latter study is of somewhat dubious applicability, however, since the so-called discussion groups contained 60 students, and in addition it was difficult to equate the performance for measures for groups thus treated differently. All in all, we may feel, there is no evidence as yet that certain methods of instruction are superior for certain ability groups of students. This claim must be considered along with the oft-expressed concern for providing a higher level of stimulation for the superior student, as in discussions of honors programs [17, 208] or in Pressey's forcible argument [217] for various educational improvements. At first glance one might think that these programs or arguments imply that small classes, special projects, independent studies, acceleration of assignments according to student readiness, rewarding each sign of intellectual progress, and so forth, are known to be more appropriate for superior students than for others. Such is not the implication, however, of the kind of evidence cited above. The best guess we can make is that *any* attempt to enhance the favorable impact of environment would be good at *all* ability levels. It is merely a practical fact that the labor and expense of special instructional arrangements seem justified, or seem to yield the greatest return, when they are provided for those students of superior ability who are obviously responsive to any method of instruction.

It has sometimes been suggested [87, 243] that improvements in instruction are to be achieved by sectioning students in large courses according to their ability. The implication is that able students can be speeded in their coverage of material or be given more extensive material; they will compete with others of their own level for marks, and be stimulated in discussions by students of approximately their own level of understanding and competence, whereas the poorer students, in sections composed of people somewhat like themselves, may for the first time feel they have a competitive chance, and therefore have reduced feelings of frustration and failure. Such data as are available [166] suggest, however, that college students prefer to be sectioned into heterogeneous groups. It may be that able students like to continue to feel more nearly uniquely superior, while poor students do not like to be classed as members of slow sections; and it may be that each extreme of student finds genuine profit in being exposed to the kinds of discussion or expressions of opinion by the group at the other extreme. For the record it should be said that Dockeray [87] has published data seeming to suggest that when students in an introductory course were sectioned according to ability (entrance examination scores, class rank, and a pre-test of ability to read or hear psychological material and pass a quiz on it) the best performance relative to ability occurred in the all-high-ability sections, next best in the all-low-ability sections, and poorest performance in the heterogeneous-ability sections. There were a number of methodological difficulties, particularly in the use of the ability data on the students, so that the study cannot be regarded as convincing. Elliott also discovered [100] that there was a tendency for both abler and less able classes of students to approve more warmly of instruction gauged at the difficulty level appropriate to the class ability level. We are left with the feeling, however, that considering how difficult it is to section students by ability in actual practice and considering also the low correlations we have reported between ability and *gains* during a course, it may not be worth the trouble to become involved in planned sectioning procedures.

PRIOR KNOWLEDGE OF PSYCHOLOGY

We often do not respond as we should to what our students already know that is accurate when they come to us, or at least, what some individuals know. True, a great deal of misbelief and firmly rooted bias is to be expected. Furthermore, such accurate knowledge as there is is likely to be spotty, for only nonsystematic reading is likely to have been indulged in (Freud, for instance), and the slight exposure to psychology sometimes available in secondary school covers but part of the field, as in a course in vocational choice or on marriage and family problems. Yet every so often we learn that an unusual individual, before he starts even an introductory course, can perform as well as the average student does on the final examination. If he is made to repeat materials he already understands he is sure to be uninterested or rebellious. Even more often we encounter a student who feels that he knows the material of the introductory course and will not believe that he is not ready to go into advanced courses.

Proficiency or anticipation examinations [as in 61] may be used for evaluation of the knowledge of such students. They may be allowed to apply for such an examination on their own initiative and then either be allowed to by-pass the course if they are ready to do so (and if institutional rules permit this), or be required to take it in accordance with objective and convincing evidence of the need for so doing. Occasional use of a recent final examination at the beginning of the course may also serve to show the areas in which the students are generally more and less deficient, so that the instructor does not dwell unduly on topics with which they are already conversant, or go to the opposite extreme of assuming "everybody knows that" when indeed everybody does not.

The use of anticipatory or classification examinations is especially desirable for transfer students. Far too often a course title or catalogue description of a course passed in another institution is taken as evidence of the student's mastery level. For his good, and the good of the instructor whose course he wishes to enter, locally obtained and objective data about just where he stands in relation to the knowledge level of his peers and fellow competitors is very desirable.

REACTIONS TO INSTRUCTION

On no topic in the academic world is there more argumentative discussion than on how to evaluate teaching. As we have indicated in Chapter 5, academic jobs are usually created because there is a demand for a particular teaching role, and success as a teacher is supposed ordinarily to have a bearing on academic status and security. Yet without question teaching adequacy—partly because there is no ready criterion by which it can be evaluated—does not often play a clear part in the formal appointment and promotional policies of an institution.

The criterion of good teaching. Guthrie [126] draws on Aristotle's *Politics* for the idea that we get a better notion of the merits of the dinner from the dinner guests than from the cook. Similarly, we should expect facts about or opinions from the students who have been taught to provide a more meaningful criterion of the quality of instruction than the opinions of those who do the teaching; and obviously those who merely teach or administer alongside cannot have direct evidence but must use rumor and hearsay in their evaluation. For many years there has been a concern about what aspects of student performance constitute a good yardstick by which to judge the teacher. Lancelot [161], for example, considers and is inclined to reject the criterion of correlation between ability measures and grades earned (which we discussed above, p. 341). He considers delayed measures of the retention of knowledge by students a good but impractical criterion. The quality of work in later courses in the same field he regards as fairly satisfactory, if the measures can be thought comparable in later and earlier courses.

It has been suggested [19, 122] that the number of students attracted to a major in the field following an introductory course might serve to evaluate that course, but this obviously applies to courses only at such a level, as does the criterion of whether an introductory course stimulates students to take later courses at all [122]. Barr [19] suggests that the basic rating of instruction ought to depend upon pupil growth and achievement, as learned from a comparison of pre- and post-tests of various kinds in each academic course or instructional unit. Barr himself points out, however, that while this procedure is sound, it does not resolve the question of what tests are valid indicators of the kinds of achievement we desire in our students. In addition Barr suggests that supervisory ratings of practice teaching are an alternative criterion of instruction, but notes that to date research studies yield low correlations between such ratings and measures of pupil change. Equally has there been a lack of noticeable correlation between personality ratings or measures of the teacher and the measures of pupil change. Barr feels, however, that this kind of approach has not yet been analytical enough, and his feeling is borne out by the finding by one group of investigators [9] that teacher style does definitely influence pupil reaction in the lower school grades.

At the college level, evaluation of instruction is in an even less satisfactory state. Certain investigators [100, 234] have carefully tried to utilize measures of student achievement, particularly achievement assessed in relation to measured ability or predicted grade. In each case the investigators have had to assume that what was being taught in the course was what ought to be taught, i.e., that the only problem was to evaluate the instructor by finding out how well his students mastered the predetermined content of the course. Visitation procedures have occasionally been used, although this has been done more for training purposes [e.g., 53, 187] than for evaluation as such. And thus we come back to evaluations of instruction by students, the case for which is made persuasively by the large Brooklyn College study [223]. As might have been anticipated, a factor analysis study reported by Guthrie [126] indicates that the impact of the instructor on his students is but one of three dimensions that are significant in the total evaluation; the other two are his impact on his profession (by way of research and scholarly productivity), and his impact on his colleagues. Impact on students (only) is the evaluation criterion we shall discuss here. Whenever it is proposed that students should be asked to rate their instructors much protest is heard from the faculty. There is presumably an underlying fear that this gives students, immature as they are, too much power over the faculty, or that freedom of faculty speech in the classroom is being invaded. These generalized implications or reactions are defensible only to the extent that specific inadequacies of student judgment are discovered, and we therefore must ask what is known about student ratings.

Kinds of student ratings of the faculty. To begin with, ratings are secured by a good many different procedures. Most commonly a given instructor trait is defined and the student asked to check one of a number of possible ratings on that trait ("Presentations clear and well organized"—"Presentations usually not well organized and hard to follow"). In another procedure [125], a form of "man-to-man" comparison is required. The student first lists names of several teachers ranging from "outstanding" to "little value to me," then by ratings compares a given instructor with his own set of reference teachers on any number of specific traits as requested. ("On 'sympathetic attitude in dealings with students,' Instructor A is like the most outstanding teacher I have ever had, but in quality of presentation he is like the next-to-poorest instructor I have had.") In still a different kind of rating scheme the student is required to make a tetrad choice [168, 195]. That is, from among four factual statements about what teachers do, he is to select the pair best characterizing the teacher being rated at the moment. (Such a tetrad might be "Has the class form committees." "Omits chapters in textbooks from lectures." "Uses an extensive vocabulary." "Tells students to have a good time in college.") Such statements have been incorporated partly because they have previously been judged to appear equally favorable (i.e., unbiased) as statements about what a teacher does in relation to his students. And some of the statements have in addition been found to discriminate between good and poor teachers, while others which do not serve as blinds, so that the student cannot deliberately choose all the bad or all the good alternatives. This form of assessment permits compilation of the number of discriminating items checked in favor of any given instructor. Sometimes ratings of aspects of the course other than the instructor's own characteristics are secured, and there is some evidence [234] that these ratings are more revealing of the quality of instruction than are direct ratings of the teacher.

Pros and cons of student ratings of the faculty. Granted that student evaluations can be secured in many ways, what reservations must we have, what interpretations must we make, concerning their accuracy or objectivity? First, it may be suggested that because of immaturity or a false conception of the nature of college instruction, students may rate high the teacher who seeks to be popular or interesting rather than the teacher who offers more substantial fare. The proposal in this form is scarcely capable of evaluation, because it joins inseparably, as it were, "popularity," which in this context is a bad word, and "interest," which presumably is central to the response a good teacher arouses. Perhaps the most nearly relevant study is that of Sartain and Waring [239], who by a careful statistical procedure studied the relation between judgments of course interest and value. First they constructed separate scales for the two dimensions, with the items making up the interest scale providing an operational definition of interest that clearly did not imply lowering of standards or other supposedly bad features of a bid for popularity. Then these two scales were utilized with students taking courses in various departments. It was found that student judgments of interest and value were moderately closely correlated (the *r*'s ranging from .38 to .75 in the various disciplines, .70 for a sample of 234 social science students). Thus, while interest is presumably related to whether the values of a course are apparent or sought, so that the two ought to be related, the correlations are not so high in the Sartain-Waring data as to suggest that the same thing is merely being measured twice. Guthrie [126], on the basis of long and close acquaintance with teachers who rated highest in the faculty evaluation program he administered at the University of Washington, came to the opinion that these high-ranking teachers were also substance teachers, not merely or simply entertainment oriented.

Student judgment have sometimes been thought undependable, changeable, and whimsical. Evidence against this comes again from Guthrie, who indicates that when as many as 25 student judgments are secured, the picture they give of the instructor becomes quite stable. Reliability coefficients are upwards of .90. The judgments themselves may be diverse, as is to be expected when any sample of opinions or judgments is collected from human beings, but the relative pattern or scatter of them is evidently rather well discerned if as many as 25 student judgments (under the Washington procedure, at least) are available.

It has been suggested that some students give judgments biased by their own position in relation to the instructor. The evidence on this point is of assorted varieties, none conclusive but all suggestive of nothing more than a to-be-expected range of variation. For example, in a relatively small sample of students, Bendig [23] found that women were somewhat more critical than men of a male instructor, rather than being swayed into simple admiration by his maleness. Advanced undergraduate students have been found to be more critical than beginners [23], undergraduates have been found to be somewhat more critical than graduate students [100] and, over all, graduate students and undergraduates have been found to give judgments correlating closely [125]. Neither majors and non-majors, nor large and small classes, differ systematically in the ratings they give, according to Guthrie's report [126]. Finally, it was Crannell's opinion [79] in reporting the widespread use of student ratings in his institution that there were no cases in which students tried to damage a faculty member by means of the ratings.

It has also been thought that the values of good instruction might not be known or appreciated until some time after a course was completed, presumably as a result of maturation or other contributors to perspective. The only study known to bear on this point [93] indicates that alumni 10 years out of college agreed very closely with undergraduates in college at the time as to what instructor traits were significant in the quality of instruction. Indeed, the first four traits (adequacy of presentation, interest, stimulation of intellectual curiosity, and a liberal and progressive attitude) were judged in exactly the same rank order of importance by both groups. Interestingly enough, the alumni put a sense of proportion and humor in fifth place, while students put it eighth. Personal appearance and peculiarities were ranked in ninth and tenth places by both groups, a perhaps reassuring fact. We learn from such a study that, while individual values must assuredly change to some extent in post-college years, the student-turned-alumnus evidently continued to feel that the same teacher traits are important, and this is not much changed by increasing maturity or perspective. (We should note explicitly that this says nothing about changes in valuation of the *content* learned in college.)

It has often been felt that the rating a student gives an instructor depends upon the mark he expects to receive, and a number of studies are pertinent to this point. That ratings of the faculty and marks earned by students are unrelated is suggested by Elliott [100], who calls the effect of marks on ratings unimportant. Guthrie [126, Figs. 5, 6] presents evidence that the generally abler students (as defined by general grade-point average) do not give higher ratings, and also that marks currently being earned by individuals in a specific course are not related to the ratings they give. In an allied study Sartain and Waring [239] found a relatively low correlation between the interest rating a student gave a course and his own mark in it. On the other hand, Anikeef [12] calculated rank-order coefficients of correlation between the mean grade a number of instructors (*ns* from 13 to 17 in various computations) gave their students and the mean rating they received from students, and found a rather close positive relationship (but a lower correlation between upper class men's ratings and their grades). There is a very technical research problem here, in that the grade the student earns is evaluated by him partly or largely in terms of what he expects to receive, and this in turn depends somehow on his perception of his ability. So it might be expected that students achieving "above" their ability level would regard the instruction very favorably, while students who were under-achievers might be very critical.

Two studies are addressed rather directly to this point, with conflicting conclusions. Elliott [100], in a study of instruction in a Chemistry 1 course at Purdue University, predicted student grades from a multiple regression equation based on aptitude and placement test scores. "Discrepancy" scores (amount the earned grade departed above or below the predicted grade) were then computed for students, and the magnitude and sign of the discrepancy compared with ratings they gave to instructors. The correlation was .239, indicating that to only a slight degree is relative achievement (after ability is removed from consideration) related to the rating given the instructor. The same kind of conclusion was reached after detailed study by Russell [234], who controlled student knowledge of grades by studying the relative over- and under-achievement of only students who earned a C grade. On the other hand, it was Russell's opinion that over the *whole* range of grades, instructor ratings by students would be found to vary. Perhaps the only conclusion we can presently reach about this is that grades are going to vary, and if it so happens that student opinion of the instructor to some extent varies correspondingly, this merely indicates a fact about students and does not invalidate the effort to find out what they think, nor reduce the importance of what they think for the way they will respond to instruction. But research is still needed to clarify this area.

It is relatively clear that students do not evaluate their instructors the way faculty colleagues do, as our mention above of the factor analysis study reported by Guthrie should imply. In addition we note Guthrie's finding [126] that research productivity, an important factor in faculty evaluation of colleagues, does not correlate at all closely with student ratings of instructors. Guthrie also reports [125] that faculty and student judgments of the quality of teaching correlated only .30, and he indicates [p. 201] that although students think mastery of subject matter is an important trait of the instructor, they are not capable of agreeing very well on whether a given instructor does in fact know his subject.

It is my own feeling that while much is obscure about the

determiners of student ratings of instruction, under certain conditions there can be a value in securing and paying attention to them. The prime requirement is that the instructor himself be willing and able to face up to what his students think of his work. I am convinced, and the Brooklyn College study [223, Chap. 10] gives support to my view, that regardless of what verbal defenses college teachers may have, very few of them can really be indifferent to what their students think. So if their defenses are not raised by having a rating system forced on them, or by knowledge that the ratings, whatever the subtleties or intricacies of their interpretation, are going to be handled blindly, statistically, and administratively, they are reasonably likely to accept student ratings as a source of personal evaluation and guidance. As we said in Chapter 7, the beginning instructor tends to be so busy with his thoughts and sentences that he does not often enough have time to observe himself in the classroom. Yet if he is to be adaptive to the task before him he should be influenced by student reaction. Rating devices make this possible if the instructor can feel that he himself has control over how the ratings are taken and interpreted.

There remains the question whether student ratings should *ever* be used for administrative evaluation of the faculty. The answer must be: It depends on local conditions and faculty attitudes; forced use of them is sure to be detrimental to faculty morale, but as Guthrie [126] indicates it is at least possible for a large majority of a faculty to approve of the practice. I do not believe, any more than anyone else, that student ratings should be overvalued in selecting, appointing, or promoting faculty members, although any information of this kind should usually be given some weight. Particularly do I think it unfortunate that the usual numerical form of ratings gives them, to many administrators, an almost spurious appearance of accuracy and solidity. If such blind faith in numbers can be prevented from influencing the interpretation of ratings, I would agree with Guthrie that there is presently no better criterion of the quality of instruction.

STUDENT TRAITS AND TEACHING METHODS

Anxiety. To an increasing degree psychologists have become concerned with the influence of basic personality variables on the way students react to various aspects of instruction. We have remarked that anxiety, as one such variable, may be aroused by examinations, relations with other students, or the behavior of the instructor. It may also be aroused to a higher degree in some students than in others. It is the latter problem, of individual differences in anxiety level, that we shall discuss here.

In a series of papers, of which only one is selected for reference here [238], Sarason and Mandler have discussed anxiety concerning examinations and tests. They developed a reliable questionnaire device for measuring test anxiety, including some 40 questions such as the following: "When you are taking a course examination, to what extent do you feel that your emotional reactions interfere with or lower your performance?" "If you know that you are going to take a group intelligence test, how do you feel beforehand?" "While taking a group intelligence test, to what extent do you perspire?" In the study under consideration this questionnaire was administered to 492 students, so that it was possible to select and compare sizable groups of students at the extremes: high-anxiety students, above the 85th percentile in weighted total score; and low-anxiety students, below the 14th percentile. (Middle groups were also studied, but the less conclusive results obtained with them will not be reported here.)

A first hypothesis of the authors had to do with the relation between degree of anxiety as they measured it and the socio-economic background of the students. It was their expectation that anxiety about intellectual matters would be less in upper-class students than in middle-class students, since intellectual values would not be primary in the upbringing of the former group. Specific indices to indicate social class were uncovered in college records and the relations of these to measured anxiety were studied. The hypothesis was confirmed in several ways. Significantly more fathers of high-anxiety students had middle-class occupations, and significantly more of the high-anxiety students were in college on a scholarship. Differences in the same direction but not statistically significant were found for the proportions of high-anxiety students attending public, rather than private, schools, and having fathers without college education. We see, then, that the Sarason-Mandler data lead us to expect somewhat different degrees of test anxiety according to the socio-economic origins of students. (It should be noted that indices such as the private vs. public school origins of a student are somewhat ambiguous. A good many private school students may typify what the authors expect to be associated with public school background, i.e., they are students who attended public school, then took only one or a few years in private school and in so doing reflected a determined middle-class motivation to enter, by means of improved preparation, a college of high standards and social standing.)

In the same paper Sarason and Mandler relate their test anxiety measures to other test performances and to academic achievement. Their hypotheses were as follows: 1. Students with a strong anxiety drive will perform more poorly than those with low anxiety drive when responses motivated by anxiety but irrelevant to the task interfere with adequate performance. 2.

When a stimulus situation contains elements specifically arousing test or achievement anxiety, this increase in anxiety drive will lead to poorer performance in students who have task-irrelevant anxiety responses in their repertoire. For individuals without such response tendencies, these stimulus elements will raise the general drive level and result in improved performance. 3. When a student with a strong anxiety drive has been rewarded for making task-relevant responses in certain situations (course examinations, doing course work), these responses will become dominant over irrelevant responses in these situations, and performance, because of the summation of drives, will be superior to that of individuals of low anxiety. One empirical prediction by the authors was that high-anxiety subjects would have significantly lower scores on scholastic aptitude tests (because of the task-irrelevant responses evoked by high anxiety during the tests, conflicting with useful responses to the test). This expectation was reliably confirmed, as was the expectation that high-anxiety subjects would have lower predicted grade averages in college (which is partly contained in the first prediction, since aptitude tests are an important component of grade prediction). The authors also predicted that high-anxiety subjects would have a significantly higher *actual* grade average, on the grounds that in an academic course the high-anxiety student has time to become familiar with the instructor, with the way examinations are handled, and so on, and thus can reinstitute anxiety-reducing and task-relevant responses. Combined with the fact of strong drive (anxiety plus achievement), these factors should produce more effective performance in courses than for low-anxiety students, and the actual-grade data reliably bear out this expectation. Several other predictions were made, and less satisfactorily borne out, probably for reasons inherent within comparisons of less than extreme groups. Possibly also, the authors suggest, at different positions on the scale of test anxiety the scores may be differentially valid because of differential distortion or masking of anxiety. For example, the results with high-anxiety students may be influenced by qualitatively different modes of defense against anxiety in examinations or in courses. But the authors show that the correlation between measured anxiety and measured intelligence, in one sample of students, is rather low (approximately .20) but significant at the .05 level of confidence. The correlation is complex to interpret (e.g., the most intelligent students all had low anxiety scores, but the least intelligent students did not necessarily have high anxiety scores), but the authors seem justified in concluding that intelligence test scores as such probably do not fairly describe individuals who have a high anxiety drive in the testing situation (or, we may generalize beyond the authors, in other kinds of performance during an academic course). Certainly the results of Sarason and Mandler are consistent with our earlier concern for measures to reduce anxiety in the classroom, in order that the student is freer to learn, or to show what he knows.

Another approach to the role of anxiety in academic performance has been made in a detailed study by Gaier [113]. Eleven students were studied; they were taking a discussion class in social science at the time. Rorschach test scores were secured on three dimensions: anxiety-readiness, rigidity, and negativism-aggression. Intelligence test data, placement examination scores, and subscores on a four-part comprehensive examination in social science were secured. In addition, Gaier utilized Bloom's method [36] for stimulating recall of thoughts during a discussion class period, by playing back a tape recording of the class meeting and stopping it at appropriate points for questioning and recall. Various content analyses were made of the recalls thus obtained. The principal results of interest to us here show that anxiety-readiness correlated −.66 with intelligence test scores; +.34 with the rote-recall or identification section of the comprehensive social science examination at the end of the course; −.48 with that portion of the comprehensive requiring analysis of familiar materials; −.61 with the part requiring comparisons of familiar and unfamiliar materials; −.42 with the subtest requiring critical evaluation of new materials; and +.60 with the number of negative thoughts about one's self exhibited in the stimulated recall of proceedings during classroom sessions. (Only *rhos* of .60 or more reach the .05 level of significance.) These results not only show that degree of anxiety-readiness relates rather predictably to aspects of academic performance, but they are complementary to the Sarason-Mandler findings in indicating that various kinds of cognitive operations are influenced in different ways, not always detrimentally, by anxiety. That is, students of high anxiety-readiness here were less able to meet demands for new and untried modes of thought in the comprehensive examination, but were reasonably able to cope with demands for recall of material previously studied in comparable form.

Gaier's findings concerning other variables serve to reinforce the findings concerning anxiety-readiness. Rigidity, as measured on the Rorschach test, correlated +.73 with scores on the rote portion of the comprehensive; only +.20 with the subtest requiring analysis and interpretation of familiar course materials; −.71 with the subtest comparing authors read in and out of the course; −.71 with the subtest requiring critical judgments on new materials; and +.52 with number of negative thoughts about one's self in the classroom. The Rorschach measure of negativism, on the other hand, did not correlate very closely at all with performance on the comprehensive examination subparts, although it did correlate +.67 with negative and critical thoughts about other people during class; +.62 with degree of criticism of ideas expressed in class; and +.52 with negative thoughts about self in class. (The *rhos* cited in this paragraph are significant at the .05 level only if .60 or above.) The content analysis of conscious thoughts during class, as used by Gaier, seems particularly interesting as a research technique and this method, together with personality analyses of students, provides an approach to the role of anxiety in the student that is a clear supplement to the approach used by Sarason and Mandler.

In connection with our mention of the variable of rigidity in Gaier's study, attention should be called to Stern's work [259]. (See also the abstract by Goldberg and Stern [119].) An inventory of beliefs, akin to a rigidity-flexibility measure, was administered to incoming college freshmen and scored to detect student extremes of three types. It was found that students having beliefs reflecting a rigid, inhibited, conforming, orderly personality, although not inferior in measured intelligence, tended to drop out of college much more often than students who were more flexible, friendly, and outgoing. This may reflect the inability of the former to accept the new ideas which college inevitably requires students to master. Such students scored lowest on a number of placement examinations, also, as in the social sciences and humanities, and exhibited vocational interests of a more concrete, instrumental, and socially unambiguous kind.

Related to what Sarason and Mandler's theorizing would lead one to expect, and Gaier's as well, is a finding of Smith [249, 250, 251]. In a small sample of students he showed that those who scored relatively lower on a special test of ability to transfer or apply their learning in introductory psychology also showed reliably more blocking and conflict (that is, signs of anxiety) in a word-association test. In another part of his research Smith made a detailed term-long study in which different classroom atmospheres were employed to manipulate student feelings of security and anxiety. These atmospheres can be described briefly as conducive to feelings of security ("positive"), apathy, or anxiety ("negative"). Smith taught all three kinds of class himself. Although the atmospheres were objectively demonstrated to be different, this independent variable in and of itself was evidently not enough to vary the over-all degree of anxiety or security in the classes. At least, on neither the applicational transfer test nor a standard achievement test did the various classes differ. However, on the *post hoc* assumption that the best index of the classroom atmosphere's affect on the student was his own report of his emotional status during the term, Smith compared nine students who became more secure under the positive method of instruction with seven students who became more anxious under the negative method. In this comparison, which is rather open to the criticism that the outcome depends on how the data are selected, it turned out that the students who became more secure under positive instruction were better able to transfer their knowledge to the new problem situations.

McKeachie, Pollie, and Speisman [193] studied the more specific notion that encountering difficult items on an objective examination increases anxiety, so that if methods of relieving this anxiety can be found the test performance of students should be improved. In a series of five minor studies, it appeared that giving students a chance to write comments about any given examination item was related to better performance. A number of follow-ups of this finding were not very conclusive, although it seems probable that one of the conditions governing it is the degree of freedom from fear that the comment, if made, might itself lead to punishment in some way. In this kind of study as in several others, it seems pertinent to remark that the analysis of anxiety itself, the defenses against it at different locations in the intensity scale, and other more detailed formulations seem necessary to more definitive experimentation.

Student personality and teaching method. In a large Social Relations course at Harvard University, Wispe [282] compared permissive and directive methods of instruction in weekly section classes of about 20 students. The teachers were assigned to the two methods by having their performance observed during the first three weeks of the term and then being instructed to be consistent and to sharpen their use of the method which came naturally. Detailed data showed that the different instructors did indeed succeed in creating different classroom atmospheres and that the students were much aware of how their own class was conducted (although Wispe himself comments that permissive teaching may not be very well done by the relatively inexperienced graduate-student instructor teaching in this course, nor is it likely to show its full effects under rather great limitations of time and cultural milieu). In addition, personality assays were made of students by means of specially constructed projective-type tests of attitudes toward, for example, college teachers, or other students, and by a sentence-completion test. These were related to their evaluations of the course and the instruction. It was found that there were a good many students who tended to be intro-punitive and to react negatively toward their instructors and their fellow students, who wanted more direction, and who particularly did not like permissive teaching —while at the same time they said they felt free to participate in the class. Another conspicuous subgroup tended to be extra-punitive and moderately favorable toward the instructor and fellow students. They preferred permissive teaching. In classes directively taught their aggression was likely to be aimed at the instructor, but in classes permissively taught it was directed at nonpersonal objects. The satisfied subgroup of students were favorably inclined toward both instructor and fellow students, showed fewer signs of punitiveness, and accepted directive or permissive teaching as it happened to fall to their lot. The conclusion of this part of the Wispe study is, then, that student personality significantly interacts with teaching method. In a measure, the instructor is in the position of needing to use different methods with different members of the same class, a situation presumably impossible to attain except in informal and small classes where adaptability is truly possible.

PATTERNS OF TEACHING

Research results of the kind found by Wispe suggest or reinforce a view about the teaching process which is perhaps inherent in this entire book, namely, that we presently know of no one method of instruction which is best for all situations, or all students, or all subject matters, or for all instructors. It is clear that although we seek laws of some degree of generality about teaching, they are relatively slow to appear in the researches available to date. Important reasons why this is so may be these: the complexity of the teaching situation, as defined by the number of variables to be isolated and manipulated; the practical difficulties of securing control over many variables which are inherent in college organization and administration; and perhaps above all, the complex interactions, in the statistical sense, which seem likely everywhere in teaching. (Wispe, for example, found that directive teaching was better than permissive for poorer students, but that there was no difference between the methods for the superior students.) It seems probable that we shall not find out whether lecture and discussion methods of instruction really differ in effectiveness until we specify the subject matter and other goals to be sought, the relevant characteristics of the instructor's own make-up, the circumstances under which the teaching is to occur, and relevant features of student make-up and history. At such a very complex and detailed level, research on teaching may finally begin to demonstrate just what kinds of lawfulness are involved in areas where, to date, the researcher's manipulations have not seemed to matter much.

In the meantime, teaching remains something of an art. It cannot very conclusively be guided by stated principles of suitable generality and validity. The individual instructor remains something of an artist. This means he must learn by personal experience to be an effective teacher, with whatever aid his peers and elders can afford him, by the gradual process of making mistakes and having successes, trying this procedure and that, with this kind of student and that, in a teaching situation about which he learns more all the time. The more analytical and flexible he is, the better the chance that teaching will in the long run be rewarding to both him and his students.

APPENDIX: EXPERIMENTAL PSYCHOLOGY

In the main body of this book we have not discussed one of the characteristic methods of instruction in psychology—the laboratory method. For a number of reasons we shall discuss it only briefly here. The principal reason is that today "the" laboratory method is evolving rapidly into many kinds of things. Use of the experimental approach has spread widely in psychology, now encompassing any area in which the critical variables can be manipulated so that subjects can be assigned to treatments at random and thus permit adequate statistical evaluations of the data. The laboratory method, in the old and narrow sense of methods applicable to what Titchener wanted to study, the normal human adult mind, has long since burst its bounds, and in the last decade or so experimental psychology has come ever closer to coinciding with the bounds of psychology itself, as experimental work in social psychology, personality, and many other areas has become feasible. The consequence of such changes is that the variety of methods of instruction in experimental psychology is very great. In most departments of psychology the procedures used are being changed practically every time an experimental course is offered, and it simply is not possible to reach firm conclusions about how to teach experimental method. (It may be remarked that the problem is no less severe at the graduate level.)

The rapidly changing nature of teaching in experimental psychology does not lessen its importance to us. If anything, it increases the necessity for the beginning instructor to know the sorts of things various teachers and departments are trying. There is practically no recent published material, and there are even fewer attempts at evaluation of instructional methods. In an effort to learn what is being done, therefore, I have corresponded with a number of Departments of Psychology where I happened to have reason to believe there was substantial teaching of the experimental method. In consequence I have to thank the following persons for lengthy replies to my questions, and in several cases their patience with repeated probings from me: Professors John W. Atkinson (Michigan), Neil Bartlett (Hobart), Edwin B. Newman (Harvard), Francis W. Irwin (Pennsylvania), Benton J. Underwood (Northwestern), Robert S. Daniel (Missouri), Eugene R. Long (North Carolina), Parker Johnson (Bowdoin), Wm. C. H. Prentice (Swarthmore), Gregory A. Kimble (Duke), and my own colleagues, Professors Kay C. Montgomery and Frederick D. Sheffield, who have done very interesting things with experimental instruction. In using the information I have gained from these men, I have decided to attempt primarily to summarize trends, and thus relieve them of responsibility for any particular statements I may make here. At the same time I must disclaim any notion that the trends found in my sample of informants are intended to be representative. It must nevertheless be said that even on paper one can perceive that enthusiastic and resourceful developments in this area of teaching are now occurring in the laboratories of these men.

OBJECTIVES AND EMPHASES

I deem it very significant that all but one or two of the men regard their teaching as oriented toward liberal arts objectives rather than pre-professional ones. There is of course no objection to having the two coincide, but it is clear that the former takes precedence in planning both content and teaching procedures. The one or two men who are exceptions to this statement are in a sense classicists. They insist that experimental psychology should be taught rigorously as a rigorous discipline; anything else is likely to be soft, a kind of pap not likely to contribute to the production of good scientists and not reflecting faithfully the nature of the field.

What liberal arts objectives are most commonly stated?

1. Nearly all who accept such objectives are concerned with teaching experimental psychology to make it generalize, not merely to other psychology courses but to the everyday lives of the students. It is the experimental mode of thought, not the particular methods, that they focus on. They quite explicitly pay no attention to whether students who take experimental psychology are majors or not, and in some instances the courses are elected by a good many non-majors.

2. The chief reason for teaching the experimental approach to psychological problems is for most instructors the same as the reason why science in general is taught in college. That is, the fact that science is historically and currently a central force in society should be fully appreciated by the liberally educated person.

3. There are varied specific phrasings of the "appreciation of science" objective. It is regarded, for example, as a proper scientific emphasis to teach both the uses of careful and planned

observation in the gathering of data and the necessity for objectivity. Respect for the canons of evidence, to borrow a phrase from one correspondent, is essential to any well-educated person's views of the natural world, of society, and of individuals—including himself. A realization that from concrete instances (data) inductions may grow helps shape the thought processes of any student. The fact that imaginativeness and disciplined thought are both essential in good science should be recognized as paralleling the emphasis on creativeness of other kinds in other disciplines. The feature of experimentation that holds the instructor himself to it, the adventure of the search, should be experienced by the student whose intellectual interests are being formed during his undergraduate years.

4. With considerably more difference of opinion, the majority of the correspondents feel that the experimental course is a good place for controlled practice at scientific reporting and writing. The actual extent to which students are required to do this depends partly on how much report-reading manpower is available in proportion to the number of reports to be read. A point of debate, however, is whether a psychology department is really responsible for the quality of expression and writing, and whether continual writing of reports does not detract from the interest value of the course, not to mention the time available for exploration of additional topical fields. The bias of this book is toward having psychologists share to a reasonable degree this responsibility for ensuring literacy among college-educated people.

5. There is rather uniform agreement that students should not be required to learn such pre-professional skills as apparatus construction, but there is no objection to a student's learning to build apparatus if this is what he wants and needs to do in order to study a problem which interests him.

6. On the other hand, the majority of instructors require considerable statistical work in the process of data analysis, or

demand careful use of graphs and tables in student reports. The fact that computation routines may require considerable time and labor does not seem to prevent their being required, the evident feeling being that such routines are basic to a feel for the nature of the data of science. There is considerable variation in whether a statistics course is prerequisite to the experimental one (this being the most common plan), co-requisite, combined with it, or, a rarely found arrangement, not directly related to it at all.

7. Although one reason for teaching the experimental course, in the eyes of several instructors, is the opportunity it can provide for individualizing the work of superior students, there is only one instance in which this feature of the course is deliberately used for recruitment purposes. In this instance, the one or two ablest students are often withdrawn from the course, if they are interested, and put to work as research assistants (often paid) in full-fledged faculty research. The high degree of involvement thus secured is felt to ensure more learning than would occur in an ordinary course, and identification with the aims of the research project and the faculty member(s) engaged in it has a definite recruitment value.

8. A number of instructors feel that the subject matter of an experimental psychology course, coming as it does in the form of problems, lends itself particularly well to two aims of the instructor: to arouse his students to active participation and active learning; and to cause, in a naturalistic way, an integration of several kinds of knowledge. For instance, to attack a problem in the formation of attitudes, students must interrelate what they know about the learning process, motivation, experimental design, statistics, interpersonal relations, and even such diverse matters as social class, role theory, and conflict. Furthermore, in any such activity the student passes from reading *about* science, as in most introductory courses, to *doing* science, which is likely to have a much greater impact on his understanding.

KINDS OF SUBJECT MATTER IN EXPERIMENTAL COURSES

One of the noteworthy things about experimental psychology is the range of levels at which it is offered. There are courses primarily for freshmen and courses primarily for seniors, although the most common level is sophomore or junior. Regardless of the level, however, most courses try to reach a balance between content devoted to method as such and content devoted to subject matter in psychology. The instructor finds this kind of balance necessary, almost inevitably, because method cannot be taught in the abstract. It must instead be method for studying *something,* and the latter is the psychological problem or subject matter area. (In one of the departments with which I have corresponded students have four or five terms of subject matter courses before they study experimental psychology. The latter is therefore taught without a special subject matter of its own, and simply draws on previously learned materials for the necessary subject matter background of any experimentation.)

When the work in experimental psychology is part of the introductory course it must reflect what is in the lectures. If the lecture course is a general survey, then the laboratory which accompanies it must include a wide variety of topics, and of necessity at this level most of them must be treated, not in a truly experimental way, but rather in some simpler manner. It is here that demonstrations are often used, and that the measurement methods, not experimentation as such, are stressed in the classical manner. Reaction time, after-images, psychophysics, the measurement of retinal color zones or the ability to localize sound sources, and the detection of "guilt" through word-association methods are common topics. It appears to be true, however, that introductory psychology courses which include laboratory work do so partly to permit their classification among the biological science offerings of the college for distributional credits, and such courses are fairly commonly slanted toward individual differences, sensory, perceptual, and associative processes to such an extent that many of the simple laboratory procedures are suitable as well as available for inclusion in the laboratory plan.

When the experimental course is offered as the single course of its kind in a department, it most commonly is given to sophomores and juniors, and here it is likely again to place most emphasis upon sensory, perceptual, and associative processes because it is thought they are most adequately taught with the aid of the laboratory. More technical treatments, or more complex methodologies, are likely to be included than in a beginner-level course. For example, psychophysics is usually elaborated to some extent, and statistical procedures receive considerably more attention than in a beginner-level course. True experimental procedures and design are likely to be studied before the course is over. Perhaps the most interesting part of each course is one in which the investigations performed are new, sometimes in the sense of a twist on a well-established procedure, but often in the sense of an exploratory piece of work in any of a great variety of subject matter areas.

Perhaps the most interesting development from the subject matter point of view is the appearance of topical courses in experimental psychology. In these courses only a limited area of content is covered, this being the only or the principal instruction in that area within the departmental curriculum. Topical courses which are substantially experimental are now offered in sensation and perception, perception, emotion, action, learning, learning and motivation combined, motivation, and personality, the last three including, because of the less advanced status of the field, considerable work in measurement methodology as such. It would appear that incorporation of experimental psychology within a series of topical courses, so that the term experimental is no longer definitive of a difference among courses, is a very natural and desirable next step from the point of view of the development of psychology and from the pedagogical or curriculum planning viewpoints as well. A number of advantages would be gained. Method and content combine naturally, not arbitrarily, in a topical type of course. When the topical label defines the course content uniquely, it is possible to create a more efficient, less repetitious kind of curriculum plan. Student interest and course selection can be focused more sharply. And finally, the range of methods covered is limited to those most useful in relation to a particular subject matter, with the result that the latter is likely to be made more meaningful by adequate attention to the methods for acquiring knowledge about it.

WORK PLANS AND PROCEDURES

In teaching experimental psychology one must plan the development of the course so that it begins with materials the student can cope with and only gradually increases its demands on him. The selection of procedures to be taught and subject matter to be mastered requires a great deal of attention, even skill, in judging what students will be ready for at any given stage of the course.

Early in the course what students do is likely to be planned mostly by the faculty. It could be called cook book experimental psychology. Experimental or measurement procedures are chosen which are quite predictable in their outcomes, and they are executed by the close following of detailed instructions. As the course progresses, however, students are expected to begin to do more of the planning. Most of the instructors expect that the latter part of the student's work in any course above the beginner level will approximate genuinely independent planning and execution. In some courses this independence is expected of a group, or a pair, rather than an individual student, and sometimes the problem continues to be assigned rather than originating with the student. But there are instructors who expect that, for instance, the last project students carry out in a course will test some idea of their own, by a procedure they themselves design and follow with only guidance and support by the instructor. It is here that the nearness of the boundaries of sure knowledge in psychology is clearly turned to pedagogical advantage, for a junior major who does a bit of independent work, be it ever so minor, on some idea of his own, is likely to have a thoroughly exciting feeling of exploring new territory. Consequently he thinks and works as he rarely has before.

A co-ordinate trend within the work plan of an experimental course is likely to be from essentially nonexperimental to truly experimental procedures. At the beginning of the course, the student is not ready for the complexities of full-fledged experimental design, so that a beginning is made with simple measurement procedures, or even demonstrations. Well before the end of most courses, however, it is expected that genuine experimentation will be done, with full attention to manipulation and control of variables, and with anticipation of statistical-analysis requirements.

Third, and less certain as a trend, there appears to be a shift during a good many experimental courses from individual or pair activities to group responsibility. Possibly related to this is the development during the course of the practice of having a whole group or class discuss and jointly plan a single, usually larger, piece of research. Whether this is consistently the course plan appears to depend on the maturity or sophistication of the students. Among less advanced students there is not likely to be the capacity for this kind of growth within the confines of one course, but in certain institutions where the students taking experimental psychology are of high intellectual quality and advanced standing, group responsibility and discussion-analysis methods are found fruitful almost from the first meeting of the course.

Finally, there seems to be in most courses a trend from emphasizing simple, even qualitative, observation as such, without much attention to data analysis and reporting, to emphasizing a more critical, analytical, statistical, and polished kind of reporting. True, this trend is not obvious in all courses, but even when it is not there tends to be an effort to do at least one report in good scientific style before the course is over. Even where there is group planning and execution of projects, individual reports are usually required on the common procedure and data.

VARIANT TEACHING PROCEDURES

Some of the great variety in experimental psychology courses stems from the inventiveness of instructors who are looking for teaching methods appropriate to the situations they face. For example, in Dr. Atkinson's course each student is required to write his half of a weekly "Dialogue," which is a form of reaction report indicating his ideas on the topics under study and his evaluation of what is going on. These are carefully read and responded to by the laboratory instructor. Emphasis is given to originality and critical thought, and students who merely rehearse the reading materials or otherwise show passivity are, in the words of the instructor, "spanked" for it. When compiled, the "Dialogues" constitute a running record of each student's development in subject matter and attitude during the course.

In Dr. Underwood's course, problem or work sheets are the center of much that is done. These are instructor-devised descriptions of experiments which have built-in flaws, concealed as such flaws may well be in actual experiments. The student is expected to analyze the experiment and detect these flaws. He must be able not merely to answer questions about the design but also to defend his answers. These work sheets are regarded by students as the real think pieces of the course and its most valuable pedagogical aspect.

Dr. Montgomery and Dr. Lloyd Beck emphasize the nature of the creative process in science. In a group setting, students are taught rules like those for free association that must be learned by the patient in psychoanalysis: "here is the problem which is to be attacked experimentally; inhibit no thoughts about it, about how to attack it, or about what is signifies," and so on. This turns out to be very embarrassing for some students, difficult for many, because they have the usual set to evaluate responses before releasing them in the classroom. The free flow of thoughts can be learned, however, with enhancement of the possibilities of genuinely new insights or hypotheses. And rich material is thereby provided for teaching the second component of the course, the disciplined modes of thought required to evaluate the ideas in the experimental tradition.

This course has at least a few elements in common with another one which is taught partly in a laissez-faire manner. In this course the instructor, after setting problems and making resources available, is especially anxious to have students learn for themselves just what is involved in making an experimental attack on a problem. He must therefore restrain himself from giving much guidance or advice, and must discipline himself to watch occasional students working hard at a project that almost certainly will fail.

In Dr. Atkinson's course, where exploratory and new studies are emphasized throughout, care is taken to do not one but two or even three studies on a topic. The instructor here is especially desirous of showing students the values of follow-up work to clinch acceptance or rejection of tentative ideas.

Considerable stress is placed on the term paper in a number of courses, but its form and content vary considerably. At one extreme, this paper is a critical methodological survey of research literature in some topical area. At the other it is a report on a major piece of independent experimentation. In several courses the term paper is completed by stages, with conferences and criticism or guidance being offered by the instructor well before the project assumes its final shape.

To give students the feeling of working intensively on their own, yet not lose the values of experience with a broad range of problems, Dr. Bartlett divides his class into pairs, each pair working actively on its own unique project and serving as subjects in all the other projects. The procedure can be cycled by the use of briefer projects and rotation of partners at the completion of each phase, thus permitting coverage of an even wider range of topics. This of course can be done only where the total number of students in the class can be regulated suitably. The instructor himself, in this kind of setting, may serve as a subject in each experiment, as part of his method of evaluating it.

A very interesting combination of procedures is used at Swarthmore, where there are two instructors and the class from the beginning utilizes group discussion and planning of experimental work. Within this department a number of different combinations of instructors have used this procedure, with a uniform feeling that it enhances the pleasure instructors get out of the problem solving process they are trying to teach at an elementary level, that it demonstrates concretely to students that ideas, not personalities or authority, are important in science, that it leads to greater stimulation of both students and instructors, and that it provides a greater range of intellectual resources for the group's activity. It helps, of course, to have enough faculty manpower available to be able to put two instructors in one class of 12 to 20 students.

Three other interest-arousing devices should be mentioned.

At Missouri, beginning laboratory students are taken on an especially planned tour of research facilities, partly to contrast their own necessarily inadequate group conditions and procedures with the way psychological science actually gets made, and partly to provide concrete examples for discussion. At Duke and at Yale independent projects are emphasized and the courses made to point toward a minor scientific convention at year's end, with other students and faculty invited to hear the reading of carefully prepared experimental papers. To enhance the effect of this sort of thing, Yale has established a prize of money and a certificate for the best undergraduate research of the year.

ON WHY SOME MEN TEACH EXPERIMENTAL METHOD WELL

To me it is revealing that both incidental remarks and planned ones indicate that men who really care about teaching experimental psychology offer considerably more to their students than the formal framework of the course. Perhaps the most distinctive thing is the opportunities they create for personal contact with students, informal discussion, or man-to-man teaching wherever this is possible. I doubt that it is accidental that what appear to be the best courses are taught by younger men with modern training in the basic nature of experimentation, with plenty of energy, and with the habit of long hours in the laboratory, evenings and weekends often being included. They keep themselves available to students. They think it important to emit ideas at a relatively high rate, feeling that this sparks the activities of their students. Often mentioned is the informal chat with students while they work, or a visit to their table or laboratory room sometime during each student session there. And a number of the correspondents quite clearly believe an enthusiastic and accepting kind of attitude to be conducive to high student motivation.

A number of additional suggestions to make for effective laboratory teaching can be made, these coming from experience with independent-research students, whether graduate or undergraduate. For example, when students first begin to have ideas of their very own, these may be overly grandiose or just plain fuzzy. (I shall never forget the girl who came to me with a bright idea of solving the nature-nurture problem by crossing chimpanzees and men, or the one who asked "What can I do with baby chicks?" because she had seen some in a store window and decided they were just right to take home to her room in the sorority house and do experimental work on.) The skillful teacher of science avoids unduly punishing these responses, but gradually must lead the student to narrow down or clarify his ideas before attempting to do research. In this way there is more likely to be sufficient reward in the process to sustain the beginner. The difficult skill here, made necessary by the hard fact that science is supposed to face up to reality, not avoid it, is to let the student make his own mistakes, or at least see what they might have been, so that there is a genuine impact of experience on the tendencies to be grandiose or unclear in grappling with scientific problems. Most teachers of experimental psychology also express a concern for teaching method at the point of need, and equally, subject matter at the point of need. Thus they tend to believe that if a student can just be gotten reasonably well under way on a project, he himself will come to see that at certain points new learning or new modes of conduct are essential to progress. The development of his understanding of science is the core to which can accrue many specific learnings as he goes along. Not the least of these is likely to be a realization that literature studies are part of the data-gathering process in science, and that new or radically different kinds of learning (new for him, that is) need not wait upon the offering of a formal course. Finally, most of the good teachers place a high value on satisfactory *completion* of a project, even in the face of unanticipated difficulties and in spite of the sometimes heavy labor. They give as much attention, supportive or critical, as is necessary to get a finished product which the student sees as primarily the result of his own work. Many of them value persistence and conscientiousness about as much as they do ability in their students.

REFERENCES

[1] Adkins, D. C., *et al. Construction and analysis of achievement tests*. Washington, D. C.: U. S. Government Printing Office, 1947.

[2] Albee, G. W. Course in human relations. *J. higher Educ.,* 1951, *22,* 43-45, 58.

[3] Albracht, M., and Gross, L. Non-directive teaching. *Sociol. and social Res.,* 1948, *32,* 874-81.

[4] Allport, G. W. *The individual and his religion, a psychological interpretation*. New York: Macmillan Co., 1950.

[5] American Association of University Professors. Academic freedom and tenure, statements of principles. *Bull., A.A.U.P.,* 1954, *40,* 81-87.

[6] American Political Science Association. *Goals for political science.* New York: Sloane Associates, 1951.

[7] American Psychological Association. *Ethical standards of psychologists*. Washington, D. C., 1953.

[8] Anastasi, A. The place of experimental psychology in the undergraduate curriculum. *Amer. Psychologist,* 1947, *2,* 57-62.

[9] Anderson, H. H., Brewer, J. E., and Reed, M. F. Studies of teachers' classroom personalities, III. *Appl. Psychol. Monogr.,* 1946, Whole No. 11.

[10] Andrews, K. R. (ed). *The case method of teaching human relations and administration.* Cambridge: Harvard Univ. Press, 1953.

[11] Andrews, T. G. Demonstrations for the introductory psychology course. *Amer. Psychologist,* 1946, *1,* 312-23.

[12] Anikeef, A. M. Factors affecting student evaluation of college faculty members. *J. appl. Psychol.,* 1953, *37,* 458-60.

[13] Asch, M. J. Non-directive teaching in psychology: an experimental study. *Psychol. Monogr.,* 1951, *65,* No. 4.

[14] Axelrod, J. The technique of group discussion in the college class. *J. gen. Educ.,* 1948, 2, 227-37.

[15] Axelrod, J. Group dynamics, non-directive therapy, and college teaching. *J. higher Educ.,* 1955, *26,* 200-07, 229-30.

[16] Axelrod, J., Bloom, B., Ginsberg, B., O'Meara, W., and Williams, J. *Teaching by discussion in the college program.* (Privately printed: The College, University of Chicago, January 1949.)

[17] Aydelotte, F. *Breaking the academic lock step.* New York: Harper and Bros., 1944.

[18] Bane, C. L. *The lecture in college teaching.* Boston: Badger Publisher, 1931.

[19] Barr, A. S. Measurement of teaching ability: impressions, trends, future research. *J. exper. Educ.,* 1946, *14,* 200-06.

[20] Barzun, J. *Teacher in America.* Boston: Little, Brown and Co., 1945.

[21] Bavelas, A. Role-playing and management training. *Sociatry,* 1947, *1,* 183-92.

[22] Beck, H. P. *Men who control our universities.* New York: King's Crown Press, 1947.

[23] Bendig, A. W. A preliminary study of the effect of academic level, sex, and course variables on student rating of psychology instructors. *J. Psychol.,* 1952, *34,* 21-26.

[24] Bendig, A. W. An inverted factor analysis study of student-rated introductory psychology instructors. *J. exper. Educ.,* 1953, *21,* 333-36.

[25] Bendig, A. W. A factor analysis of student ratings of psychology instructors on the Purdue scale. *J. educ. Psychol.,* 1954, *45,* 385-93.

[26] Berg, I. A. The use of human subjects in psychological research. *Amer. Psychologist,* 1954, *9,* 108-11.

[27] Berg, I. A., and Murphy, R. J. Final examination performance in traditional and cross-disciplinary courses. *J. educ. Psychol.,* 1954, *45,* 365-71.

[28] Bernard, L. L. Teaching of sociology in the United States in the last fifty years. *Amer. J. Sociol.,* 1945, *50,* 534-48.

[29] Berrien, F. K. A new type of elementary course. *Amer. Psychologist,* 1947, *2,* 148-50.

[30] Berrien, F. K. General education and psychology. *Sch. and Soc.,* 1951, *73,* 353-57.

[31] Berrien, F. K. *Cases and comments on human relations.* New York: Harper and Bros., 1951.

[32] Bestor, A. E. *Educational wastelands.* Urbana: Univ. Illinois Press, 1953.

[33] Bills, R. E. Investigation of student centered teaching. *J. educ. Res.,* 1952, *46,* 313-19.

[34] Birney, R., and McKeachie, W. The teaching of psychology: a survey of research since 1942. *Psychol. Bull.,* 1955, *52,* 51-68.

[35] Blauch, L. E., *et al. Teaching in colleges and universities.* Indianapolis: Amer. Assoc. of Dental Schools, 1945 (Chap. 18).

[36] Bloom, B. S. Thought-processes in lectures and discussions. *J. gen. Educ.,* 1953, *7,* 160-69.

[37] Bloom, B. S., and Ward, F. C. The Chicago Bachelor of Arts degree after ten years. *J. higher Educ.,* 1952, *23,* 459-67.

[38] Bogardus, E. S. Behavior patterns of college teachers. *Sociol. and social Res.,* 1945-46, *30,* 484-90.

[39] Bogardus, E. S. Obtaining a position in sociology. *Sociol. and soc. Res.,* 1953, *38,* 38-45.

[40] Bogardus, E. S. Teaching problems of young sociologists. *Sociol. and soc. Res.,* 1954, *38,* 174-82.

[41] Bogardus, E. S. Special problems of young sociologists. *Sociol. and soc. Res.,* 1954, *38,* 242-52.

[42] Bousfield, W. A. The use of laboratory sections in the teaching of introductory psychology. *J. Psychol.,* 1948, *26,* 289-97.

[43] Bovard, E. W., Jr. The psychology of classroom interaction. *J. educ. Res.,* 1951, *45,* 215-24.

[44] Bovard, E. W., Jr. Group structure and perception. *J. abnorm., soc. Psychol.,* 1951, *46,* 398-405.

[45] Bowman, C. C. The administrator and the professor. *Bull., A.A.U.P.,* 1946, *32,* 678-86.

[46] Bowman, C. C. The psychodramatic method in collegiate instruction, a case study. *Sociatry,* 1948, *1,* 421-30.

[47] Brayfield, A. H. (ed.) *Readings in modern methods of counseling.* New York: Appleton-Century-Crofts, Inc., 1950.

[48] Brigham, C. C. *Examining fellowship applicants.* S.S.R.C. Bulletin, No. 23. Princeton, N. J.: Princeton Univ. Press, 1935.

[49] Brown, W. F., Abeles, N., and Iscoe, I. Motivational differences between high and low scholarship college students. *J. educ. Psychol.*, 1954, *45*, 215-23.

[50] Buck, P. H. The college teacher and faculty organization. (In Cronkhite, B. B. *A handbook for college teachers.* Cambridge: Harvard Univ. Press, 1950, Chap. 10.)

[51] Burnham, P. S. *Study of academic performance of Directed Studies students, classes of 1950-53. Report of research division, Student Appointment Bureau, Yale University.* Research paper No. 143 (Parts I, II, III), 1954.

[52] Buxton, C. E. Planning the introductory course. *Amer. Psychologist*, 1946, *1*, 303-11.

[53] Buxton, C. E. The pros and cons of training for college teachers of psychology. *Amer. Psychologist*, 1949, *4*, 414-17.

[54] Buxton, C. E. Teacher training in the graduate school. *Amer. J. Physics*, 1949, *17*, 571-76.

[55] Buxton, C. E. Teaching: have your cake and eat it too? *Amer. Psychologist*, 1951, *6*, 111-18.

[56] Buxton, C. E. Issues in undergraduate education in psychology. *Amer. Psychologist*, 1956, *11*, 84-94.

[57] Buxton, C. E., and Albaugh, W. P. A selected bibliography for the college teacher of psychology. *J. gen. Psychol.*, 1950, *43*, 275-81.

[58] Cantor, N. *The dynamics of learning.* (2nd ed.) Buffalo, N. Y.: Foster and Stewart, 1950.

[59] Cantor, N. *Learning through discussion.* Buffalo, N. Y.: Human Relations for Industry (443 Delaware Ave.), 1951.

[60] Cantor, N. Function and focus in the learning process. *J. educ. Res.*, 1951, *45*, 225-31.

[61] Carlson, H. B., Fischer, R. P., and Young, P. T. Improvement in elementary psychology as related to intelligence. *Psychol. Bull.*, 1945, *42*, 27-34.

[62] Cason, H. An intelligent-question method of teaching and testing. *J. genet. Psychol.*, 1939, *54*, 359-90.

[63] Castore, G. F. Attitudes of students toward the case method of instruction in a human relations course. *J. educ. Res.*, 1951, *45*, 201-13.

[64] Castore, G. F., and Berrien, F. K. A student evaluation of a case method course. *Amer. Psychologist*, 1950, *5*, 149-51.

[65] Cattell, J. McK. The psychological laboratory. *Psychol. Rev.*, 1898, *5*, 655-58.

[66] Chicago, University of. *Announcement: a comprehensive program of undergraduate education*. Chicago, 1952.

[67] Chicago, University of. *Announcements: the college; for sessions of 1952-53*. Chicago, 1952.

[68] Chicago, University of, Board of Examinations. *Manual of examination methods*. Univ. Chicago Bookstore, 1937.

[69] Coffman, W. E. Determining students' concepts of effective teaching from their ratings of instructors. *J. educ. Psychol.*, 1954, *45*, 277-86.

[70] Cohen, I. B., and Watson, F. G. (eds.) *General education in science*. Cambridge: Harvard Univ. Press, 1950.

[71] Cole, L. *The background for college teaching*. New York: Farrar and Rinehart, Inc., 1940.

[72] Coleman, W. Role playing as an instructional aid. *J. educ. Psychol.*, 1948, *39*, 427-33.

[73] Committee. *General education in school and college*. Cambridge: Harvard Univ. Press, 1952.

[74] Committee of Fifteen. *The graduate school today and tomorrow*. New York: Fund for the Advancement of Education, 1955.

[75] Committee on General Education. *Report*. New Haven: Yale Univ., 1953 (lithoprint).

[76] Conant, J. B. *Science and common sense*. New Haven: Yale Univ. Press, 1951.

[77] Conant, J. B. *Education and liberty*. Cambridge: Harvard Univ. Press, 1953.

[78] Conklin, E. S. Superstitious beliefs and practices among college students. *Amer. J. Psychol.*, 1919, *30*, 83-102.

[79] Crannell, C. W. An experiment in the rating of instructors by their students. *Coll. and Univ.*, 1948, *24*, 5-11.

[80] Crannell, C. W. The responses of college students to a questionnaire on animistic thinking. *Sci. Mo.*, 1954, *78*, 54-56.

[81] Creager, J. A. A multiple factor analysis of the Purdue Rating Scale for Instructors. *Purdue Univ. Stud. in higher Educ.*, 1950, *70*, 75-99.

[82] Daniel, R. S., and Louttit, C. M. *Professional problems in psychology*. New York: Prentice Hall, Inc., 1953 (Chap. 13).

[83] Delabarre, E. B. Les laboratoires de psychologie en Amérique. *L'Année psychologique,* 1894, *1,* 209-55.

[84] Dennis, W. Animistic thinking among college and university students. *Sci. Mo.,* 1953, *76,* 247-49.

[85] Deutsch, M. Social relations in the classroom and grading procedures. *J. educ. Res.,* 1951, *45,* 145-60.

[86] Di Vesta, F. J. Instructor-centered and student-centered approaches in teaching a human relations course. *J. appl. Psychol.,* 1954, *38,* 329-35.

[87] Dockeray, F. C. Psychology for beginners. (In *Ohio State Univ. Stud., Bur. of educ. Res., 1932.* No. 15, Chap. 10.)

[88] Dockeray, F. C., and Valentine, W. L. An analysis of the elementary psychology course at the Ohio State University. *J. appl. Psychol.,* 1935, *19,* 503-20.

[89] Donham, W. B. Why experiment? The case system in college teaching of social science. *J. gen. Educ.,* 1949, *3,* 145-56.

[90] Dressel, P. L. *Evaluation in general education.* Dubuque, Ia.: Wm. C. Brown Co., 1954.

[91] Dressel, P. L. With candor and caution. *J. gen. Educ.,* 1955, *8,* 195-97.

[92] Dressel, P. L., and Mayhew, L. B. *General education: explorations in evaluation.* Washington, D. C.: Amer. Council on Educ., 1954.

[93] Drucker, A. J., and Remmers, H. H. Do alumni and students differ in their attitudes toward instructors? *Purdue Univ. Stud. in higher Educ.,* 1950, *70,* 62-74.

[94] Dudycha, G. J. The superstitious beliefs of college students. *J. abnorm., soc. Psychol.,* 1933, *27,* 457-64.

[95] Duncan, C. P., Bell, G., Bradt, K. H., and Newman, S. E. How the poorer student studies: a research report. *J. educ. Res.,* 1951, *45,* 287-92.

[96] Dyer, H. S. Can general education courses in the sciences be evaluated? (In Cohen, J. B., and Watson, F. G., eds. *General education in science.* Cambridge: Harvard Univ. Press, 1952.)

[97] Dysinger, D. W., and Gregory, W. S. A preliminary study of some factors related to student achievement and grades in the beginning course in psychology. *J. gen. Psychol.,* 1941, *24,* 195-209.

[98] Eels, W. C. Reliability of repeated grading of essay type examinations. *J. educ. Psychol.,* 1930, *21,* 48-52.

[99] Eglash, A. A group discussion method of teaching psychology. *J. educ. Psychol.,* 1954, *45,* 257-67.

[100] Elliott, D. N. Characteristics and relationships of various criteria of college and university teaching. *Purdue Univ. Stud. in higher Educ.*, 1950, *70*, 5-61.

[101] English, H. B. Why students register for psychology. *J. appl. Psychol.*, 1928, *12*, 242-44.

[102] Ericksen, S. C. A terminal course for psychology majors. *Amer. Psychologist*, 1955, *10*, 22-24.

[103] Evans, J. *Three men.* New York: Alfred Knopf, 1954.

[104] Faw, V. A psychotherapeutic method of teaching psychology. *Amer. Psychologist*, 1949, *4*, 104-09.

[105] Federighi, H., and Leuba, C. The proper study of mankind is man; a two-year course on man and his relation to the living world. *J. gen. Educ.*, 1948, *2*, 193-98.

[106] Field, P. E. First report of an attempt to standardize the introductory course in psychology. *Amer. Psychologist*, 1949, *4*, 215-16.

[107] Fisher, M. B. Comparison of performance of freshmen and sophomores in general psychology. *J. exper. Educ.*, 1941, *10*, 29-32.

[108] Fitch, M. L., Drucker, A. J., and Norton, J. A., Jr. Frequent testing as a motivating factor in large lecture classes. *J. educ. Psychol.*, 1951, *42*, 1-20.

[109] Flexner, A. *Universities, American, English, German.* New York: Oxford Univ. Press, 1930.

[110] Fox, W. M. Additional notes on the case method of instruction. *Amer. Psychologist*, 1954, *9*, 242-43.

[111] Freeburne, C. M. A practice-teaching program for M.A. candididates in psychology. *Amer. Psychologist*, 1952, *7*, 22-23.

[112] French, F. C. The place of experimental psychology in the undergraduate course. *Psychol. Rev.*, 1898, *5*, 510-12.

[113] Gaier, E. L. Selected personality variables and the learning process. *Psychol. Monogr.*, 1952, *66*, No. 17.

[114] Garrett, H. E., and Fisher, T. R. The prevalence of certain popular misconceptions. *J. appl. Psychol.*, 1926, *10*, 411-20.

[115] Gibb, C. A. Classroom behavior of the college teacher. *Educ., psychol. Meas.*, 1955, *15*, 254-63.

[116] Gibb, L. M., and Gibb, J. R. The effects of the use of "participative action" groups in a course in general psychology. *Amer. Psychologist*, 1952, *7*, 247 (abstr.).

[117] Gilliland, A. R. A study of admission requirements in general psychology. *J. appl. Psychol.*, 1941, *25*, 171-75.

[118] Gilmer, B. von H. Evaluating the criteria for higher education. *J. higher Educ.*, 1949, *20*, 473-79.

[119] Goldberg, S., and Stern, G. G. The authoritarian personality and general education. *Amer. Psychologist*, 1952, *7*, 375 (abstr.).

[120] Grambs, J. D. Dynamics of psychodrama in the teaching situation. *Sociatry*, 1948, *1*, 383-99.

[121] Gross, L. An experimental study of the validity of the non-directive method of teaching. *J. Psychol.*, 1948, *26*, 243-48.

[122] Guetzkow, H., Kelly, E. L., and McKeachie, W. J. An experimental comparison of recitation, discussion, and tutorial methods in college teaching. *J. educ. Psychol.*, 1954, *45*, 193-207.

[123] Gustav, A. A follow-up of undergraduate psychology majors. *Amer. Psychologist*, 1952, *7*, 510-12.

[124] Guthrie, E. R. *The psychology of learning*. New York: Harper and Bros., 1935.

[125] Guthrie, E. R. The evaluation of teaching. *Informational Bull., Training Analysis and Development Division, Air Training Command, Scott Air Force Base, Ill.*, 1953, *4*, 199-206.

[126] Guthrie, E. R. *The evaluation of teaching: a progress report*. Seattle: University of Washington, 1954 (lithoprint).

[127] Hahn, P. B. Johnny Rocco—teaching material for elementary students. *J. abnorm., soc. Psychol.*, 1948, *43*, 384-90.

[128] Hannay, N. C. The instructor and effective speech. (In Cronkhite, B. B. *A handbook for college teachers*. Cambridge: Harvard Univ. Press, 1951, Ch. 9.)

[129] Harper, R. S. The first course in psychology. *Amer. Psychologist*, 1952, *7*, 722-27.

[130] Harper, R. S. The Knox conference on the relation of psychology to general education. *Amer. Psychologist*, 1954, *9*, 803-04.

[131] Hartstein, J. I. Preparing psychology teachers at Long Island University. *Sch. and Soc.*, 1954, *79*, 155-56.

[132] Harvard Committee. *General education in a free society*. Cambridge: Harvard Univ. Press, 1945.

[133] Hawkes, H. E., Lindquist, E. F., and Mann, C. P. *The construction and use of achievement examinations*. Boston: Houghton Mifflin Co., 1936.

[134] Hayes, A. McH. (ed.) The discussion method in teaching: a symposium. *J. gen. Educ.*, 1954, *8*, 1-71.

[135] Hendry, C. E., Lippitt, R., and Zander, A. Reality practice as educational method. *Psychodr. Monogr.*, 1944, No. 9.

[136] Hilgard, E. R. *Introduction to psychology.* New York: Harcourt, Brace and Co., 1953.

[137] Hofstadter, R., and Hardy, C. DeW. *The development and scope of higher education in the United States.* New York: Columbia Univ. Press, 1952.

[138] Hofstadter, R., and Metzger, W. P. *The development of academic freedom in the United States.* New York: Columbia Univ. Press, 1955.

[139] Holland, B. F. The effect of class size on scholastic acquirement in educational psychology. *Sch. and Soc.,* 1928, *27,* 668-70.

[140] Holland, J. B. The image of the instructor as it is related to class size. *J. exper. Educ.,* 1954, *23,* 171-77.

[141] Holley, J. W., and Buxton, C. E. A factorial study of belief. *Educ., psychol. Meas.,* 1950, *10,* 400-10.

[142] Holtzman, W. H., Brown, W. F., and Farquhar, W. G. The survey of study habits and attitudes: a new instrument for the prediction of academic success. *Educ., psychol. Meas.,* 1954, *14,* 726-32.

[143] Horrocks, J. E., and Nagy, G. The relationship between the ability to make a diagnosis and to select appropriate remedial procedures. *J. gen. Psychol.,* 1948, *38,* 139-45.

[144] Horrocks, J. R., and Troyer, M. E. Case study tests of ability to use knowledge of human growth and development. *Educ., psychol. Meas.,* 1947, *7,* 23-36.

[145] Hudelson, E. *Class size at the college level.* Minneapolis: Univ. Minnesota Press, 1928.

[146] Hunt, P. The case method of instruction. *Harvard educ. Rev.,* 1951, *21,* 175-92.

[147] Husband, R. W. A statistical comparison of the efficacy of large lecture vs. smaller recitation sections upon achievement in general psychology. *J. Psychol.,* 1951, *31,* 297-300.

[148] James, H. W. The effect of handwriting upon grading. *English J.,* 1927, *16,* 180-85.

[149] James, W. *Psychology.* (Living Library Ed.) New York: World Publ. Co., 1948.

[150] Johnson, D. M., and Smith, H. C. Democratic leadership in the college classroom. *Psychol. Monogr.,* 1953, *67,* No. 11.

[151] Jones, H. M. The role of higher education in America. (In Cronkhite, B. B. *A handbook for college teachers.* Cambridge: Harvard Univ. Press, 1950, Chap. 16.)

[152] Jordan, W. K. The college teacher in relation to research and publication. (In Cronkhite, B. B. *A handbook for college teachers.* Cambridge: Harvard Univ. Press, 1950, Chap. 13.)

[153] Kay, L. W. Role-playing as a teaching aid. *Sociometry,* 1946, *9,* 263-74.

[154] Keller, F. S., and Schoenfeld, W. N. The psychology curriculum at Columbia College. *Amer. Psychologist,* 1949, *4,* 165-72.

[155] Keller, F. S., and Schoenfeld, W. N. *Principles of psychology.* New York: Appleton-Century-Crofts, Inc., 1950.

[156] Kelley, H., and Pepitone, A. An evaluation of a college course in human relations. *J. educ. Psychol.,* 1952, *43,* 193-209.

[157] Kelley, T. J. *Toward better college teaching.* Washington, D. C.: U. S. Government Printing Office, 1950.

[158] Kimpton, L. A. The state of the university. *Tower Topics, Univer. of Chicago Alumni Bull.,* 1953, *20,* No. 3.

[159] Knapp, R. H., and Greenbaum, J. J. *The younger American scholar: his collegiate origins.* Chicago: Univ. Chicago Press, 1953.

[160] Krohn, W. O. Facilities in experimental psychology in the colleges of the U. S. *Report, U. S. Commissioner of Educ.,* 1890-91, 1139-51.

[161] Lancelot, W. H. Standards of measurement of teaching ability. *Sch. and Soc.,* 1931, *34,* 236-38.

[162] Landsman, T. *An experimental study of a student-centered learning method.* Ph.D. Dissertation, Syracuse University, 1950.

[163] Landsman, T., and deMartino, M. F. Some areas of caution for the psychology student. *Amer. Psychologist,* 1947, 2, 145-47.

[164] Leuba, C., and Federighi, H. A course in the life sciences. *Amer. Psychologist,* 1948, *3,* 30-34.

[165] Levit, G., and Jennings, H. H. Learning through role playing. *Adult Leadership,* 1953, 2, 9-16.

[166] Longstaff, H. P. Analysis of some factors conditioning learning in general psychology. *J. appl. Psychol.,* 1932, *16,* 9-48, 131-66.

[167] Lorge, I. If they know not, teach. *Teach. Coll. Record,* 1954, *56,* 165-68.

[168] Lovell, G. D., and Haner, C. F. Forced-choice applied to college faculty rating. *Educ., psychol. Meas.,* 1955, *15,* 291-304.

[169] Lowell, A. L. *At war with academic traditions in America.* Cambridge: Harvard Univ. Press, 1934.

[170] MacIver, R. M. *Academic freedom in our time.* New York: Columbia Univ. Press, 1955.

[171] MacLeod, R. B. *Religious perspectives of college teaching in experimental psychology.* New Haven: Edw. W. Hazen Foundation, 1951.

[172] Magaret, A., and Sherriffs, A. C. Personal factors influencing the learning of the first course in psychology. *J. gen. Psychol.,* 1947, *37,* 67-77.

[173] Maier, N. R. F. *Principles of human relations.* New York: Wiley and Sons, 1952.

[174] Marcuse, F. L. Objective and subjective examinations. *Sch. and Soc.,* 1950, *72,* 136-37.

[175] Marcuse, F. L. Objective and subjective examinations—a rejoinder. *Sch. and Soc.,* 1950, *72,* 394-95.

[176] Marcuse, F. L. On methods of teaching elementary psychology. *J. educ. Psychol.,* 1951, *42,* 236-40.

[177] Marsh, C. J. Student opinions on the importance and attainment of course objectives in psychology. *J. genet. Psychol.,* 1944, *64,* 305-09.

[178] May, M. A. *Toward a science of human behavior; a survey of the work of the Institute of Human Relations through two decades, 1929-1949.* New Haven: Yale Univ., 1950.

[179] McClelland, D. C. The recruitment of scientific psychologists. *Amer. Psychologist,* 1954, *9,* 811-13.

[180] McConnell, T. R. Liberal education and specialization. (In Valentine, P. F. *The American college.* New York: Philosophical Library, 1949, Ch. 3.)

[181] McDonald, F. Confused allies: teaching and research. *J. higher Educ.,* 1952, *23,* 319-22.

[182] McDonald, R. W. Fundamental issues in general education. *J. gen. Educ.,* 1949-50, *4,* 32-39.

[183] McGarvey, J. W. Transfer of learning in elementary psychology (1) to popular misconceptions, and (2) to social science courses. *Psychol. Bull.,* 1937, *34,* 704 (abstr.).

[184] McGrath, E. J., The control of higher education in America. *Educ. Record,* 1936, *17,* 259-72.

[185] McGrath, E. J., *et al. Toward general education.* New York: Macmillan Co., 1948.

[186] McKeachie, W. J. Anxiety in the college classroom. *J. educ. Res.,* 1951, *45,* 153-60.

[187] McKeachie, W. J. A program for training teachers of psychology. *Amer. Psychologist,* 1951, *6,* 119-21.

[188] McKeachie, W. J. Student-centered versus instructor-centered instruction. *J. educ. Psychol.,* 1954, *45,* 143-50.

[189] McKeachie, W. J. Individual conformity to attitudes of classroom groups. *J. abnorm., soc. Psychol.,* 1954, *49,* 282-89.

[190] McKeachie, W. J., DeValois, R. L., Dulaney, D. E., Jr., Beardslee, D. C., and Winterbottom, M. Objectives of the general psychology course. *Amer. Psychologist,* 1954, *9,* 140-42.

[191] McKeachie, W. J., and Hiler, W. The problem-oriented approach to teaching psychology. *J. educ. Psychol.,* 1954, *45,* 224-32.

[192] McKeachie, W. J., and Kimble, G. A. *Teaching tips* (2nd ed.). Ann Arbor: Wahr Publishing Co., 1953.

[193] McKeachie, W. J., Pollie, D., and Speisman, J. Relieving anxiety in classroom examinations. *J. abnorm., soc. Psychol.,* 1955, *50,* 93-98.

[194] Meyer, G. An experimental study of the old and new type examination. *J. educ. Psychol.,* 1934, *25,* 641-61; 1935, *26,* 30-40.

[195] Meyer, P. R., and Patton, R. M. Can student ratings of instructors be painless and foolproof? *Sch. and Soc.,* 1954, *80,* 200-01.

[196] Michigan State College. *Catalog,* 1953, *48,* No. 11.

[197] Miller, E. O. Teaching psychology in the small liberal arts college. *Amer. Psychologist,* 1953, *8,* 475-78.

[198] Milner, E. Student preferences concerning teaching method and class structuring. *Amer. Psychologist,* 1948, *3,* 233-34 (abstr.).

[199] Muenzinger, K. F. *Psychology: the science of behavior.* New York: Harper and Bros., 1942.

[200] Munn, N. L. *Psychology, the fundamentals of human adjustment.* Boston: Houghton Mifflin Co., 1946.

[201] Newman, S. E., Duncan, C. P., Bell, G. B., and Bradt, K. H. Predicting student performance in the first course in psychology. *J. educ. Psychol.,* 1952, *43,* 243-47.

[202] New York *Times,* July 29, 1953, p. 21.

[203] Nixon, H. K. Popular answers to some psychological questions. *Amer. J. Psychol.,* 1952, *36,* 418-25.

[204] Oeser, O. A. Psychology applied to the teaching of psychology: sketch of a recently developed department of psychology. *Amer. Psychologist,* 1951, *6,* 172-76.

[205] Owen, D. The graduate student in search of a teaching position. (In Cronkhite, B. B. *A handbook for college teachers.* Cambridge: Harvard Univ. Press, 1950, Chap. 15.)

[206] Owen, J. E. This pressure to publish. *Bull., A.A.U.P.*, 1954-55, *40*, 638-42.

[207] Palmquist, E. M., and Drummond, D. F. (eds.) *Toward better teaching*. Columbia: Univ. of Missouri, 1951 (lithoprint).

[208] Pennock, J. R. The Swarthmore honors system. *J. higher Educ.*, 1953, *24*, 57-63, 106.

[209] Phillips, J. D. Report on discussion 66. *Adult Educ. J.*, 1948, *7*, 181-82.

[210] Pierson, G. W. The elective system and the difficulties of college planning, 1870-1940. *J. gen. Educ.*, 1950, *4*, 165-74.

[211] Pierson, G. W. *Yale College, an educational history, 1871-1921*. New Haven: Yale Univ. Press, 1952.

[212] Portenier, L. G. Predicting success in introductory psychology. *Educ., psychol. Meas.*, 1948, *8*, 117-26.

[213] Present and Former Members of the Faculty. *The idea and practice of general education*. Chicago: Univ. Chicago Press, 1950.

[214] Pressey, S. L. Fundamentalism, isolationism and biological pedantry versus socio-cultural orientation, in psychology. *J. gen. Psychol.*, 1940, *23*, 393-99.

[215] Pressey, S. L. The place and functions of psychology in undergraduate programs. *Amer. Psychologist*, 1949, *4*, 148-50.

[216] Pressey, S. L. Development and appraisal of devices providing immediate automatic scoring of objective tests and concomitant self-instruction. *J. Psychol.*, 1950, *29*, 417-47.

[217] Pressey, S. L. Concerning the nature and nurture of genius. *Sci. Mo.*, 1955, *81*, 123-29.

[218] Pusey, N. M. Harvard and religious faith. *Harvard Alumni Bull.*, 1953-54, *56*, 71, 78-80.

[219] Ralya, L. L. Beliefs of senior premedical psychology students. *J. appl. Psychol.*, 1944, *28*, 35-42.

[220] Reid, L. D. How to improve classroom lectures. *Bull., A.A.U.P.*, 1948, *34*, 576-83.

[221] Remmers, H. H. Learning, effort and attitudes as affected by three methods of instruction in elementary psychology. *Purdue Univ. Stud. in higher Educ.*, 1933, No. 21.

[222] Remmers, H. H. Psychology—some unfinished business. *Psychol. Bull.*, 1944, *41*, 713-24.

[223] Riley, J. W., Ryan, B. F., and Lifshitz, M. *The student looks at his teacher*. New Brunswick, N. J.: Rutgers Univ. Press, 1950.

[224] Robinson, F. P. *Effective study.* New York: Harper and Bros., 1946.

[225] Rogers, C. R., *et al. Client-centered therapy, its current practice, implications and theory.* Boston: Houghton-Mifflin Co., 1951.

[226] Rogers, C. R. Persons or Science? A philosophical question. *Amer. Psychologist,* 1955, *10,* 267-78.

[227] Roy, H. L. A comparison of the performance of freshmen and sophomores in general psychology. *Psychol. Bull.,* 1945, *42,* 371-75.

[228] Ruch, F. L. *Psychology and life.* Chicago: Scott, Foresman Co., 1937.

[229] Ruckmich, C. A. The history and status of psychology in the United States. *Amer. J. Psychol.,* 1912, *23,* 517-31.

[230] Ruja, H. Content of the first course in psychology. *Psychol. Bull.,* 1943, *40,* 488-96.

[231] Ruja, H. The order of topics in general psychology. *Amer. Psychologist,* 1948, *3,* 199-202.

[232] Ruja, H. Defining "discussion." *Sch. and Soc.,* 1953, *78,* 6-8.

[233] Ruja, H. Nondirective teaching and self-insight: a statistical addendum. *J. gen. Psychol.,* 1954, *51,* 331-32.

[234] Russell, H. E. *Interrelations of some indices of instructor effectiveness: an exploratory study.* Ph.D. Dissertation, Univ. of Pittsburgh, 1951.

[235] Sanford, F. H., and Fleishman, E. A. A survey of undergraduate psychology courses in American colleges and universities. *Amer. Psychologist,* 1950, *5,* 33-37.

[236] Sanford, F. H., and Hemphill, J. K. An evaluation of a brief course in psychology at the U. S. Naval Academy. *Educ., psychol. Meas.,* 1952, *12,* 194-216.

[237] Sarah Lawrence College. *Bulletin, 1953-54.* Bronxville, N. Y., 1953.

[238] Sarason, S. B., and Mandler, G. Some correlates of test anxiety. *J. abnorm., soc. Psychol.,* 1952, *47,* 810-17.

[239] Sartain, A. Q., and Waring, E. G. Interest in and value of college courses. *J. appl. Psychol.,* 1944, *28,* 520-26.

[240] Schlosberg, H. A laboratory period in the first course in psychology. *Amer. Psychologist,* 1947, *2,* 384-87.

[241] Schoen, M. The elementary course in psychology. *Amer. J. Psychol.,* 1926, *37,* 592-99.

[242] Scott, C. W., and Hill, C. M. *Public education under criticism.* New York: Prentice-Hall, Inc., 1954.

[243] Seashore, C. E. Trial and error in the development of the elementary course in psychology. *Sch. and Soc.,* 1931, *33,* 782-86.

[244] Seashore, C. E., *et al.* Report of the committee of the American Psychological Association on the teaching of psychology. *Psychol. Monogr.,* 1910, *12,* No. 4.

[245] Selle, R. M. "Reasons why my mark should be raised"—by a pre-med. *Sch. and Soc.,* 1954, *79,* 153.

[246] Sinick, D. Comments on "The use of human subjects in psychological research." *Amer. Psychologist,* 1954, *9,* 589.

[247] Skinner, B. F. *Science and human behavior.* New York: Macmillan Co., 1953.

[248] Skinner, B. F. Freedom and the control of men. *Amer. Scholar,* 1955-56, *25,* 47-65.

[249] Smith, D. E. *Applicational transfer: its nature, measurement and improvement.* Ph.D. Dissertation, Cornell University, 1952.

[250] Smith, D. E. P. Applicational transfer and inhibition. *J. educ. Psychol.,* 1954, *45,* 169-74.

[251] Smith, D. E., and Glock, M. D. Measuring knowledge and application: an experimental investigation. *J. exper. Educ.,* 1953, *21,* 327-32.

[252] Smith, D. E. P., and Wood, R. L. *Help yourself to efficient reading.* Ann Arbor: Univ. Michigan Press, 1953.

[253] Smith, H. C., and Dunbar, D. S. The personality and achievement of the classroom participant. *J. educ. Psychol.,* 1951, *42,* 65-84.

[254] Smith, M. B. Psychology in a liberal education. *J. higher Educ.,* 1951, *22,* 181-87.

[255] Spence, R. B. Lecture and class discussion in teaching educational psychology. *J. educ. Psychol.,* 1928, *19,* 454-62.

[256] Starch, D., and Elliott, E. C. The reliability of grading of high school work in English. *Sch. Rev.,* 1912, *20,* 442-57.

[257] Starch, D., and Elliott, E. C. The reliability of grading high school work in mathematics. *Sch. Rev.,* 1913, *21,* 254-59.

[258] Steiner, L. R. *Where do people take their troubles?* Boston: Houghton-Mifflin Co., 1945.

[259] Stern, G. G. Studies in personality typologies. The N, R, and S syndromes. (Paper presented at Midwestern Psychological Association, 1953. Incorporated in: *Methods in Personality Assessment.* Glencoe, Ill.: Free Press, 1956.)

[260] Stripling, R. O. Orientation practices for new college faculty members. *Bull., A.A.U.P.*, 1954-55, *40*, 555-62.

[261] Taylor, H. (ed.) The teaching of undergraduate economics. *Amer. Econ. Rev.*, 1950, *40*, Suppl., Part 2.

[262] Terry, P. W. How students study for three types of objective tests. *J. educ. Res.*, 1934, *27*, 333-43.

[263] Tozzer, A. M. *Social origins and social continuities.* New York: Macmillan Co., 1925.

[264] Travers, R. M. W. *How to make achievement tests.* New York: Odyssey Press, 1950.

[265] Triggs, F. O. *Improve your reading.* Minneapolis: Univ. Minnesota Press, 1942.

[266] Tussing, L. What students want from the elementary course in psychology. *J. appl. Psychol.*, 1938, *2*, 282-87.

[267] United Nations Educational, Scientific and Cultural Organization. *Teaching in the social sciences. The teaching of the social sciences in the United States.* Paris: UNESCO, 1954.

[268] United States Office of Education. *Biennial survey of education in the United States, 1950-52.* Chap. 1 (Table 34, p. 41).

[269] Valentine, W. L. Common misconceptions of college students. *J. appl. Psychol.*, 1936, *20*, 633-58.

[270] Voegelin, E. W. Anthropology in American universities. *Amer. Anthropol.*, 1950, *52*, 350-91.

[271] Voeks, V. Ridicule and other detriments to effective teaching. *Bull., A.A.U.P.*, 1954-55, *40*, 621-30.

[272] Ward, F. C. The program at the University of Chicago. (In Stickler, W. H. *Organization and administration of general education.* Dubuque, Ia.: Wm. C. Brown Co., 1951, Chap. 10.)

[273] Webb, W. B. The problem of teaching interneships. *Amer. Psychologist*, 1952, *7*, 20-21.

[274] Weitzman, E. Misconceptions of entering college freshmen. *J. educ. Res.*, 1948, *42*, 224-27.

[275] Wendt, G. R. The development of a psychological cult. *Amer. Psychologist*, 1949, *4*, 426.

[276] Whitaker, J. R. The college teacher's search. *J. higher Educ.*, 1947, *18*, 244-48.

[277] White, R. W. *Lives in progress, a study of the natural growth of personality.* New York: Dryden Press, 1952.

[278] Whyte, W. F. Leadership and group participation. Cornell University, Ithaca, N. Y.: New York State School of Industrial and Labor Relations, Bull. No. 24, 1953.

[279] Williamson, E. G. *Counselling for adolescents.* New York: McGraw-Hill Co., 1950.

[280] Wilson, L. *The academic man.* New York: Oxford Univ. Press, 1942.

[281] Wisconsin, University of. *College of Letters and Science: General announcement of courses,* 1952-54. Madison, 1952.

[282] Wispe, L. G. Evaluating section teaching methods in the introductory course. *J. educ. Res.,* 1951, *45,* 161-86.

[283] Wispe, L. G. Teaching methods research. *Amer. Psychologist,* 1953, *8,* 147-50.

[284] Wolfe, H. K. The new psychology in undergraduate work. *Psychol. Rev.,* 1895, 2, 382-87.

[285] Wolfle, D. The first course in psychology. *Psychol. Bull.,* 1942, *39,* 685-712.

[286] Wolfle, D. The sensible organization of courses in psychology. *Amer. Psychologist,* 1947, 2, 437-45.

[287] Wolfle, D. *America's resources of specialized talent.* (*Report of the commission on human resources and advanced training.*) New York: Harper and Bros., 1954.

[288] Wolfle, D., Buxton, C. E., Cofer, C. N., Gustad, J. W., MacLeod, R. B., and McKeachie, W. J. *Improving undergraduate instruction in psychology.* New York: Macmillan Co., 1952.

[289] Woodburne, L. S. *Faculty personnel policies in higher education.* New York: Harper and Bros., 1950.

[290] Wrenn, C. G. *Student personnel work in college.* Ronald Press Co., New York, 1951.

[291] Yale University. *Undergraduate Courses of Study, 1955-56.* Bull. Ser. *51,* No. 6, 1955.

[292] Young, K. Some problems of interdisciplinary courses in the social sciences. *J. gen. Educ.,* 1953, 7, 201-08.

[293] Young, K. Psychology as a general social science course. *Amer. Psychologist,* 1955, *10,* 25-28.

[294] Zander, A. F. Role playing: a technique for training the necessarily dominating leader. *Sociatry,* 1947, *1,* 225-35.

[295] Zander, A. F., and Lippitt, R. Reality-practice as educational method. *Sociometry,* 1944, 7, 129-51.

INDEX